The King's Finances II

Translated by Haena Lee

A third-generation Christian, Haena Lee received her bachelor's degree from Grove City College, a Christian liberal arts college in Grove City, Pennsylvania. She attended the Graduate School of Translation and Interpretation at Ewha Womans University in Seoul, Korea.

THE KING'S FINANCES II

copyright © 2021 by Kim MiJin
All rights reserved.

1st edition is printed in March 16, 2021
Published by Kyujang Publishing Company
Edited and Designed by Kyujang Publishing Company
Phone : +822-578-0003
Email : kyujang0691@gmail.com
HomePage : www.kyujang.com
Address: 20, Maeheon-ro 16-gil, Seocho-gu, Seoul 06770, Republic of Korea

Originally published in Korean under the title
왕의 재정 2 (which means The King's Finances II)

No part of this book may be reproduced in any form without permission in writing from the publisher, except in the case of brief quotations embodied in critical articles or reviews.

Scripture quotations are taken from The Holy Bible, New International Version® NIV®
Copyright © 1973, 1978, 1984, 2011 by Biblica, Inc.TM Used by permission.
All rights reserved worldwide.

Scripture quotations are taken from The ESV® Bible (The Holy Bible, English Standard Version®), copyright © 2001 by Crossway, a publishing ministry of Good News Publishers. Used by permission. All rights reserved.

Scripture quotations are taken from the Holy Bible, New Living Translation, copyright © 1996, 2004, 2015 by Tyndale House Foundation. Used by permission of Tyndale House Publishers, a Division of Tyndale House Ministries, Carol Stream, Illinois 60188. All rights reserved.

Scripture taken from the New King James Version®. Copyright © 1982 by Thomas Nelson. Used by permission. All rights reserved.

Scriptures and additional materials quoted are from the Good News Bible © 1994 published by the Bible Societies/HarperCollins Publishers Ltd UK, Good News Bible© American Bible Society 1966, 1971, 1976, 1992. Used with permission.

Scripture quotations marked MSG are taken from THE MESSAGE, copyright © 1993, 2002, 2018 by Eugene H. Peterson. Used by permission of NavPress, represented by Tyndale House Publishers. All rights reserved.

ISBN 979-11-6504-189-2-03230

BREAKING OUT OF THE BONDAGE OF DEBT AND LIVING THE LIFE OF THE HOLY RICH

THE KING'S FINANCES II

Kim MiJin

Edited by Dr. SungGun Hong
Translated by Haena Lee

Explanatory Notes

All Bible quotes are from the New International Version of the Bible unless otherwise noted.

All testimonies in this book, under both real names and pseudonyms, have been recorded with the consent of the individual.

Editor's Notes

The Key to Revival in the Korean Church Is in Finances

Why a Biblical Understanding of Finances Is Absolutely Necessary

People mistakenly think that when "one has a lot of money," it means that "one is rich because of that money." They then apply such logic to the following equation: "Having a lot of money means one is rich and, therefore, happy." Likewise, people then also say: "Not having money means one is poor and, therefore, unhappy." But such are the words of people who do not fully understand money.

In fact, some people are unhappy despite having a lot of money, and some are happy despite having no money. This is because money is not what determines one's happiness.

And yet this logic, which equates money to happiness, burdens the hearts of many.

Mammon's powerful influence plants a false understanding of money within people. Mammon makes people value money in and of itself, causing them to chase after it. And from this mammon brings ruin to the lives of those who chase after money.

Ultimately, these are the equations that people are left with:

Lots of money = rich = happy

No money = poor = unhappy

Tricked by such formulas, people become easily tempted by money and chase after it. However, once we clearly understand money, we live life not with love of it, but instead with a love of God; we learn to love God in all His greatness and thus learn how to handle money. It is my hope that the readers of this book begin a journey of reflection and learn to see who is truly happy, who is rich, who is unhappy, and who is poor. I hope that through this journey, readers will gain an understanding of the real function and value of money.

Will You Serve God, or Will You Serve Mammon?

No one can serve two masters. Either you will hate the one and love the other, or you will be devoted to the one and

despise the other. You cannot serve both God and money
Matt. 6:24

In the above verse, the Aramaic word used for 'money' is 'mammon.' Mammon was an idol of the ancient Near East that was worshipped in the land of Canaan. It was a divine being that specifically dealt with wealth. Mammon itself is a deity. Mammon seeks to take God's place on His throne. Unbelievable!

Mammon creates misunderstanding of wealth in people. He then pulls these people under his influence so that they are unable to carry out the works of God. Under his powerful control, people are made to love money and live their lives in pursuit of it. It is for this reason that we must absolutely learn how to cut off and fight against the spirit of mammon: to learn how to handle money the right way. God entrusted each of us with wealth because He wants to use us. To some, He entrusted 1 billion won[1], and to others, 100 million won. Some, He entrusted with 10 million won, and with others, 10,000 won.

Wealth does not only refer to fiat currency, it also encompasses a great many goods. Hence, anything we own, such as clothes, shoes, watches, cars, houses, is all a part of our wealth. God tests us through the wealth we possess. We

---

[1] One U.S. dollar is approximately 1,000 won.

must always be mindful of the fact that we are being tested.

For example, God calls us "faithful" when we create 1 billion won with the 100 million won He entrusted to us. But fear keeps us from taking action, and we bring the 100 million won back to God exactly as it was given to us. Thus, He calls us "wicked and lazy." God wants us to put the 100 million won to work and multiply this amount. God makes this very clear in Luke Chapter 19 and Matthew Chapter 25.

Mammon Makes Us Go into Debt

This happened during the initial stages of our ministry when Sister Kim MiJin and I attended a joint conference in the Busan region. Three hundred people, including 30 pastors, attended the conference at which I gave all-day lectures over two days. I spoke very strongly about debt during my lectures. I explained how the Bible describes indebtedness in detail and provided additional explanations to elaborate on this further.

"I have never been in debt in my entire life, not even a single won."

Hearing this, Kim MiJin rose from her seat, came up to the podium and said:

"Reverend Hong, if you put things that way, who from the audience could your words possibly encourage? Most of them are in debt."

"Sister MiJin, the people here can't have that much debt. Why would you say that?"

"Reverend Hong, how many from the audience would you say are in debt?"

"I would say around 30 percent, at most."

"No, most are in debt."

I looked to the audience and said, "Sister MiJin, do not underestimate our audience here today."

She responded, addressing the audience: "I want you all to close your eyes. Those who have debt, including those who do not have the means to make their next credit card payment, please raise your hand. If you have even a little bit of debt, raise your hand high."

She continued, "Now, Reverend Hong, I want you to open your eyes and see."

I was stunned by what I saw that day. I could not believe my eyes. Every single one, 100 percent of the audience, had their hand raised (What I saw that day changed how I viewed and understood the world).

Sister Kim MiJin said, speaking to the audience:

"Ladies and gentlemen, I went into an immense amount of debt when my business went bankrupt. I sold everything I owned to pay it back, but even after all that, I still had 5 billion won in debt to repay. Debt collectors harassed me every single day. I was so despondent that I twice tried to kill myself. I spent my days in despair. Then one day, my husband gave me a cassette tape of Reverend Hong SungGun's lecture on finances. The lecture addressed finances from a biblical perspective. I was desperate, and so I began living according to the teachings of the Bible.

And to my amazement, in just four and a half years, I had paid off all 5 billion won of my debt. When I began living according to the Word of God, I began to see His words unfold in my life exactly as He said."

As she finished speaking, I turned my eyes to the audience. I could see that they had switched sides, from Team Hong SungGun to Team Kim MiJin. As I observed them, I sensed the following cry emanating from their hearts:

How could Hong SungGun—a pastor, a man who has never been in debt—understand what is weighing on our hearts! Kim MiJin, the woman who has suffered immensely under huge debt, but repaid it all by obeying the Word, will be able to understand us.

From that day forward, I began receiving fewer and fewer requests for lectures on finances while requests for Sister Kim MiJin's lectures came flooding in!

I happened to meet a well-respected and robust church elder, renowned as one of the world's top 100 scientists. When I spoke with him on the issue of debt, he asked me this question:

"Reverend Hong, do you think it is possible to do business without debt in today's capitalist world?"

"Taking on debt to do business goes against the principles of God's Word," I said sternly.

But in reality, debt is a severe problem. The church elder's question is a glaring one presented to every Christian living in this modern world.

In the kingdom of Hell, the devil relentlessly presses his advisors to come up with strategies so that he might strengthen his domain. To achieve his goal, the devil needs a strategy capable of eliminating the threat which the church and Christians pose to his kingdom. The devil's advisers have presented numerous strategies over the past two millennia with no success. But an adviser named 'mammon,' who was held in the highest regard among all of the devil's advisers, put forth a new strategy: to put the church and Christians in debt.

"I read the Bible (Demons also read the Bible; it is simply that they do not obey. see Jas. 2:19), and the best way is for us to put them in debt. Once they are indebted, they will become slaves to the lender. In Proverbs 22:7, it is stated, 'the borrower is slave to the lender.' Once they are in debt, neither can they be slaves of Christ Jesus, nor a threat to our kingdom. So let us put make them go into debt," said mammon.

His words angered the devil.

"That makes no sense! The Bible states its principles clearly. This will never work!"

"Let me try once," mammon responded. "I will start by pulling one man into debt, then one more, and then another. I will make it normal for people to be in debt."

His strategy worked. At first, people were terrified about going into debt. Yet slowly but surely, debt became the norm. And today we find ourselves asking questions like, "Is it even possible to do business without debt?" This is precisely mammon's strategy.

God's Command to Breathe Life Back into the Christians and Churches of This Age

A church invited Kim MiJin to speak.

"Could you come to speak at our church? We will provide you with two hours on Sunday afternoon."

"Two hours is not enough."

"Then how many hours will you need for your lecture?"

"At least two 90-minute sessions over four days."

The church administrator was surprised by the request, asking if there really was so much to say about money. The second request—that the title of the event be "finance revival" and not "finance seminar"—shocked the administrator even further. No "finance revivals" had ever been held at that church.

When Sister Kim MiJin was at a church in Busan for a lecture, an elder from the church pulled her aside.

"You've come to tell us the things our senior pastor cannot say to our faces, haven't you?"

She replied, "Elder, please sit in the very front row. And if you hear me mention the word 'offering' even once, tell me."

Following her lecture, that very elder became a staunch supporter of Kim MiJin. These are some examples of the ways we are changing the nature of church gatherings.

The financial lecture videos uploaded on YouTube have accrued more than 100 million views to date. All this is only possible because the Holy Spirit is moving the heart of His church. It is He, the Holy Spirit, who moves the church.

Currently, the Korean church stands at a critical fork

in the road and must choose a direction. Will the Korean church revive itself, or will it collapse; will it be used in God's works, or will it be rendered powerless? The Lord has said that the key to revival in the church is in 'finances.' This is the command God has given to breathe life back into the Christians and churches of this age.

Four Editing Guidelines

First, is it biblical?

Whether it be NCMN (Nations-Changer Movement & Network)'s school or seminars, or any of its other ministries, all NCMN ministries are carried out based on a biblical foundation. In this book, as well, we prioritized a biblical foundation above all else.

When people share their testimonies, they will often quote the Bible to support what is being said. But in writing this book, our first priority was to listen to God's words through the Bible; it began with obedience to His Word. This book is an account of the events that took place in the lives of people as a result of their obedience. In sound faith, Scripture and obedience always come before all else.

Second, is it the truth?

I scrutinized the events that occurred in the lives of people who had heard Kim MiJin and her lectures and then lived out these teachings in their lives exactly as they were taught. Everything had to be the truth. Half-truths or even exaggerations were strictly forbidden. The testimonies enclosed in this book are all 100 percent truth.

Third, are they living in obedience to the Word?

Some make grandiose claims but remain just that. This is true on both an individual and a community level. I have no interest in such words. God's kingdom is not in words but in power. The author of this book works closely with me as a ministry partner, serving as OD (Operation Director) in NCMN. As a result, I can examine her life up close. What is striking about her life is its transparency. She treasures truthfulness above all else. In other words, she speaks what she is living.

Fourth, can this book be beneficial for all?

Jesus tells us, "I have come that they may have life, and have it to the full" (John 10:10). This is the power of the Gospel and the spirit of Christianity. This book will not only bring tremendous benefit to individuals, families, communities, and businesses, it will even benefit entire nations.

NCMN is an organization that leads the Christian Civilization Reform Movement. Its purpose is to establish God's kingdom on this earth. Its mission is to fulfill this purpose together with churches and various Christian organizations. This book will make the greatest contribution to achieving this purpose.

The first book of *The King's Finances* influenced many

lives. In this second book, we recorded the stories of those who were influenced by *The King's Finances* and of those who, through training, lived it out in their lives. I have high hopes for this book. I foresee that this book will spark a revival in the Korean church, not only paving the way to reunification of the Koreas, but also enabling the Korean church to play a major role in creating a Korea which serves the world.

Hong SungGun

> Prologue

Stories from the Lives of Those Who Have Lived Out the King's Finances

The Return of the Unbelievers and the Disheartened
In the first volume of *The King's Finances*, I explained the purpose of writing the book. It was because God had told me that, through this book, the disheartened and the unbelieving would return to Him. He said that He would be their hope and that He would perform new work through them. Below is the last paragraph from the foreword of the first book.

"This book is the first account of *The King's Finances* written by Kim MiJin, a student of Rev. Hong SungGun. The second account will be continued by new students who have heard Rev. Hong's and my lectures. It will contain the stories of how they witnessed God's promises unfold precisely as written, how they were able to break the chains of wealth, and how the structure of their wealth was transformed by living a life of faith. Let us wait in anticipation of the wondrous expansion of the kingdom of God that will take place through them!"

Five years have passed since.

This happened during a King's Finances Revival Conference at the Onnuri Love Church in Daegu. Among the audience on the first day of the conference, there was a devout Buddhist mystic from Palgongsan Mountain. She said that she had come to see Kim MiJin in person after having come across her book and videos. She decided to become a believer of Christ at the conference and now attends church.

On the second day of the conference, another devout Buddhist mystic came to listen to the lecture. On the third day, a very highly respected Buddhist mystic from Taebaeksan Mountain was also in the audience. And on the fourth day, a mystic called the "Shaman of Applause" came to listen to the lecture as well.

On the third day, Reverend Hong SungGun invited these mystics to the stage and anointed them with prayer. We all stretched out our hands and joined the prayer. During this prayer, the eyes of the Buddhist mystic from Palgongsan Mountain opened wide before shutting again. She repeated this three times; my spiritual senses could feel that the Lord had done something to her.

When I asked her what happened during the prayer, she told me:

"The ground shook and split open; my body fell through the earth and then rose back to the sky." She asked what it was that she was seeing: when she opened her eyes out of fear, she could see that the ground was still there but as soon as closed her eyes she would experience the same thing again.

Since this experience, she has repented for converting people to Buddhism. She also bought 100 copies of *The King's Finances*, giving them out and sharing the Gospel with Buddhists as an evangelist.

I saw God's stunning plan and His goodness in how transforming one mystic led then to the return of many mystics back to the Lord (I now call our former mystic attendees Christian sisters and use the term "Auntie": Auntie Palgongsan, Auntie Taebaeksan, Auntie Gyeryongsan, Auntie Gayasan, Auntie Sokrisan, Auntie Seoraksan, Auntie Myanmar, and Auntie Toronto). They have written down their testimonies and sent them to us.

30 Years a Buddhist, Auntie Palgongsan Returns — Kim YangSook

I am SiYeon (granddaughter)'s 73-year-old grandmother. I met the Lord after 30 years of attending Buddhist temples. My husband is a pharmacist and we led a comfortable life until he was the victim of fraud and we went into great financial hardship. It was because of this experience that every word of Kim MiJin's lectures struck a chord with me.

I stood with great remorse before the Lord for having led most of my acquaintances to Buddhism throughout my life. My entire family is Buddhist, so I began evangelizing my family by sending a copy of The King's Finances to my older sister and her husband and telling them about the lecture videos. But she was a more devout Buddhist than I was; I assumed that it would be impossible to lead her to church.

While this continued, my older sister was suddenly hospitalized at a big medical center in Seoul. I sent a request to Sister Kim MiJin for her to visit my sister in the hospital. After her visit, Kim MiJin left an envelope with my sister. Inside this envelope, she had enclosed one million won. Shocked, my sister said to me:

"Is Kim MiJin an angel? How do Christians live like that?"

That very day, my sister began reading her book and watching her videos.

"God is a much greater god than Buddha. I should believe in this Jesus god," my sister said after she had watched and read everything. She and her husband have been faithfully attending church since her release from the hospital.

I have now evangelized my son, daughter-in-law, grandchildren, and siblings and am living in inexpressible joy. Throughout my remaining life, my mission is to spread the Gospel to the ends of the earth.

— One day, Auntie Palgongsan came to meet Reverend

Hong and me in order to share her testimony. Her hands were full of the food that she had cooked for us. "Pastor, I have been sharing the book and videos with Buddhists, and one by one, as though it were a chain reaction, they have been attending church. God is amazing. She is using me, a mystic, to evangelize other mystics." SiYeon's grandmother is an elegant beauty who is incredibly loyal. She never fails to say, "Thank you. Thank you," every time she sees me and still makes food for Reverend Hong and me every week.

Seven YouTube students (people who have received finance training through my YouTube videos) attended my lecture at the Tongyeong Modern Church. They had formed a small group through which they were training themselves financially. As I sat and ate with them, I heard an amazing testimony. They told me that a deaconess among them was leading prayer meetings so that they could put the lessons from the YouTube videos into action. Moreover, they were putting into practice God's command which tells us, "Do not focus on money. First, seek His kingdom and His righteousness in your life."

The seven students told me that each of them had taken on the responsibility of praying for and serving one Buddhist both materially and emotionally. They told me that six of the seven Buddhists have returned to the Lord and the remaining one was at the lecture. I was greatly encouraged to hear that the remaining one also returned to the Lord following the lecture.

I received news that some YouTube students would be attending the lecture at the Daegu Full Gospel Church with a few Buddhist mystics. But it was not just a few mystics: 20 of them, from all over the country had come to listen to the lecture. After the talk, a small group gathered in the senior pastor's room for fellowship. The room was filled with Buddhist mystics. Thinking about that day still puts a smile on my face. That day, I got a glimpse of God's heart, His heart which values a single soul more than the entire universe.

I met a Buddhist mystic during a conference at the Toronto Korean Presbyterian Church. She was also a businesswoman: she was the owner of a massage parlor. She had brought over numerous Buddha statues from Korea to Canada as her dream was to build a Buddhist temple in Toronto. The wife of the pastor of that church had always kept the mystic in her prayers. But after reading *The King's Finances* herself, she gifted a copy to the mystic and prayed for her fervently.

She asked the mystic to attend the King's Finances Revival for just one day, but the mystic never came. Instead, she read the book and took a liking to the author, Kim MiJin. The mystic told the pastor's wife that she would like to offer a free 90-minute massage to the author so as to help with travel fatigue and asked if the author would be okay receiving a massage from a mystic.

I immediately thought, This is my chance. I went to the

massage parlor with the pastor and his wife. When I got there, I said to the mystic: "I'm not here for the massage; I am here to see you in person. You promised me 90-minutes, so how about we talk for that time over a cup of tea?"

We began talking, sitting across from each other. During our conversation, the Lord showed me the mystic's past and future. I saw the hardships she had endured; I saw the scars of how people had hurt her. I told her exactly what the Lord had placed on my heart.

"You are not meant to build a Buddhist temple; you are meant to build a church as a believer of Jesus Christ."

Tears began rolling down her face. I urged her to attend the conference later that night before returning to my hotel. When I arrived to give my lecture, I saw that the mystic was there, sitting in the front row. She had changed her ways as a mystic and returned as a child of God on that very day! Today, she is living a beautiful life of faith, diligently attending every single church service, even including the dawn services at her church.

Auntie Toronto, Who Gave Up on Building a Buddhist Temple
Park GyeongEun

Ten years ago, I arrived in Canada with many Buddha statues intending to build a small temple in Toronto. But as soon as I arrived, I was defrauded and lost everything I owned. As a result, I was in immense economic hardship.

Living through those troubled days, I had to postpone my plans to build a temple.

Then one day, the wife of the pastor of the Korean church, who I had known for some time, handed me *The King's Finances* and told me I should read it and attend the revival conference where the author herself would be speaking. I was not interested and declined. But reading through the book, I came to understand that she is a good person who does good deeds. I wanted to treat her to a massage to help ease her travel fatigue. So, I invited her to my massage parlor.

When she came to my shop, I listened to her stories. I then attended her lecture at the church that very night. I sat in an empty seat at the very front. The author's words about 'Abraham's seed' made their way straight into my heart. From a distance, I heard a sound.

What do you have to show for yourself?

I mumbled to myself, Yes, what do I have to show for myself? That instant, tears began streaming uncontrollably down my face. I bowed my head, and out of habit, I began quietly chanting a prayer to Avalokiteśvara.[2] It had become such an ingrained habit that I forgot I was in a church and continued to chant the prayer quietly for some time. I had never been inside a church in my life; I did not know what I was supposed to do.

---

[2] A bodhisattva who embodies the compassion of all Buddhas.

Quite sometime later, when I lifted my head back up, I felt as though the cross hanging in the sanctuary was coming towards me at great speed. Suddenly, I heard another sound.

'It's okay, be still!'

I returned home after the tearful lecture. Feeling like I must do something, I began by inviting the church pastor to dispose of all the Buddha statues that I owned. Having gotten rid of the statues, when I prayed I felt as though I sensed a voice saying, 'Read the Bible,' 'Save your mother,' 'Save your siblings.' Any time I had a question, the Holy Spirit answered with Scripture and showed me God's kingdom as a kind counselor would.

God forgave and accepted me; me, a woman who was planning on building a Buddhist temple. Now, I am getting to know His endless and abounding love. I am living a life of faith, still attending the church where Kim MiJin gave her lectures. My son and daughter in Korea have also accepted the Lord Jesus as their Christ and Savior. I will spread Jesus' Gospel until my dying breath.

— Auntie Toronto came to visit the King's Finances School in Seoul briefly. She told me that she was in Korea to share the Gospel with her mother who was sick in the hospital. She then thanked me for introducing her to the joy of salvation. We still keep in touch from time to time.

As the Lord said in *The King's Finances* Volume I, we are witnessing the fruit of our work in the return of the unbelievers and the disheartened. All glory belongs to, and only to, our Lord.

My Son Returns from a Cult Lee ChoonJa

I am Chinese of Korean descent. The Lord that I knew of was a scary and fearsome God who punishes and mercilessly whips people for their transgressions. That was the only God I knew, so I taught my children the same. As a result, my son joined a cult, drank and smoked, and there was not a day of peace or joy in our home. Every day, I felt an immense sense of guilt, emptiness. There was a tremendous heaviness weighing on my heart.

In 2017, I heard Sister Kim MiJin's moving testimony in an online lecture. Through it, I rediscovered a God who is kind, gracious, and loving in nature. I cried and cried. I listened to her lectures every day and began implementing the teachings in my life. I trained to live as a faithful servant with whom the Lord would be pleased. I wanted to become a disciple of Christ and dreamed of healing my family.

Then, I began taking courses at the King's Finances School and embarked upon the "Living It Out Project." The Lord is pleased when we serve the poor. As much as my means would allow, I served the poor by cooking meals at home and taking them to the less fortunate. I began addressing my husband and children with Jesus' gracious character. This "project" transformed my family in just eight months. My husband was promoted from his position as a subcontractor to a regular position at a large conglomerate, K Motors.

Moreover, my son, who had been involved in a cult for three years, came back to the Lord. After my children experienced the Holy Spirit in NCMN's Hero Camp, they quit drinking and smoking and used their extra money to serve the poor. My daughter is now serving as a project leader in a relief ministry.

One time, we walked out of our home with only five rice balls. That was all we had at the time. We met five homeless people. And those five rice balls were neither too much nor too little; they were just enough. It was God's way of encouraging us. Although it may seem insignificant, the experience helped my children mature in their faith.

I have faith that my children will be a good influence on society and will be used as part of a generation that changes the culture of the world to one of Christian values. We will continue to spread the Gospel faithfully to those who do not know Christ. I praise the Lord, who healed and completely transformed my family.

— Sister Lee ChoonJa is a woman of astonishing faith. It broke my heart to see her get hurt as a result of the unhealthy words that she would receive in her interactions with other Chinese of Korean descent. But at the same time, I am thankful that the Korean church continues to serve that community. I experienced firsthand that it is the Lord who can free her son from the powerful hold of cults. I hope that the example of this family provides hope to other families that are currently struggling with family members who are members of cults.

Observing Cheondojae[3] for Eight Years Jung JiSoo

I grew up in a family of devout Buddhists. My grandfather even built a Buddhist temple. During the Asian Financial Crisis, my family struggled to make ends meet as a result of the debts for which we were the guarantor. Although we diligently observed cheondojae several times a year for eight years hoping that it would turn our financial distress around, our struggles persisted.

Around that time, a friend of mine strongly recommended that I read *The King's Finances*. I bought the book, hoping that maybe it could provide some insight into ways of earning money. I finished the entire book in one sitting and learned some truths that I would never have come across as a Buddhist.

The first of these truths was that Christianity is a religion that believes not in man but in an almighty God who is real. Second, salvation only comes from Jesus. Third, that if I repent and return to the Lord, I too will be saved and eligible to receive Abraham's blessing. Fourth was

---

[3] A Buddhist rite that is held to send the spirit of the dead to the afterlife.

the biblical way of earning and spending money. Fifth, I understood the reasons my struggles did not stop despite the fact that I was making money.

While reading *The King's Finances*, I discovered the secret of the kingdom of Heaven. I was drawn to lectures on biblical financial principles. After searching and seeking out these videos, I became a Christian. Converting to Christianity, an amazing religion that teaches belief in God Almighty, filled me with immense hope.

In one of her lectures, Kim MiJin said: "The faithful one is the one that multiplies." I wanted to be faithful to God. I could not just sit and watch my family members going to Hell. This stirred up a passion up in for saving souls. I became determined to evangelize my husband, my youngest daughter, as well as my mother and sister, who were both devout Buddhists. I wanted to multiply the salvation that had been given to me so that I may help wipe away the tears God was shedding for lost souls.

I prayed and prayed again, longing for God's grace. The Lord answered my prayers, and now my entire family is attending church and serving the Lord. I am radically changing my master to God and God only through NCMN's King's Finances School and seminars, which I began attending to gain a deeper understanding of God.

My financial situation also began to improve slowly as I started implementing the biblical principles I had learned in the King's Finances School. But most importantly, I thank the Lord for graciously allowing my entire family to return

to Him.
— I met Sister Jung JiSoo in person. Many around me have heard stories proving the truth of her testimony. Hallelujah!

I will continue to share the stories of people who overcame their financial obstacles and began to dream of the kingdom of God with the King's Finances training program in the main text of this book. The total volume of testimonies collected in NCMN alone numbers close to 50,000. We could produce volumes and volumes of books if we attempted to record them all in a series.

I would like to thank my teacher, Reverend Hong, who set up all the biblical foundations for the King's Finances ministries. I thank my family, NCMN ministry partners, and all the King's Finances School and YouTube students for living out the teachings diligently together.

The Lord has said that *The King's Finances II* is His gift to the Korean church. It is my deepest wish that the Korean church is strengthened with the King's Finances and that this country prepares for reunification, becoming a Korea that serves to the ends of the earth.

Kim MiJin

Editor's Notes 5
Prologue 16

Part I Experience God's Supernatural Provision

Chapter 1 Supernatural Movement of Wealth 38
- Feed My Sheep 39
- Dedicating My All in the Wilderness 43
- 210 Million 46
- The Movement of Wealth for a 30-Pyeong Apartment 50
- The Movement of a Wealth of 15 Billion 51
- The Movement of Wealth Through Relationships 54
- He Opens the Doors to a New Business 57
- OREGIN, A Gift from God 59
- God Owns 100 Percent 62

Chapter 2 Do You Truly Want to Become Rich (A Holy Rich Person)? 64
- Reborn a True Rich Ma 65
- From Debtor to Holy Rich 67
- God's Mathematical Equation 72
- Breakthroughs Come from Training 75
- Becoming a Kitchen Aide 80
- From Owner to Employee 84
- Rainbow 87
- Be in the Place of and Within the Methods of God's Provision 89
- The Courage to Stand on the Edge of a Cliff 93

Contents

Chapter 3 A Life of Faith — 100
    God Shows the Next Step to Those Who Obey — 101
    How a Luxury Watch Became a Luxury Car — 104
    What People Whom God Uses Have in Common — 106
    The Turning Point in My Ministry — 109
    Do Not Limit the Power of God — 115
    Carried in on the Back of Another, Walked out on One's Own Feet — 118
    The God Who Brought Me Back to Life — 119

    A Brief Introduction to The King's Finances Implementation Workbook — 123

Part II Restore a Life of the Altar and the Tent

Chapter 1 There Are Three Seasons to God's Provision — 136
    The Season for Supernatural Provision — 137
    The Season in Which He Feeds Me the Work of Others' Hands — 140
    The Season to Harvest and Eat What I Have Sown — 141
    A Budget Plan of Faith — 143

Chapter 2	**Abraham's Seed, Solomon the Worldly Rich, David the Godly Rich**	150
	Transplant Abraham's Spiritual DNA	151
	Two Strands of DNA in Abraham's Life (A Life of the Altar and the Tent)	152
	Two Strands of Abraham's Spiritual DNA (Faith and Faithfulness)	154
	Why Did I Fail?	156
	Single Determination	161
	The Worldly Rich Solomon's Attitude Toward Riches	166
	The Holy Rich David's Attitude Toward Riches	169
	My Life as a Holy Rich Person Finally Begins	172
Chapter 3	**The Six Rules of Life**	176
	The Correct Relationship with God, People, and Riches	177
	Two Rules on Our Relationship with God	177
	Two Rules on Our Relationship with People	181
	Two Rules on Our Relationship with Riches	184
	Becoming a Multiplier of the King's Finances	185
Chapter 4	**Is My Arm Too Short?**	198
	Remove the Foreign Rabble Within Yourselves	199
	Now Is Not the Time to Ask for Meat	200
	You Will Eat Meat when He Has Enlarged Your Territory	202
	The Mighty Power of the Execution Workbook	206
	Things Just Seem to Work Out for You	210
Chapter 5	**The Heavenly Bank = Good Soil**	214
	The Poor	215
	Tithes	221

3.3 Percent — The Blessing of "the Other Tithes"	225
The Two Blessings of Tithes	227

Part III Look After the Poor

Chapter 1 The Miracle of the Five Loaves and Two Fishes Continues to This Day — 232

- Give Them Something to Eat — 233
- The Lord Does Not Take What You Do Not Have — 235
- Must I Close Shop on Sundays? — 239
- King's Finances Training for the Whole Family — 243
- About This Time Tomorrow, I Will Turn Around and See You — 252
- Taking Ownership of God's Promise in Faith — 255
- Treating My Leprous Spirit by Restoring the Love I First Had — 258
- The Characteristics of the Wilderness — 260

Chapter 2 Solicit a Visit from God — 264

- A Cry of Desperation — 265
- The Way God Works: He Sends the Hornets — 266
- Train! Train! And Train Again! — 269
- Characteristics of God-Given Riches — 273
- Keywords for Moving the Riches of Heaven – Uprightness — 277
- Keywords for Moving the Riches of Heaven – Diligence — 279
- God Rebukes My Dishonesty — 281

Chapter 3 Those Under Mammon's Captivity 284
    Judas Iscariot 285
    Achan 285
    Gehazi: The Servant of Elisha 288
    Ananias and Sapphira 291
    Give Me Back My Donations 292
    The Worldly Rich 2 293
    The Life of the Worldly Rich Who Have Been Captured by Mammon 298

Part IV Awaken the Next Generation of Faith

Chapter 1 The Secret to a Life of Contentment 304
    Be Content 305
    Stop Practicing Usury 308
    Be Faithful with Others' Wealth 311
    The Equity of God's Kingdom 314
    Out of Debt into the Light 318
    Having Certainty with Faith 321
    Awaken the Goodness in Korea's Heart 324
    Let's Walk Together — MY 5K 326
    Fruit of the 5K Share Love Movement 332

Chapter 2 The Kingdom of God vs. the Kingdom of the World 336
    There is No Middle Ground for the Believer 337
    Pass on the Inheritance of Holy Riches to Your Children 338
    Awaken the Next and Not a Different Generation 339

The Obedience of Sacrificing Isaac	341
The Heroes of the Hero Camp	343
The Light of the Word Looses Bound Children	345
I Have Been Transformed by the King's Finances School for Kids	347
Children Who Come as Unbelievers and Return as Devotees	349
Heroes Come to Camp Prepared	351
The Name That Was Not Erased for Three Days	354

Epilogue 358
Final Words 366
About NCMN Ministries 376

Part I
Experience God's Supernatural Provision

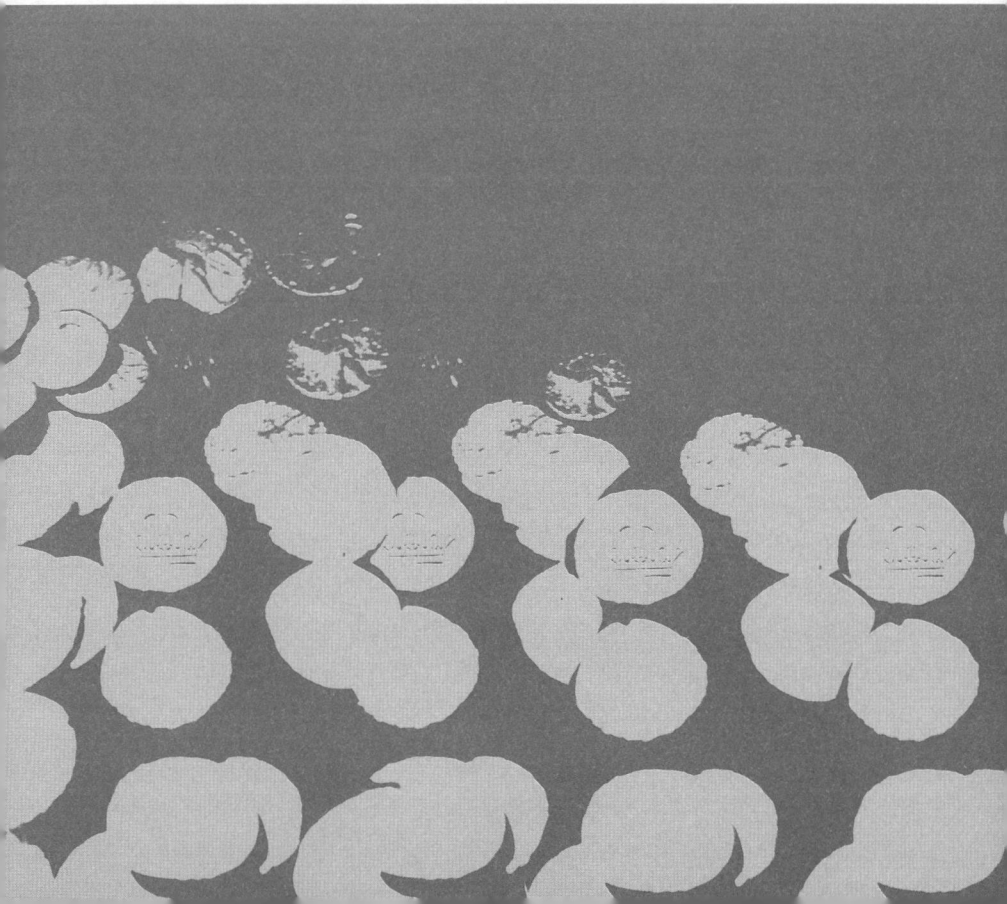

CHATPER 1

Supernatural Movement of Wealth

PART I Experience God's Supernatural Provision

Do you believe in the supernatural movement of wealth? I do. I know from experience.

Feed My Sheep
For ten years, I was taught humility in the wilderness of life. My greatest gain from the experience was that I became a seed of Abraham. I declared:

"I am the one who will carry on Abraham's inheritance; I have inherited all of Abraham's blessings!"

One day in the wilderness, God encouraged me with these words: My daughter, I will make you prosper. You will sit with the nobles.

> The Lord sends poverty and wealth; he humbles and he exalts. He raises the poor from the dust and lifts the needy from the ash heap; he seats them with princes and has them inherit thrones of honor. For the foundations of the earth are the Lord's; on them he has set the world 1 Sam. 2:7-8

In my destitution and desperation out in the middle of the wilderness, the Lord visited me. One day, He asked me this question: Do you love me? Then feed my sheep.

The first thought that came to my mind was, How should I feed them? I have nothing. But God told me to feed the sheep with the Word and nutritious food. When I first heard this, it weighed heavily on my heart; I had no choice but to pray.

During my prayers, the Lord showed me a vision of me traveling to the ends of the earth with a large suitcase. In hindsight, the wilderness was where I restored a closeness with God and received a new vision.

> This is what the Lord says to his anointed, to Cyrus, whose right hand I take hold of to subdue nations before him and to strip kings of their armor, to open doors before him so that gates will not be shut: I will go before you and will level the mountains; I will break down gates of bronze and cut through bars of iron. I will give you hidden treasures, riches stored in secret places, so that you may know that I am the Lord, the God of Israel, who summons you by name Isa. 45:1-3

'How do I provide them nutritious food?'

I labored over this question but did not have a solution. Yet through His Word, God instructed me to continue to meditate quietly on His being God.

> When the Lord your God brings you into the land he swore to your fathers, to Abraham, Isaac and Jacob, to give you— a land with large, flourishing cities you did not build, houses filled with all kinds of good things you did not provide, wells you did not dig, and vineyards and olive groves you did not plant—then when you eat and are satisfied Deut. 6:10-11

When this happens, Scripture tells us not to forget the Lord, to fear Him, and not to follow other Gods (see Deut. 6:12-15). God promised us four things through this Scripture.

> First, you will receive flourishing cities you did not build.
> Second, you will receive houses filled with all kinds of good things you did not provide.
> Third, you will receive wells you did not dig.
> Fourth, you will receive vineyards and olive groves you did not plant.

I needed to strengthen and magnify my faith to seize His promises.

'From where to begin?'

I began by studying and researching the Bible for over ten hours every day so that I could feed His sheep with the Word. Every time I had some money, I bought vitamins and sent them to the mission field. I did this for ten years, but nothing changed. Oppressed by my circumstances, I eventually grew disheartened and weary.

'Do I need to continue doing this?'

Whenever I felt that my will was breaking, I would open up my prayer journal and pick myself back up. Enduring the ten years I spent in the wilderness with no exit in sight was no easy task. But I continually resolved to find the strength in myself, held on tightly to the vision God had given me, and consistently did what was required of me every day.

Then one day, I received my first request for a lecture from Country C. I paid for the rather expensive flight ticket and made it to Country C. However, when I got to the classroom, I saw only two elderly women sitting there. In spite of the initial disappointment, I lectured about intercessory prayer and spiritual warfare for six hours a day over five days, for a total of 30 hours. After I was done with the final lecture, I asked the two elderly ladies:

"Grandma, what is intercessory prayer? What is spiritual warfare?"

She summed up my 30-hour lecture with a straightforward statement and a blank stare.

"I don't know."

I was devastated by their answer. But I did not accept defeat. When I studied how our Lord gave His sermons, I found out that the Lord delivered His sermons in such a way that everyone, from young children to old grandmothers, could easily understand and enjoy His sermons. I also paid close attention to the sermons of my teacher, Reverend Hong. His sermons had three distinct characteristics.

First, they are fun and easy to understand.
Second, he provides background information to help with understanding.

Third, for important messages, he uses reiteration by paraphrasing from different perspectives in order to convince the audience and facilitate understanding.

'Will I be able to do the same in my future lectures?'

I implemented the things I learned from my teacher in my own lectures. Although I had prepared diligently and was completely ready for my first lecture, the Lord wanted to teach me humility through the failure of my first lecture. Then, slowly and gradually, He built me up as a lecturer. After my first lecture, the classroom size increased to four, then eight, and then to 16.

For four years, I gave only four lectures. Mr. Ha GapCheon (Director of Maum Care Hospital), who was sitting in that classroom of eight students, is now the leader of the King's Business Group in NCMN. Now, we reminisce and laugh about that day from time to time.

Dedicating My All in the Wilderness

I felt that I needed to make a considerable sacrifice to pass through the wilderness as quickly as possible. Not knowing the Lord well at the time, I dedicated everything to the Lord without much thought.

'Lord, if you let me pass through the wilderness and give me another chance, I will give everything I have back to you except for this house I am living in before my son is married.'

I thought my offering to be quite an impressive one. At the time I made this dedication, my son, YuJin, was not yet in elementary school. Time passed, and one day in October 2017, my son said to me:

"Mother, there is a lady I would like to marry."

"YuJin, how old are you now?"

"I will be 24 next year."

I could not object as I had always told him to get married at 24. And so, his wedding date was set for April 21, 2018.

'How have the years passed by so quickly?'

Something did not feel right. Every time I prayed for my son's marriage, I would be reminded of the offering I promised to make way back when. I felt that I could not delay it any longer. I began to sort out the wealth the Lord had entrusted to me. I emptied all my bank accounts and offered the money to the Lord. Any jewelry or luxury goods that were worth anything, I also offered up to the Lord. But there was one more thing the Lord had entrusted to me through supernatural ways. I did not feel comfortable keeping that either, so I returned it to the Lord.

After it was all said and done, I had less than one million won in my bank account. My son was still in college, and he did not have a home to live in once he was married. About four months before my son's wedding date, I made 20 million won through the fruits of my hard work. I told my son, who was working part-time to save up for a wedding ring:

"YuJin, all I have to give you is 20 million won. Use this money to rent a home."

"I was not expecting this, Mother. Thank you so much."

My son, YuJin, and daughter-in-law, JuHee, were touched by my gesture and very grateful. These two had seen me dispose of all my wealth and thus had not been expecting to receive anything from me. I asked a fellow believer who was a realtor to help me find a home for my son. She found a 15 pyeong[4] apartment for long-term lease for 240 million won and said that she could get the price down to 230 million won. I told her I did not have the money, so we settled on a deposit of 20 million won, and a monthly rent of 600,000 won. After we had sorted out the apartment, my son and daughter-in-law bought the necessities for their home with the two million won that my mother had earned selling pickled seafood and sent to them. A missionary friend gave them her old bed and closet, and anything else that was needed for the house my son and daughter-in-law bought secondhand. They did the interior work on their own and, after spending only 1.8 million won on their home in total, had done an excellent job of tidying up the place. I thought they had done an admirable job.

Then, out of the blue, the landlord called me and said that the rent agreement needed to be changed to a long-term lease agreement as her daughter had suddenly decided

---

[4] A *pyeong* is a Korean unit of area and floorspace, equal to 3.3058 m^2.

to get married. As I had already given her 20 million won as the deposit, she asked that I pay her an additional 210 million won. I did not have it in me to tell my child to look for a different home.

210 Million

I began to pray systematically and wrote down my prayer requests in my prayer journal.

⟨March 1st, 2018 Prayer⟩

First,	Father, give me 210 million won.
Second,	I believe that you have answered my prayers for the 210 million won. I dedicate myself to you.
	Show me grace so that I, too, may be a channel through which a house flows to one of your servants. (until March 1st, 2019)
Third,	Provide me with 35 million won to pay for the venue rental fees and other expenses for the wedding.

I wrapped up my prayer with, 'Father, please withdraw the deposits I have made into the Heavenly Bank until now.' As the wedding date drew closer, I grew more and more anxious. And toward the end of March, I received a "flowing card" while running the King's Finances School.

Item	210 million won
Recipient	Sister Kim MiJin
Purpose	I flow 210 million won to Sister Kim MiJin for Brother YuJin's long-term lease deposit

My heart skipped a beat when I saw the card. Up until that point, I had told no one that I had been praying for 210 million won.

'But how…? I've told no one but the Lord.'

I found the person who wrote that card. Hearing their story, I was nothing short of shocked.

They had registered in the 12th session of the King's Finances School as a couple in Fall 2017. The husband could not complete the coursework due to his work schedule, but the wife had completed the course. After she had graduated, the couple began their training on finances. Then one day, the wife and husband heard the voice of the Lord.

'Who is your master? Where do you place your sense of stability?'

The couple replied, "Jesus, You are our master. Our stability lies only in You, Jesus."

But while engaging in prayer, they came to realize that their sense of stability lay in their total assets of 400 million won. Upon this realization, they came clean before the Lord.

"Lord, our sense of stability comes from our net worth of

400 million won."

The Lord spoke to the couple.

'Bring it to me. From now on, I will be your sense of stability.'

The two pondered upon the best way to respond to God's voice. The couple decided that they would pray separately and if they heard the same voice during their prayers they would both know that it was the voice of God and give the money to whom the Lord directed.

"Father, to whom should we give our entire net worth of 400 million won?"

Prayer Notes ⟨400 million⟩

	Wife	Husband
Amount	210 million won	Two hundred and ten million
To Whom	Brother YuJin	

The wife spoke:

"I heard the Lord say that we should give 210 of the 400 million won to Sister MiJin's son Brother YuJin."

The husband responded:

"Whenever I prayed, 'Two hundred and ten million' came to my mind so that I thought 'Give it to Lee EokCheon (This name has the same pronunciation with Two hundred and ten million in Korean).' However, from what you are saying, it was Two hundred and ten million won. Now I got it."

At that time, my husband belonged to a small group and

his leader's name was 'Lee EokCheon.'

The husband and wife told me that they gained a much deeper understanding of God's wondrous ways by praying and sharing their prayers with each other.

All I could do after hearing what the couple had to say was to be in awe of God's provision. I was touched by God's attention to detail. I started praying on March 1st, 2018. The couple had been praying since after they had heard the voice of God in late Fall 2017. This experience strengthened my trust in Him, He who provides the best for me when I obey Him in everything.

I was endlessly grateful to the couple who had allowed me to relive the joy of The God of Sulwhasoo (*The King's Finances I*, English translation, p.106). When I showed my prayer journal to the husband, his eyes welled up with tears. He said that they were not, at first, able to understand God's voice.

"Sister Kim MiJin is a holy rich woman. Why would she need the money?"

"Why, of all people, is the Lord directing us to give the money to her?"

The Lord was not telling them to give the money to the poor, a church in need of funds, or a mission project, but to give it to me. They felt quite uncomfortable doing so. Nevertheless, they obeyed the Lord, and the Lord created a beautiful and amazing testimony through the couple.

This experience also challenged me and provided the opportunity for me to improve my understanding of what it means to live by faith.

The Movement of Wealth for a 30-Pyeong Apartment

The second prayer request in the March 2018 entry of my prayer journal says, "I believe that you have answered my prayers for the 210 million won. I dedicate myself to you. Show me grace that I too may be a channel that flows a house to one of your servants (by March 1st, 2019)."

The reason that I could pray so boldly was that I had saved in the Heavenly Bank throughout my life, and I believed that God would surely answer all my needs. God provides for the lives of those who give even more generously. And I believed in His promise.

"Give, and you will receive. Your gift will return to you in full—pressed down, shaken together to make room for more, running over, and poured into your lap. The amount you give will determine the amount you get back" (Luke 6:38, New Living Translation).

God answered in miraculous ways, and in December 2018, I was able to purchase and gift a 30 pyeong apartment. The holy poor person, who had the apartment flowed to them through me, experienced a **supernatural movement of wealth** (There is a witness to this story. A believer was in charge of the entire process, from the purchase of the property to the transfer of the property title).

My third prayer request was, "Provide me with 35 million won for venue rental fees and other expenses for the wedding." God provided for this in surprising ways as well. I was at a church to lecture at their mission school when the senior pastor of the church, whom I had always admired, handed me five million won to use for my son's wedding on top of the speaking fee. I did not know how to respond. A holy poor person was flowing his wealth to me. Thanks to the generosity of such people, my son was able to have a wedding under the grace of God.

In the King's Finances School, there are many who lead dynamic lives. Such small and large movements of wealth have taken place over 10,000 times until now.

The Movement of Wealth Worth 15 Billion

One day, a Chinese person who was not very fluent in Korean came to see me. After introducing himself as the secretary of the CEO of a Chinese company, he told me that he had a message for me from the CEO.

Around five years ago, the CEO and his family had been planning to end their own lives because the company filed for bankruptcy. At that time, someone told the CEO about The King's Finances and lecture videos. The CEO's mother was of Korean descent and the father Han Chinese, so the CEO was able to speak a little Korean.

The CEO read the book after having it translated into Chinese. Then, he watched and studied the videos, which ultimately moved him so much that he decided to give life another try.

Then, he made this promise to God: I will become a holy rich man and dedicate an offering of ten million won to the kingdom of God for every single lecture I have watched. The CEO stored my lecture videos on a USB and watched one every day for three years. And now, his secretary was in my office to pay for the lectures.

The secretary told me that he had come to Korea to transfer the deeds of seven buildings, each of which was worth around 2 billion won. I was shocked! What magnanimity! I collected the documents and took them to Reverend Hong.

"Pastor Hong, this is the payment I've received for my lectures. Please use it where you see fit."

Pastor Hong and I even have a picture holding the seven documents in memory of that day. After spending some time in prayer, Pastor Hong said, "We must use this money for Chinese and global missions." And like that, 100 percent of that wealth was flown to China and other nations.

"Lead the Christian Civilization Reform Movement!"

This is NCMN's mission statement. To achieve this mission, NCMN bought a 50,000 pyeong parcel of land in Gosung, Gangwondo, on which it will build a vision center. Currently, specific projects for the founding of ministries such as the Youth and Young Adult Hero Camp, ministers' training, pastors' training, Christian elementary, middle, and high schools are underway. Although NCMN is also in need of funds, Pastor Hong decided it best to use the money to spread the Gospel in China. After I witnessed him make such a tough decision, my respect for him grew even more profound.

These testimonies are only a fraction of all the amazing events that have taken place. Praise the Lord, who does amazing work among us! I look forward to offering seven trillion won to the kingdom of God so that it may be used for reunification ministries. Even on this very day, I am working hard and striving towards this goal.

How would we define a supernatural movement of wealth? It is not wealth that suddenly lands in our laps. It is wealth that is supplied from beyond our capabilities. For example, a businessman who was never able to make a net profit of over ten million won, no matter how well he ran his business relying on his own strength and skills, is able to accumulate a monthly profit of 50 million or even 100 million won when God gives him the ability to produce wealth.

God sends us the wealth of foreign nations. He moves hidden treasures and riches stored in secret places.

"But remember the Lord your God, for it is he who gives you the ability to produce wealth" (Deut. 8:18).

"With my great power and outstretched arm I made the earth and its people and the animals that are on it, and I give it to anyone I please" (Jer. 27:5).

If we are seen as upright in God's eyes, there will most certainly be a breakthrough in our finances.

The Movement of Wealth Through Relationships   Kim NamYeon

I left the company in Tokyo I had been working in for 23 years to start my own business. While I was preparing for this new venture, I learned about the King's Finance School through Kim HyeYoung who was involved in the school. During training, I saw how little faith I had and realized just how great the scale of my debt was. The training, however, was extremely intense, and I was continuously looking for excuses to get out of the program. Suddenly, I found my opportunity to escape. The economic association I was involved in was holding a global conference in Korea, and I also had some business I needed to attend to in Korea.

Moreover, attempting to attend all the training and outreach programs meant that I would have to return to Japan three times throughout my business trip to Korea. Regardless, I could not bring myself to skip the training and thus completed the coursework with the 1st session of the King's Finances School, albeit with much difficulty and at great cost.

I then prayed that I would become a holy rich person so that I might aid in finding a new sanctuary for our church that was holding services in less than ideal conditions. I also prayed that God would place the people I need for my business in my life and that He would provide me with a brilliant business idea.

This happened while I was attending a seminar in Osaka for the ultrasound machines I am currently selling. When the seminar ended, I wanted to get dinner with two former

PART I Experience God's Supernatural Provision

colleagues. We stepped out of the hotel and stood by a crosswalk, waiting for a taxi.

Next to me, there was a little control box for the traffic lights, and sitting on top of that box, was a bag, a perfectly normal-looking bag. I thought it was strange that someone would leave such a nice bag there. My colleague suggested that we immediately take it to the police station, but I felt a need to check its contents first. Inside the bag, there was a contract in English, a Hong Kong ID card, and a stack of business cards, which I assumed belonged to the owner of the bag.

This person could be leaving the country tomorrow. Not having this ID with him could pose a big problem for him, I thought.

As someone who often travels abroad for business, I could not just ignore the bag. So I dialed the number on the business card. The owner of the bag told me he was in a state of complete panic due to the loss of his bag. I told him the location of the hotel I was staying at, and the bag's owner was there in 15 minutes. Looking quite flustered, he began checking the contents of his bag as soon as he arrived. His expression changed to one of relief at seeing everything was there. Then finally, he checked inside a pocket in the interior of the bag.

Inside the pocket, there was what appeared to be quite a large sum of money. The exact amount was 300,000 yen (three million won), and he handed me 30,000 yen as a gesture of gratitude. I declined many times, but upon his insistence,

THE KING'S FINANCES II

I accepted the money and split it three ways with my coworkers and then paid for dinner with my 10,000 yen.

The following day, I received a call from him as I was about to board the Shinkansen[5] back to Tokyo. He told me he too would be in Tokyo for a meeting and said that he would like to see me there. We later met up in Tokyo, and I was surprised to hear why he had come to Japan. He had come looking for medical device items he could sell in his new business.

So I took the time to explain the different devices I was selling, and he seemed to be quite interested in what I had to say. He proposed that we try doing business together as he would not only be selling new products but also used medical devices.

Not long after our meeting in Tokyo, he placed an order. The purchase order was quite extensive, so I called Hong Kong to confirm this. When I asked him if he needed one of each item, he told me that he would need at least ten of each. Although it was not easy to find every product on the list, God, in his wondrous way, sent the necessary helping hands at the right time, and I was able to make the delivery. Ever since I began trying to live by the principles I learned in the King's Finances School, God has been guiding me in the most mysterious ways. In the year after I started my own business, I have come to experience numerous

---

5 The *Shinkansen*, colloquially known in English as the 'bullet train', is a network of high-speed railway lines in Japan.

miracles.

I was also able to evangelize two friends to whom I thought I would never be able to get through. All these experiences have taught me that God is indeed at work. I am looking forward to seeing how things play out in the future as I continue to live a God-centered life. I want to live this life to the fullest, so that God may be glorified through my life.

He Opens the Doors to a New Business

I founded the NC Group while praying for God's hand in starting a company that would belong to Him. The first item we produced was an "immune belt," a cordless, no-charging-necessary abdominal belt that would heat up on its own to raise body temperatures. But due to the market being flooded with knockoffs, we suffered huge losses. We could not possibly keep up with the incredibly low prices of the knockoffs; inventory overstock became a problem, and we had to fold the business and accept defeat after two consecutive years of losses.

I was humbled, thinking that the first business of a company owned by the Lord Himself had failed. Fortunately, the company had zero debt and this gave me the room to plan and prepare for the company's next venture. I took some time to stand before the Lord and analyze just why the business had failed.

"But remember the Lord your God, for it is he who gives you the ability to produce wealth" (Deut. 8:18).

As I meditated on this verse, I built up the courage to try again. Right about that time, the Lord gave me another new business opportunity. I met a YouTube student who had returned to Korea after working in the U.S. as an expatriate. The Lord told me that this student would act as a bridge for His work in the future.

As I was praying and preparing for the next season, this student arranged a meeting with the director of an American company. Although I did not know much about the man, he was introduced to me as "a man filled with the Holy Spirit who does business only for the kingdom of God."

Reverend Hong and my husband were with me when I met with Director Sam Caster for the first time. Although it was the first time I had seen him, the Lord whispered into my heart, This man is your spiritual father. Later, he took me in as his adopted daughter and we formed a father-daughter relationship. I will never forget this one question he asked me while we were talking in English.

"Sister MiJin, what is your vision?"

I answered without hesitation.

"It is to strengthen the kingdom of God through the Word, and to provide nutritious food to children around the world who are in absolute need."

Although our time together was short, it was all part of God's perfect timing. After our meeting, I discovered that he is a very well-known person around the world. He had achieved success in the global markets by producing supplements and had founded MannaRelief, a nonprofit organization providing proper nutrition to malnourished children in 140 countries around the world.

But, he told me, when the company grew, and the nutrition project came to an unexpected halt due to certain investors' lack of understanding about the project, he had no choice but to leave the company. He said that he had been praying for a ministry partner when someone told him about me. He told me that he had already developed supplements of a much higher quality and that he was looking for a business partner with the same vision. It was truly a work of God's amazing guidance!

OREGIN, A Gift from God

I prayed and deliberated for a long time over this business proposal. I approached it with caution as it was an undertaking that would require a substantial investment.

I muttered to myself: "But God can heal the sick in supernatural ways... That doesn't require money, and no one suffers..."

But when I meditated on the Word, God spoke from the deepest corners of my heart.

"Fruit trees of all kinds will grow on both banks of the river. Their leaves will not wither, nor will their fruit fail. Every month they will bear fruit, because the water from the sanctuary flows to them. Their fruit will serve for food and their leaves for healing" (Ezek. 47:12).

It was a piece of Scripture I was already familiar with, explaining the works of the Holy Spirit. But whenever I prayed about the business, the Lord continuously led me to the following verses.

"In those days Hezekiah became ill and was at the point of death. The prophet Isaiah son of Amoz went to him and said, 'This is what the Lord says: Put your house in order, because you are going to die; you will not recover.' Hezekiah turned his face to the wall and prayed to the Lord, 'Remember, Lord, how I have walked before you faithfully and with wholehearted devotion and have done what is good in your eyes.' And Hezekiah wept bitterly" (2 Kgs. 20:1-3).

"Go back and tell Hezekiah, the ruler of my people, 'This is what the Lord, the God of your father David, says: I have heard your prayer and seen your tears; I will heal you. On the third day from now you will go up to the temple of the Lord. I will add fifteen years to your life. And I will deliver you and this city from the hand of the king of Assyria. I will defend this city for my sake and for the sake of my servant David'" (2 Kgs. 20:5-6).

These verses explain that God healed Hezekiah. They seemed to confirm my thoughts when I read them, but then God drew my attention to the following verse.

"Then Isaiah said, 'Prepare a poultice of figs.' They did so and applied it to the boil, and he recovered" (2 Kgs. 20:7).

It was indeed God who had healed Hezekiah, but He

healed him through a poultice of figs!

I heard the Lord's voice: 'My daughter, this is how I heal people. Oregin is my gift to you. Receive it.'

That is how Oregin began, as a gift from God. Supplements became NC Group's second business. The Lord told me to feed the children of the world through this business. The whole process was nothing short of wonderful.

The most recent research and academic studies from the U.S. revealed that food is one of the main causes of chronic infections, obesity, and other diseases, and they proposed a dietary guideline to change our bodies from one which burns sugar to one that uses fat for energy.

Oregin's Ace Balance Bar was the only product to pass all the standards proposed in the guidelines and did so with outstanding marks. The product that came in second received points far below Ace Balance Bar's stellar marks.

Besides Ace Balance Bar, Director Sam also developed Acemeta, Aceimmune, and Acegenol (made with natural extracts from the purest regions of New Zealand). He told me that many illnesses are rooted in chronic infections and that these supplements, which help boost the immune system, are effective tools for combatting infections.

Genol is an ingredient that helps treat cerebropathy. Director Sam added that the genol made from natural extracts which can penetrate the blood–brain barrier used in Acegenol is several times more expensive than other types of genol. Despite this, he insists on using the natural kind, meaning that not all supplements that use genol as an ingredient are equally as effective.

The success of a business lies in making "truthful products." Director Sam was implementing biblical financial principles in his business. He prayed and gave us all the Oregin supplements he had free of charge.

God Owns 100 Percent

We decided that Oregin would feed all the malnourished children of the world through MannaRelief. We reduced the company profit margins and created the "1:1:1 Project," in which the sale of one bottle of supplement provides nutrition for a malnourished child for one month. We are feeding the children of close to 100 countries. I had decided to dedicate 90 percent of Oregin's supplement business profits to the Lord and to live on only 10 percent. But my husband, the co-CEO of Oregin, proposed that we donate all of Oregin to NCMN, a non-profit, and offer up all of the company's earnings to the kingdom of God. Of course, I agreed with a joyous heart.

As a private enterprise, Oregin used to only supply its products to hospitals. But after becoming part of a non-profit collective, even individuals were able to purchase Oregin products either through sales representatives (called LCs, or "Life Changers") or the company website.

I never spoke of Oregin when it was just a private enterprise, as I did not want people to misunderstand and think that I was out to sell supplements. But after donating the company to a non-profit, I can proudly speak about Oregin wherever I go.

"Ladies and gentlemen, every bottle of Oregin sold gives life to an undernourished child. You are expanding God's kingdom with every purchase!"

Oregin's many LCs are all there within a single vision. The Lord is sending His blessings in amazing ways (www.oregin.com).

CHATPER 2

Do You Truly Want to Become Rich
(A Holy Rich Person)?

PART I Experience God's Supernatural Provision

Reborn a True Rich Man

Hear the testimonies of the many who are living completely renewed lives after training and implementing the biblical approaches proposed in *The King's Finances*. Men and women who have paid back their debts of 200 million won in three years, 1.2 billion won in two years, and 2 billion won in a single year; those who have paid off their debt of tens of millions of won and were reborn after finding the King's Finances videos and training at the very moment they had decided to give up on everything. These men and women that took ownership of their money were reborn as the truly rich.

There is an easy way to become rich. That is, "to live it out" (the "Let us live it out! Live it out! Live it Out Project" is enclosed in the revised version of *The King's Finances Workbook*). To change today's reality, you must first transform your thinking and actions. Action! Only by taking action can we erase the deficits in our households and corporate budgets and turn our finances around to begin saving money.

We need to live it out in order to change the negative balance in our account to a positive one. The King's Finances programs are not complicated. They speak a simple truth. The moment you change your thinking and actions and decide to live out these changes, your life will be transformed from the very core!

I invite you to a life of higher standards. The methods mentioned in *The King's Finances* may be simple, but they are potent. This is because these methods are not my own, but the Lord's. If you are sick and tired of being a slave to money and want to take ownership over money, live out the principles laid out in *The King's Finances Volumes I & II* as well as the workbook. Whether it is a family, business, or a church and regardless of the size of money in question, the same principle applies. Put the teachings of this book into action!

When we live it out, we will no longer be a slave to money. Instead, money will become our slave. The message of the King's Finances strikes at the conscience of many who read it. Thus, they criticize and leave hurtful comments about me online. Yet I pay no attention to them. All that I testify are works that the Lord has done within me. The Lord is my guarantor; the words I speak are His, and the message I spread is truth. Many are giving glory to the Lord for experiences that are similar to mine

> If you do not have the will to take action, put the book down! It is a waste of time.
> Only through action can you change the remaining balance in your accounts.
> Only action will transform your life from its very core!

From Debtor to Holy Rich Kim JaeSung

I found out about Sister Kim MiJin for the first time in October of 2017 through an online video. At first, I was convinced that she was a cult leader, so I just wanted to find out what she had to say. But a few minutes into the video, tears began running down my face. I was overwhelmed, hearing the deeply moving message of the true Gospel. Wanting to live out the teachings of the videos, I cut through the fierce competition and registered for the 12th session of the NCMN's King's Finances School in October of 2017.

I met God on a personal level 14 years ago. Whenever I got my hands on some money, I offered it up to the Lord. My desire to dedicate to the Lord was so great that I constantly borrowed from friends and even took out a bank loan to make offerings. At the time, I thought that going into debt for the Lord was a sign of strength. The total value of my offerings to the Lord was greater than three billion won.

Then, in January 2018, my debts surpassed two billion won. Yet it was not the debt I found upsetting; I was sad that I could no longer make monetary offerings. As happens naturally with such a sizable debt, my business began spiraling into crisis. It was a challenge to bring myself to go to church or go out and meet people. What troubled me most, however, was that I could no longer dedicate anything to the Lord.

As I attended the lectures of Rev. Hong and Sister MiJin at the King's Finance School, I made a final resolution and understood that it was my last chance.

"My son, if you have put up security for your neighbor... you have been trapped by what you said, ensnared by the words of your mouth. So do this, my son... Free yourself, like a gazelle from the hand of the hunter, like a bird from the snare of the fowler" (Prov. 6:1-5).

Being in debt, I was no different than a gazelle or bird in the hands of a hunter. What people saw from the outside and how I felt inside were two completely different people. At church people appreciated me, and at work my employees admired me. Although people saw me as a successful businessman, all I wanted to do was flee abroad. But I could not have solved my problems by running away; I had to change. All the content and processes of the King's Finances School are centered on the idea of "living it out." Members of small groups and leaders alike were all engrossed in the "Let's Live It Out Project". I had to pay off all my debt by offering full tithes and putting forth my "best 1." I declared my resolution before my small group and Sister MiJin.

"I will pay back my debt of two billion won in one year!"

I obeyed God's teaching and put every won I owned towards repaying my debts and cutting back on myself. I did not buy any new clothes, refrained from eating out, and spent only what was absolutely necessary for my three children. I restructured my company and cut down on costs. I sold everything I could to pay off my debts. Then, I stopped taking any more loans. My only true wish was to become a slave of the Lord, not of money. After I did all this, my debts began to decrease. It was amazing; my debts, which had only grown in size for the past ten years, were suddenly being paid off at immense speed. It was all happening much, much more rapidly than I ever could have imagined. How could this be, you may ask?

Even when I was paying off my debts, I offered every material thing the Holy Spirit led me to give within my means. Even when it seemed impossible, when the Lord moved me to make a material offering, I did not hesitate to give. I only obeyed and gave as the Lord directed.

And just as I had declared I would before my small group, I completely paid off my debt of two billion won in one year. I do not owe anyone a single won! I feel as light as a feather. I promised the Lord two trillion won for the unification of Korea. I vowed to build 1000 churches in the most difficult mission fields around the world. So far, I have built ten. I put these words into action each month. The King's Finances training has transformed my life from its very core.

The EB-1 visa I received during the finances training was another amazing gift I received from God. My three children had been studying abroad in the U.S. for the past three years. Their tuition and living expenses were extremely high. Although I too had wanted to expand my business in the U.S., it was not a decision I could readily make with my massive debts and business operations in Korea.

Moreover, after the Trump administration came into office, it became nearly impossible for green card applications to get approval. But it was during this time the Lord moved my heart to apply for a U.S. green card.

Is it really the Lord that has placed this in my heart? I began questioning the idea.

As I stood before the Lord asking for His guidance, He spoke with greater clarity.

'Apply for a green card with an EB-1 visa.'

I was dumbfounded; I was not even eligible to apply for an EB-1 visa—a special visa only given to those who have demonstrated extraordinary ability in certain academic fields and gained international acclaim. So objectively, it was nearly impossible to prove that I was deserving of this visa.

One thing I learned at the King's Finances School that stuck with me the most was, "Be a man of faith, not a religious fanatic." So I decided to obey what God had laid in my heart and tried what I had been instructed to do. I gathered all the documents I could and applied for a U.S. green card with an EB-1 visa in August 2018. Getting the green card would also mean that I no longer had to worry about my children's tuition.

The agent who was handling my papers told me that it was impossible for my application to be approved. The people around me laughed when I told them that I had applied for a visa after hearing God's voice. I felt that they were laughing at our Lord when they laughed at me. I immersed myself in prayer and desperately called out to the Lord. Then, I remembered something they had taught us at the King's Finances School.

"When you feel that you cannot hear God's voice, do the 'fleece test.' But remember, once you do the test, you must obey God's will 100 percent, no matter what the result."

So, to understand God's will, just as Abraham's old servant (Gen. 24:42-49) and Gideon (Judg. 6:36-40) had, I did the fleece test.

'Lord, if it really is Your will that I move to the U.S., issue the EB-1 visa by December 2018. If my application is approved, I will know that You are sending me to the States to expand my business. If it is rejected, I will know that it is not Your will, and I will remain here. I will bring my children back, as well.'

My family agreed that we would fully obey God's will no matter what His answer; we put everything in His hands. From that point on, I began doing what I needed to do and started putting forth my "best 1". I prepared for both possible cases: approval and rejection. I sorted out business ideas and strategies for company expansion in case the visa was approved. I also looked up schools for my children as they would need to return to Korea if the visa was rejected.

I held on tightly to the Scriptures God gave me during my prayers. Deciding that God's will would be my anchor no matter where I was, no matter what I was doing, and leaving everything in His hands, I was freed and at peace with myself.

"Enlarge the place of your tent, stretch your tent curtains wide, do not hold back; lengthen your cords, strengthen your stakes" (Isa. 54:2).

Then, on the morning of December 6, 2018, I received a text message from my immigration lawyer.

"Congratulations. Your visa has been approved."

My application for an EB-1 visa had been accepted! And just four months after I had submitted the documents! It was a miracle.

Both the repayment of all two billion won of debt in one year and the miracle of the EB-1 visa had all happened while I was enrolled in the King's Finances School. To express my gratitude to Rev. Hong and Sister Kim MiJin for teaching my family how to live by faith, I visited them and handed them an offering of thanks. But they declined, telling me to serve the church I was attending with the offering. Their honest humility once again humbled me.

Going forward, I will give 100 percent of what God, my master, has given me toward further expansion of His kingdom. I will dedicate my life to the work of bringing about the Christian Civilization Reform Movement in the heart of New York.

God's Mathematical Equation

$5+2=7$

$5+2=5000+12$

What is your answer to this mathematical equation?

Is it seven? If so, you are no different than the ten men who went to explore the land of Canaan and in their faithlessness gave a bad report upon their return. Just as the Lord said, Canaan was a land flowing with milk and honey. To prove just how fertile the lands were, the men carried back a single cluster of grapes, which only two men could carry. The 12 explorers' report was based on actual truth (see Num. Chapters 13, 14).

First, these cities, including Jericho, are impregnable fortresses. Environmentally, it was impossible to conquer them. Archaeologists say that the top of the wall of Jericho was thick enough for two trains to pass side-by-side. The city walls were very thick all the way from the bottom to the top.

Second, the military strength of the people who live there is phenomenal. Militarily, too, we are inferior in absolute terms.

Third, among them are giants, the descendants of Anak. We are like grasshoppers to them. Their size is much greater than ours (Goliath, a descendant of Anak, was 2.7 to 3.1 meters tall).

In summary, this was the explorers' report: "Environmentally, militarily, and size-wise, they are impossible to conquer." The Israelites began to weep aloud after hearing the report. Seeing the people, Caleb, who had explored with them, responded:

"Listen to me. What the ten men say is the truth. But their calculations are all off. Our God has said that we will take possession of the land. Our God is almighty. God, who has spoken, will give us the land. Therefore, do not be afraid; let us take possession of the land. We will devour them!" (see Num. 13:30, 14:6-9).

The Israelites grew spiteful at Caleb's words and debated stoning him. Right then, the glory of the Lord appeared among them.

"You ten without faith will not be able to enter the land and die in the wilderness as you believe. And every one of you who did not believe me and disobeyed me after hearing their words will also die in the wilderness. Your children, born in the wilderness, will enter the land. But Caleb, I will bring into the land according to his faith, and he will take possession of the land" (see Num. 14:10-24).

What is faith? It is to overcome limits; it is to experience God's power by faith. Men and women of faith should answer, "5+2=5000+12." This answer will act as the channel that draws God's power to this earth.

Faith does not mean having our wishes granted, nor does it mean believing in what we want to have happen. Faith is believing in God's covenants and promises; it is to obey God in all that one does and to trust wholly that He is able.

Breakthroughs Come from Training   Goh JaeJin

I was enrolled in the 2nd session of the King's Finances School in Gwangju. My father has a grade one disability[6], and my mother left us when I was in the sixth grade. I despised my poverty-stricken life and wanted an escape. Looking to make a quick buck, I started a business selling golf club memberships at the age of 27.

Although I had studied biblical financial principles in 2009, I ignored the teachings, thinking, Only pastors who have no idea about how the world operates could say, don't go into debt. Who does business with their own money? Being able to get a loan is a skill in and of itself. My business did well. To make even more money, I took out a loan and partnered up with a non-believer to invest in new business opportunities. But the new business I had started on loans struggled. I soon began borrowing from whomever and wherever I could. I took out as many daily installment loans, auto loans, and private loans I could get my hands on, even going as far as to borrow from the *kkongji*[7]. Eventually, I had to file for bankruptcy. The lawyer handling my case told me that I could be facing three to five years in prison.

I attempted to kill myself twice, but each time I tried the faces of my three children lingered before my eyes and

---

6 In Korea, the grades of disability range from one to six: grade one disability is the severest, while grade six is the least serious.

7 *Kkongji* is the name given to Korean casino loan sharks.

stopped me from going through with it. I was living but not truly alive. It was during this period that I read *The King's Finances* and signed up for the King's Finances School in Gwangju. There, I resolved to give life another try, giving it all that I had.

My circumstances did not change while I was attending school. Every day without fail, another check would bounce and I found myself taking out more loans, one after the other. This went on until I could not possibly go on any longer. Every day, I would go to bed at night, hoping that I would not wake up to see the morning. But each morning, I woke up to a new day.

At the King's Finances School, they told us to create a budget. I did not know where to even begin. I would say to my study group, "Even Sister MiJin could not set up a budget if she were in the situation I am in." At the time, I had racked up a debt of over 2.2 billion won. 1.5 billion of that debt was money that had to be paid back urgently. I finished the program, but nothing changed and still I saw no exit ahead.

After the program ended, my small group leader advised me to join the NCMN King's Business Group in Seoul for further training. I worried that bad things would happen to me if I did not get out of Gwangju and the NCMN King's Business Group was the perfect excuse. Every third Friday of the month, we would meet for worship, prayer, small group meetings, and all-day lectures from 9 am to 5 pm.

Rev. Hong and Sister Kim MiJin presented biblical financial

principles using the Bible. I would start driving at three in the morning to get to Seoul from Gwangju on Fridays. But my situation kept on getting worse. At one of the meetings, Brother Jung WonSuk gave a lecture on brand identity. I remember thinking to myself, Brand? Identity? What are you talking about? My company has gone bankrupt. Why don't you try teaching me something useful, like how to make money? I shut my ears. I was engulfed in paralyzing worry and anxiety; I felt suffocated.

On one Friday, I was at a King's Business Group meeting listening to a lecture as I did on every third Friday of the month. But on that day, I had the feeling someone was asking me a question, 'Will you choose to live, or will you choose to die?'

"Then the sword you fear will overtake you there, and the famine you dread will follow you into Egypt, and there you will die" (Jer. 42:16).

This verse rebukes the faithlessness of those who are running away to Egypt out of fear of war and famine (hunger).

"Do not be afraid of the king of Babylon, whom you now fear. Do not be afraid of him, declares the Lord, for I am with you and will save you and deliver you from his hands" (Jer. 42:11).

For me, the "king of Babylon" represented everything that was pressuring me at the time.

'Do not be afraid of him. It is the Lord who will deliver you from his hands.'

That lecture completely changed my perspective. With the help of a fellow small group member, I started performing devotions again; all of a sudden, I began hearing what the three lecturers were saying. And then to escape the vicious cycle of despair and live out the teachings in my life, I devised a budget of faith.

First, I needed to structure my finances such that my income exceeded my expenses. I sold everything I could get money for, including the last bit that was left of my pride—my car. I trained as hard as I could, and I gave it my "best 1". I desperately needed the Lord's hand to intervene in my situation.

God also showed me a reflection of my inner self during a King's Business Group's joint worship. I saw my vanity, my need to compare and compete with others as well as the arrogance that kept me from obeying the leaders. I realized, despite all my smugness, I had nothing to show for myself.

I had to let go of everything to survive. I decided that I would obey the leaders at my church and the King's Business Group. I took on my church's and the King's Business Group's visions as my own. Slowly, I began building up the strength to train.

The results of my training with *The King's Finances Workbook* were genuinely amazing. When I was enrolled in NCMN's Changer Leadership School in Gwangju in August of last year, there was a day when I absolutely had to pay back 22 million won by 6 pm or risk losing everything. At 5 pm, I did not even have one million won in my hands.

I shuffled through my phone, muttering, "I need the money now. Who can I call?" Up until that point, I had fought so hard to keep what I had left. But on that day, my heart changed. I declared:

"Lord, if You tell me, 'Enough!' I will stop here. I cannot fix my situation by borrowing more money. Besides, I have no one left to borrow from."

When I let go of everything, including my own life, I felt a strange sense of relief. But at 5:45 pm, I received a phone call from one of my employees.

"Mr. Goh, I just heard back from the customer we met last week. He's sending us the down payment."

"Oh yeah? How much is that?"

"It's 22 million won, Mr. Goh."

Tears gushed from my eyes. I made a resolution that day.

'I will now cross the River Jordan. I will no longer live with the wealth that comes from grace but with the wealth that He gives through truth!'

Since that day until now, I have not once borrowed money from anyone; I have paid off all my personal and corporate debts. This breakthrough happened after 2.5 years. I began serving my church with even greater vigor. I was transformed into someone who prioritizes taking care of the poor. I now live in abundance and drive an even better car.

I will make this confession: "Lord, only You are my master." Furthermore, I will dedicate 90 percent of my income for use in the kingdom of God for as long as I live.

Becoming a Kitchen Aide

The words of Proverbs Chapter 6, Verses 1-5:

"My son, if you have put up security for your neighbor" (verse 1).

My son, if you are in debt

"You have been trapped by what you said, ensnared by the words of your mouth" (verse 2).

You have been trapped. You can no longer live a life of influence.

"So do this, my son, to free yourself, since you have fallen into your neighbor's hands: Go and humble yourself, and give your neighbor no rest!" (verse 3).

Do this! Free yourself!

"Allow no sleep to your eyes, no slumber to your eyelids" (verse 4).

Do not be lazy!

"Free yourself, like a gazelle from the hand of the hunter, like a bird from the snare of the fowler" (verse 5).

Put forth your "best 1" to pay off your debts.

These words are powerful words for the indebted. All debtors have been trapped. In whose hands, you ask? Just like a gazelle in the hand of the hunter, like a bird in the snare of the fowler, the debtor is trapped in the hand of his creditor. His life has no influence. That is why the debtor must pay back his debt as though he is running for his life.

This is the debt repayment strategy the Lord has given to

PART I Experience God's Supernatural Provision

us.

First, twice (in verses 3 and 5), He tells us, "Free yourself." It is not about waiting on someone else to help free us. We cannot just sit there doing nothing, just waiting for the Lord to come to our aid. We cannot afford to be passive and resigned. Instead, we must have an active and enthusiastic mindset.

Second, be diligent.

Proverbs Chapter 6 verses 6-11 give us a strategy for paying off our debts.

Third, put forth your "best 1."

The following equation puts this idea into perspective.

0×100 million $= 0$ (I do nothing and wait on good fortune)
1×100 million $= 100$ million (I experience God's power when I do my best)

I found the debt repayment method explained in these verses to be quite shocking at first. The simple strategy of "be diligent and free yourself" placed a heavy burden on my heart. I started my first business with funds from an outside investor, so that was what I had planned on doing once I got back on my feet. But through these verses from Proverbs, God told me to free myself from debt as though my life depended on it! I had to take this business plan

THE KING'S FINANCES II

humbly before the Lord.

What could I, a woman with nothing in her name but debts of five billion won, possibly do? I was devastated. But I had no other choice; I made the decision to put forth my "best 1." I headed out to start looking for a way to make money when I saw a flyer stuck on a wall.

"Restaurant kitchen aide/ wait staff needed. 1.2 million won/ month."

I called them and agreed to start working immediately.

- Change Your Master Project Execution Guidelines

    1. Identify the source of your debt and eliminate it.

        (e.g., compulsive shopping, excessive spending, extravagance, etc.)

    2. Immediately stop taking out more debt, starting today.

    3. Immediately begin paying back the principal even if it is just 10,000 won, starting today.

    4. Before buying anything, ask yourself three times, "Do I really need this?"

- My Debt Repayment Project

    Principal: Five billion won

    Income: Pay from the waitressing job 1.2 million won

    Monthly debt repayment: One million won

    Rent: 200,000 won

    Food Expenses: Ask for leftovers from the restaurant

This crushed my spirit. My calculations showed that it would take me 500 years to pay off all my debt at this rate. But at the time, working as a kitchen aide was the "best 1" that I could put forward.

I started work at the restaurant the next day.

"Excuse me, waitress?"

Before this, people had always addressed me as "Boss," "CEO," or "Director". Even after my company had shut down, people still called me "Mrs. Kim." It felt so foreign to hear someone call me "waitress." Nevertheless, I did the best I could to do my job well.

After lunch, the owner of the restaurant handed me half a day's pay and asked me not to come back. He said something about how he could not keep the business afloat if everyone in the restaurant kept the water running like I did while doing the dishes.

But I am not one to back down. I called another restaurant; they told me they were looking for someone with experience. A half-day experience is still experience. I started to work there. I worked hard all day, but in the evening, the owner handed me the day's wage and said not to come back. Again, it was because I had kept the water running while doing the dishes. Still, I refused to give up. I started at another restaurant, but they too told me to stop coming for the same reason.

I had been fired from three restaurants. I went before the Lord to reflect on what it was that I was doing wrong.

'Am I in the place of and within the methods of God's

provision?'

At the time, I did not know what it truly meant to live a life that hears God. I could not hear His voice. But every time I prayed, there was one thought that always came back. I wanted to work as an employee at the optician's shop I had sold at half the value when I filed for bankruptcy.

From Owner to Employee

I told the gentleman who had bought the shop from me about my situation. Because I was a certified optician, I was able to start work there with a starting wage of three million won. Only a few employees remained from the time when I was the owner of the shop, and most of the employees were new. The store manager had changed, as well. Many employees with high salaries were being let go as this was during the Asian Financial Crisis. As the shop's losses continued, the new owner of the opticians, my boss, told me that he would have to let go of a middle manager who had been there since I was the owner of the store. He had a family to take care of, with two children in elementary school. I said to my boss:

"Don't let him go. I will split my salary with him; we'll get 1.5 million won each. And if we make good sales and get your profits up, then, you can pay us three million won each and give us a ten percent bonus if we sell above a certain amount."

My boss agreed, but the sales target he set was impossible

to achieve. The middle manager and I clung desperately to the Lord; we prayed that He would send crowds of customers to us. The middle manager was not a believer at the time.

If sales were to go down any more, we would both be fired. We did our best; we treated each customer who walked through our doors with respect and kindness. Our customers were pleased with our service and recommended our shop to others. Some customers even brought in their family members. God did not just allow us to meet our sales targets but allowed us to exceed them by so much that we even received bonuses starting from the very first month. The middle manager became a believer and started going to church after this incident.

There was a lady who lived in a small alley behind the opticians. Her husband had left her, and she lived in poverty with her son who has a grade one disability. Back when I owned the opticians, I allowed her to set up a small ice-cream stall in front of my shop and each month I would give her rice and some money, ranging from half a million to a million won, to cover her living expenses.

But after I sold the business, she was not allowed to set up her stall. Unable to sell anything, she was really struggling. My heart broke for her. As I did not have the means to help her, I thought of another way that I could. I saved the lunch and dinner money of 20,000 won I received from work for her, and I brought my meals from home instead. All I could afford to pack was kimchi and rice every day.

One day, when I was eating inside a storage space attached to the shop, the new senior manager walked in and slammed the lid of my lunch container shut.

"We're giving you money for lunch. Why do you have to stink up the place with your packed lunches?" he yelled.

I had no choice but to go the street behind the storage space and sit on top of some boxes to finish my lunch. The new manager was quite displeased with my presence in the shop. He already had a boss he was working for, and he was unhappy that the old boss had returned as well. He did everything he could to get me fired. One day, one of my old customers came to the shop. Thinking I was still the owner of the opticians, she referred to the shop as "your shop" while we were talking. I did not see a need to tell her that I had gone bankrupt, so I did not correct her. But the new store manager, who was listening in on our conversation, interrupted us.

"Mrs. Kim isn't the owner of this shop anymore. She went bankrupt, so she sold the place. We have a new owner now. I'd appreciate it if you could refer to her as Mrs. Kim from now on."

I was mortified and heartbroken. Though the manager really hurt my pride, I held back my tears. I said to myself, 'The moment you let him get to you, you lose.' Although he continued to try to embarrass me in front of customers in order to get me to leave, I continued to smile. I knew that was the only way I could survive. He spent all day disrespecting and bullying me. From 9 am when we started work until 10 pm when the shop closed, he bullied me for 13 hours every day.

Rainbow

Brokenhearted, I came home, put my boy YuJin to sleep, and headed to church. It was 30 minutes past midnight. I locked the doors of the sanctuary and made my way to the altar. When I kneeled before the cross, all the emotions I had kept inside came flooding out. I clenched my fists and shook as I cried out loud.

"Hey, you! You're nothing but a manager! I am the boss! I'm the boss!"

I was still burning with rage.

"I will not forgive you, you horrible, terrible, awful man!"

I yelled like that as loud as I could for a good while. When I ran out of energy to scream, I collapsed onto the floor and began bawling. I could see that the hands of the clock were pointing to 1:30 am. In between my sobs, I heard a voice coming from a distance.

"Boss? Boss, are you there?"

I was so scared I hid inside the pulpit. But I heard the same voice again.

"Boss, are you there?"

I answered, my voice trembling with fear.

"Is someone there? Who are you?"

I realized that it was my dear friend Lee KyoungHee, the wife of our church's associate pastor at the time.

"MiJin, please don't cry. You'll always be my boss lady. Kim MiJin is the boss!"

KyeongHee told me she had gotten there before me but had fallen asleep underneath the pews until I woke her up with all my screaming. I could not tell you how long we cried together, holding onto each other tightly. When I needed a shoulder to lean on, this friend became that shoulder for me.

Not too many days after that, we saw a rainbow while praying together. KyoungHee said to me:

"MiJin, I think the Lord is going to give you back your opticians."

I did not believe her. I would need a lot of money to buy the shop back. How on earth could I make that shop mine again? Even after seeing such a rainbow of promise, which I did not believe, going in to work at the shop felt like stepping into hell every day because of the senior manager. About three months later, I was still at church praying with a broken spirit. The Lord placed the words "obey authority" on my heart. He told me that, as a clerk, I needed to respect him as my manager. Truth be told, even at that point, I had not yet been able to come to terms with the fact that I was now just a clerk.

In every corner of the store I saw the touches of interior design that I had created, the little details I had built with my own hands. They were all still there. I had fooled myself into thinking that I was still the owner of the opticians. So, I obeyed the Lord. The very next day, I apologized to the senior manager and told him that I would respect his authority. But still, my heart was torn in pieces.

A few more months passed. One day, a very elegant and refined-looking lady, the wife of the shop owner, came into the store. She seemed to be furious about something. Something terrible had obviously happened between the couple.

The Lord intervened once again in His amazing way. Without a dollar to my name, I was able to get my opticians back. Just as my friend had said, the shop was mine again. Although I had placed limitations on God's power by focusing only on my impossible circumstances, my dear friend KyoungHee supported me when I lacked faith.

Be in the Place of and Within the Methods of God's Provision

> Then the word of the Lord came to Elijah: "Leave here, turn eastward and hide in the Kerith Ravine, east of the Jordan. You will drink from the brook, and I have directed the ravens to supply you with food there." So he did what the Lord had told him. He went to the Kerith Ravine, east of the Jordan, and stayed there. The ravens brought him bread and meat in the morning and bread and meat in the evening, and he drank from the brook. Sometime later the brook dried up because there had been no rain in the land   1 Kgs. 17:2-7

God told Elijah that the place of His provision is the "Kerith Ravine," and that the method of His provision is "ravens." Elijah obeyed immediately. But due to the drought, the brook dried up soon after. It is in these moments that we need to be spiritually awake. Because it is when God finds us in the place He has commanded that He begins His work.

When there was not enough water, God solved the problem by changing the place and method of His provision. We must not make the mistake of relying on the ravens as the source our remedy. We must not look to people who make large donations to us (ravens), but look only to God, the One that sends us the ravens. We must rely on God and God alone instead of turning to those around us for help.

> Then the word of the Lord came to him: "Go at once to Zarephath in the region of Sidon and stay there. I have directed a widow there to supply you with food" 1 Kgs. 17:8-9

God changes the place of provision from the Kerith Ravine to "Zarephath" and the method of provision from ravens to "a widow." God's love for the poor widow of Zarephath asked of her everything she had. How could she possibly have known of God's plans to show her the miracle of the five loaves and two fishes?

At times, we may find ourselves in a situation just like the widow did. Sometimes, when we cannot understand why,

God requires us to give up everything. God did the same thing to the young man who was seeking eternal life. When the young man came to Him, Jesus said, "Sell everything you have and give it to the poor." The young man who loved his money left Jesus after hearing these words. But what Jesus really wanted was not the young man's money; He required his heart.

Jesus wanted to give the young man eternal life and an eternal reward. But the rich young man caved before money. He was a man poor in faith. Conversely, the poor widow of Zarephath became rich in both flesh and spirit by obeying God's command. Due to severe drought and famine, all the poor widow had left was a handful of flour and a little olive oil in a jug. The widow tells Elijah that she is planning to die with her son after eating one last meal (see 1 Kgs. 17:8-13). It was in such dire circumstances that God asked the widow to show faith.

> Elijah said to her, "Don't be afraid. Go home and do as you have said. But first make a small loaf of bread for me from what you have and bring it to me, and then make something for yourself and your son. For this is what the Lord, the God of Israel, says: 'The jar of flour will not be used up and the jug of oil will not run dry until the day the Lord sends rain on the land.'" She went away and did as Elijah had told her. So there was food every day for Elijah and for the woman and her family. For the jar of flour was not used up and the jug of oil did not run dry, in keeping with the word of the Lord spoken

THE KING'S FINANCES II

by Elijah 1 Kgs. 17:13-16

Do you wish to experience God? Have the courage and be prepared to stand at the edge of a cliff should the Lord ask. Elijah and the widow experienced God's works through obedience. The miracle of the flour that was not used up and the jug of oil that did not run dry was possible because of the widow's obedience to the Word of God.

If you knew that your current work is God's place of provision and that your boss is the method of provision in this season, you could not possibly be careless at work. And then for some, God's provision is through the businesses they are running. Those who believe that only the supernatural is God's way of providing run the risk of becoming religious fanatics who fail to do their own part.

I, too, frequently experienced changes in the place and method of provision throughout my life. I have worked for companies, worked in wholesale and retail, conducted international trade, and even manufactured, sold, and distributed goods. Now God has led me to produce supplements. This is why we must be vigilant in noticing these changes by always listening for the voice of God in our lives.

Do you feel like you are hitting a wall in everything you do? Are you drowning in piling losses? Then come before the Lord, take time to self-reflect, and then ask yourself this question:

PART I Experience God's Supernatural Provision

> "Am I in God's place of provision right now?"
> "Is this God's method of provision?"

Then pray and rely on the Lord with a yearning heart.

I once provided business consulting services for a client. Stuck in the memories of the heyday of his company, he was struggling to close down his business, even though his company had already been in the red for the past seven or eight years and showed no hope of recovery. We must be aware that the place and method of God's provision can change at any given time. (Recommended Seminar: NCMN "Hearing God's Voice Seminar" / Recommended Book: *The King's Voice*, co-authored by Hong SungGun & Kim MiJin)

The Courage to Stand on the Edge of a Cliff   Kwon HyeHyuk

I dedicated my life to the Lord in college and was actively involved in campus evangelism ministries. I wanted to change the world through the Gospel. But, primarily driven by passion, I reached the limits of what is achievable with my own efforts and means. I wanted to become the 'Nation-Changer' NCMN talks about but was not able to figure out a way to live with influence.

Upon graduation, I started working in the field of economics, an area completely dominated by mammon. At that point, I had yet to learn about the biblical financial principles of handling money. Thus, I approached life with a worldly mindset forged by mammon, feeling overwhelmed by a sense of failure and defeat. On the one hand, my faith felt like a burden: I was serving and sacrificing for the Lord, but only out of the sense of obligation that I had to repay the Lord for my salvation.

Then one day, I learned about the biblical principles of economics through a King's Finances video lecture. I was shocked. Through the lecture, I learned that God is master, provider, and ruler, even in the realm of economics. In one part of the lecture, Sister Kim MiJin told the story of how she confronted the Lord, demanding to know how it was fair that she had gone completely bankrupt.

When she listed all the monetary offerings made for the Lord and asked, 'How could you make me go bankrupt?' the Lord replied, 'Have I ever demanded that you must donate?' She said that she almost felt betrayed by the Lord's answer.

Her confession completely freed me from the pressures I was feeling. I started listening to her lectures every day, over and over again. Unless I was talking with someone, I was almost always listening to one of these lectures. And the more I listened, the more I began to realize that the core of Sister Kim MiJin's message is not in fact money. She was challenging her audience with this simple question, "Who is your master?" Her core message was for us to live a life of faith.

I signed up for the 3rd session of the NCMN King's Finances School in order to receive formal training on living

PART I Experience God's Supernatural Provision

a life of faith. I started my own debt repayment project with information from online lectures even before the classes had begun. I did not eat out, nor did I buy any new clothes for myself. I saved and cut down and was able to pay back my mortgage and all my student loans.

Soon, training began in the King's Finances School. I first had to make right the wealth I had acquired through unjust means to eliminate mammon's influence in my life. I started with the company that had been handed down to me. In the process of developing the company, I had forged some papers to earn certifications and government contracts. I canceled all of them. I purified my company, making honest payment for any unjust favorable treatment my company had previously received.

During the course of my training, I began to understand the reason behind my debts. The problem was that I was spending without any limits. I came to thoroughly understand that I needed to turn away from a life in which I was master, doing with my money as I please, and turn to a life in which God is the only master, and in which I manage as a steward. I began asking my master before I spent anything. As a result, my life has become abundant, allowing me to serve, enjoy, and share more than ever before.

The best training for hearing the voice of God was learning to "flow" (giving as the Lord's voice directs). The training, which began in the second week of classes, consisted of bringing "arrogant goods" (goods that were outside of my means and purchased with debt) before the Lord. For me, this was two bicycles I had sitting at home. However, I was not able to hear the Lord's voice specifying a recipient, so I took it to the school as an "undesignated flowing." With an undesignated flowing, a person who has prayed for the item steps out, humbly tells everyone that he or she has been praying for it, and takes it, accepting it as God's provision.

Surprisingly, Sister Kim MiJin raised her hand, saying that she had prayed for two bicycles, one for men and one for women. I can never forget the exhilaration and joy that comes having the confirmation that I heard God's voice correctly when someone who has prayed for the very thing which the voice of God directed me to give comes forward. Sister MiJin received the bicycles and then, instantly, flowed them again to two other students who had each been praying separately for a bike.

After completing all the required courses at the King's Finances School, I packed my bags to leave for the 1-Week Implementation Outreach Program. As I was about to head out, I felt a compelling urge to give my computer to the outreach leader. Wanting to confirm that it was indeed God's voice, I asked our outreach leader about it. He told me that he had prayed to the Lord, saying, "I will know it is your provision if the computer I receive is white in color." Truly amazing! My computer was white.

The King's Finances School taught me to become more sensitive to God's voice through learning to flow. I also learned how to stand with courage before the Lord, who sometimes placed me on a cliff edge.

"Jesus looked at him and loved him. 'One thing you lack,' he said. 'Go, sell everything you have and give to the poor, and you will have treasure in heaven. Then come, follow me'" (Mark 10:21).

God called me with these words. Though I chose to obey, it was not a decision I could make on my own. So I decided to do the fleece test. I prayed, "Lord, I have said I will not speak to my wife about the words you have given to me. If you speak to her with the same words, I will know that you have called us a couple and obey."

It was one week later. My wife told me that she had heard the voice of the Lord and shared with me the exact same message I had received from the Lord! Together, we decided to stand at the edge of the cliff. We sold everything we owned, our apartment, and first paid off all our debts. With what was left, we flowed it to the kingdom of God (the poor).

One day, God told me to give my car (an SM5 model)[8] to someone. The more I trained, the more I began to understand Sister Kim MiJin's teaching, "Living by faith is the easiest thing you can do; the most difficult thing is to live without faith." I had already made the Lord master over everything I owned through training and did not hesitate to flow the car to the person as the Lord had directed. I willingly gave

---

8 The Renault Samsung SM5 is a mid-size car or large family car.

up what was asked of me.

Not too much longer after that, something amazing happened. In front of the 500 students in the 11th graduating class of the King's Finances School as my witness, the Lord provided me with an almost brand new luxury car (Mercedes E350). Sister MiJin's 'God of Sulwhasoo' is the living God whom I serve!

He also gave me new business ideas. But of course, I needed to make sure that the ideas were indeed from God. I needed funds to turn the ideas into an actual business; to do so without going into debt, I had no choice but to ask from the Lord. We decided that we would tell no one about the necessary funds.

Then one day, my father-in-law invited me to his home. He gave me 150 million won, saying that he had not yet been able to thank me for when I worked for him, a time during which the Lord had blessed and multiplied his company. I was at a loss for words. We moved from a studio apartment to a small apartment where we currently live. We started our own small business and are working hard with hope for the future.

But that was not the end of God's amazing work. For ten years since our marriage, my wife and I had not been able to have children. We were told that it was nearly impossible for us. All we did was obey the Word and serve the poor, but God allowed us an unbelievable return on our faith and gave us a beautiful boy as a gift.

While in training at the King's Finances School, neither

my company nor my family had any money after we had paid off all our debts. But in only a couple years, we found ourselves with a wealth of 400 million won that had been given to us in supernatural ways. After praying about it, my wife and I decided to donate the entire amount to the projects of the kingdom of God. All glory be to God who gives us the strength to obey; glory be to Him who gives in abundance.

− I have watched this couple from up close. I was tremendously encouraged and thankful to see them training and living it out so diligently. This couple, who serve the homeless from their hearts, radiate the sweet aroma of Christ with their lives.

CHATPER 3

A Life of Faith

God Shows the Next Step to Those Who Obey

A life of faith does not happen on its own.

First, it is not achieved through a position of spiritual authority.
For example, being a pastor, a missionary, or a deaconess does not automatically make you a person of faith.

Second, it is not achieved by the number of years a person has been a believer.
Even if you have been a believer for decades, even if you were born into a Christian home, no one can automatically become a person of faith.

Third, it is not achieved by having a lot of biblical knowledge.
Knowing a lot about the Bible does not automatically make someone a person of faith.

A life of faith must be proven with "action that displays obedience to the Word of God." When we live by faith, we experience God, and our trust in Him grows. This is why the Lord tells us, "The last shall be first and the first last."

Even if you have been a believer for just one year, you can be a person of faith who obeys the Word. One cannot simply "become" a person of faith. Therefore, we must always be alert and come before the Lord with fearful and trembling hearts. No matter the domain in our lives, if we do not have a new testimony that is the end of our faith. A minister who tries to continue his ministry with the testimony of ten years past is a pitiful one indeed. One cannot handle the ministry of today with the anointing of yesterday!

> Your word is a lamp for my feet, a light on my path.
> Psa. 119:105

Take note of God's style of delivery. When God calls Abraham, He tells him, "Go from your country, your people and your father's household." He does not tell Abraham exactly where to go; instead, He says, "Go to the land I will show you" (see Gen. 12:1).

"By faith Abraham, when called to go to a place he would later receive as his inheritance, obeyed and went, even though he did not know where he was going" (Heb. 11:8).

Though he had no clue as to where he was headed, he simply obeyed and left.

How about Samuel?

"After removing Saul, he made David their king. God testified concerning him: 'I have found David son of Jesse, a man after my own heart; he will do everything I want him to do'" (Act. 13:22).

God planned to remove Saul and place David as king.

The Lord says to Samuel, "I am sending you to Jesse of Bethlehem. I have chosen a king from that household. You are to anoint for me the one I indicate and make him king" (see 1 Sam. 16:1-3). So Samuel arrived in Jesse's house, completely clueless as to whom he was to anoint.

When Samuel saw Jesse's eldest son, Eliab, he thought that he must be the one.

"When they arrived, Samuel saw Eliab and thought, 'Surely the Lord's anointed stands here before the Lord.' But the Lord said to Samuel, 'Do not consider his appearance or his height, for I have rejected him. The Lord does not look at the things people look at. People look at the outward appearance, but the Lord looks at the heart'" (1 Sam. 16:6-7).

First, God does not look at our outward appearance, but at our hearts. I found hope in these words. Blessed be our God who gives equal opportunity to everyone.

- Outward appearance: educational background, skills, wealth, family background, face, height, etc. These are the criteria the world uses to judge.
- Heart: faith, loyalty, meekness, humility, honesty, etc. These are the traits by which God judges.

Even Samuel, a man of God, was nearly fooled by Eliab's outward appearance.

Second, God works through those who obey him.

Samuel, who obeyed the Lord and went to Jesse's house without a clue about whom to anoint, got very close to making a mistake. But in the end, Samuel's obedience allowed him to see David, who God would anoint as king.

Third, God shows the next step to those who obey.

What Abraham and Samuel had in common was that neither of them knew anything from the start to the finish. God did not tell them where to go or whom they should anoint. But with every step of obedience, God led Abraham to the land of Canaan (Gen. 12:5) and Samuel straight to the one he must anoint (1 Sam. 16:6-12).

Do you want to know God's will in your life? The Lord will lead you to exactly where you need to be when you obey and take the first step. God does not tell us everything, from beginning to end. It is when we take that first step of faith that he lets us know where our next step is. As though hunting for treasure, search for His direction in *The King's Finances Volumes I & II*.

How a Luxury Watch Became a Luxury Car

I suddenly had a thought during prayer.

'Do you not think a student would want to have what his teacher has?'

This was true; I wanted to have what was Rev. Hong's as well. When he gave me his iPad, I felt as happy as I imagine

PART I Experience God's Supernatural Provision

Elisha had felt when Elijah anointed him. So I began sharing my possessions with my students. But there was one thing I could not bring myself to share, so I kept it hidden from the Lord.

A few months passed. The luxury watch I had kept stowed away began to weigh heavily on my heart. Reluctantly, I took the watch out and brought it before the Lord. He told me to give it to Lee JaeHee, a beloved student of mine. He was deeply moved when he received the watch and was able to obey gladly and flow his Mercedes when the Lord asked. It is students like him who make me proud to be a teacher.

Some more time passed. The car I had at the time was an average car with more than 200,000 km on the clock. But having spent all my money on my son's wedding, I was not able to get a new car. My car was the most important thing I owned, as I spent an average of more than three hours on the highway to get to my lectures.

A teacher who saw the state of my ride flowed five million won to me so I could start saving for a new one. Immediately after, two other students flowed me additional amounts. Still, it was not nearly enough to buy a new car. I was praying to the Lord and saving funds for a new car when I remembered the teachings of my mother, "My dear daughter, always look after the servants of God before anything else."

I remembered a missionary who was working very hard. With help from another believer who works with cars,

I bought a small car and sent it to that missionary. This brought joy to my heart. After, I tightened my belt once again and began saving to buy a car for myself.

Not too long after that, I received a flowing message from a beloved student who was an ophthalmologist. He told me that the Lord had spoken to him during his morning prayer.

"I want to become your feet Sister MiJin. Buy the best car; I will wire the money to your account."

Then he sent me a sum enough to buy a luxury car. Amazing things were happening in my life. I had always been the giver, but in 2018, God allowed me to receive tremendous gifts. Because I had always been told to be faithful with others' money, I ordered a car in the same vehicle size class as the one I had always driven. But I ended up buying a mid-sized car after being told that the car I had ordered would not be available for a while due to new government regulations on diesel cars.

The luxury watch I had kept hidden away after wearing only a few times, the new luxury car, my teacher's and students' obedience; all these humbled me before the Lord. With big and little events like these that take place in my life, I am learning and growing every day. I want to praise my generous Lord who transformed my luxury watch into a luxury car.

What People Whom God Uses Have in Common

God only uses those who have met Him on a personal

level. It is through fellowship with such people that I experience the depth of God's love for me. When we come face to face with God's power, we become strong men and women of faith and change into people with an unwavering trust in the Lord.

Before he was used for God's work, Moses first had to meet the God of power through miracles. This is because all that God would do in the future through Moses was only possible through His power.

When Moses threw his staff as the Lord directed, it turned into a snake. And when he took it by its tail, the snake turned back into a staff. When Moses put his hand inside his cloak, his hand was leprous; when he put it back into his cloak and took it out again, his skin was restored (see Exo. 3:1-12).

Joseph saw the vision of divine providence through his experiences in the pit, the slave market, Potiphar's house, and Pharaoh's prison. He met the God of protection who held a shield over him in all situations.

Abraham started in faith, but due to his fear he faltered and failed, sending his wife as the wife of another on two different occasions (see Gen. 12:10-20, 20:1-11). But through his experiences, he met the God of mercy, the God who gives another chance.

To save Lot from captivity, Abraham attacked four nations with the 318 men born in his household whom he had trained. He recovered his relative Lot, other captives, and all his possessions. Through this experience, Abraham learned that war belongs to God and that only God is the owner of history (see Gen. 14:14-16).

Before God began using Gideon for His work for the people, Gideon first met a God who was with him on a personal level. When Gideon prayed, "Let there be dew only on the fleece and all the ground be dry," the Lord did as he asked. When he prayed, "Make the fleece dry and let the ground be covered with dew," again, the Lord did as he asked. Gideon, who experienced God through this fleece test, became a military leader and fulfilled God's mission (see Judg. 6:36-40).

Elijah experienced the power of God, which brought the Widow of Zarephath's dead son back to life. Later, Elijah took on 450 prophets of Baal and was victorious. He experienced God's fire of power (see 1 Kgs. 17-18).

David experienced the power of the name of the Jehovah of armies through the Goliath incident. He learned that war belongs only to God. Then, he obeyed the God who took away his son as a result of the Bathsheba incident. Through this experience, David gained a profound understanding of what sin and forgiveness mean to God.

What about the story of Daniel and his three friends? The Bible cannot record the accounts of each individual witness. Listen to the stories in the Bible and the stories of those who have been used to serve people in the past 2000 years of church history in the New Covenant. Every single one of them was a person who had met God on a deeply personal level.

To meet God on a personal level, we must set apart time to spend with Him.

First, the best way to achieve this is consistently reading and meditating on the Bible every single day.

Second, by obeying His Word, we too can experience God.

Third, make time to learn about God and receive training through good seminars and training schools.

Give God the time He deserves and get to know Him more!

The Turning Point in My Ministry Jung CheolHan

On September 15, 1997, God led me to the city of Daegu. With absolutely no ties to the city, I struggled to find a ministry and spent my days and nights kneeling before the Lord. After starting as a church of eight people, the Daegu Onnuri Love Church grew to a church of 150 members. Out of a desire to serve the Korean church, we bought a big van, purchased sound and visual equipment, and created a worship team that led revival conferences all around the country. Everywhere we went, there was healing; stumbling small churches were brought back on their feet. However, the massive financial investment caused some problems, big and small, to arise in our church.

Spending so much time leading revival conferences outside of our church, the revival of my own church began to stall. The financial problems the church was facing caused many to leave. As a result, after 15 years, I had to leave the revival ministry behind. Then in 2014, though I spent every waking hour desperately shouting to the Lord on Juamsan Mountain in Daegu, the change I yearned for in our church never took place and my body grew ill.

It began with a chronic cough at the end of September of that year, and by the beginning of October, I had lost eight kilos. I thought it was just due to malnutrition, but a health check-up found abnormalities in my lungs, pancreas, and thymus glands as well as symptoms of rheumatism. The doctor referred me to Dr. Park JaeYong, the director of the pulmonary medicine department at the Kyungpook National University Hospital. After undergoing some tests there, the doctors diagnosed me with terminal cancer, saying that cancer had already spread throughout my body. Dr. Park called my wife to his office. "Your husband only has about three to six months left to live. Make sure he eats delicious food and sees good things; perhaps the two of you could go traveling together. There is nothing we can do for him at the hospital." I was distraught. Was this what I deserved for all my hard work as a pastor and revival ministry leader? Members had left our church, it was on the brink of bankruptcy with all the debt, and my body was ill; I would soon be dead. My entire world was crumbling before my eyes. But I needed to hold myself together.

Who is my God? Is he not the God almighty who breathed life back into the putrefying corpse of Lazarus, who had already been dead for four days? Is the kingdom of God not the kingdom of miracles where lepers heal, the dumb speak, the blind see, and the lame walk? "Your faith has saved you." Yes, faith! This is the kingdom of God. I cannot die like this. I will live!

The members of our church joined me in tearful fasting and prayer. After two months, I went to the hospital for another check-up. The results came back a few days later, and I was shocked.

"All the tumors in your lungs and pancreas have disappeared!"

The doctors were in greater shock than I was. The few members who had remained in our church witnessed the power of God firsthand. God saved me and gave me a second chance at life. With a renewed heart to start my ministry afresh, I waited for God's guidance.

It was around that time that a close pastor friend of mine told me about NCMN. I enrolled in the 6th session of the King's Finances School. From day one, I felt quite uncomfortable. Lecturer Cho, who looked more like a member of the mafia than anything else, had the audacity to call me "Brother Park." Calling a pastor and revival ministry leader of 20 years a "brother?" I tried to remain calm. I felt as though my authority was being trampled on.

When I told him, "I'm a pastor," he replied, "Pastor, can't

I just call you brother?" The nerve! At the end of the first lecture, we were asked to sign papers stating that we would comply with the course requirements, but in my anger I walked out and drove straight back down to Daegu. When I got to my church, I kneeled before the altar with a heavy heart.

'Lord, You've led me to the King's Finances School in prayers for a new ministry, but do I have to keep attending? A lecturer with the face of a mafia member calls me, a pastor of 20 years, brother.'

I knelt before the Lord with my wounded ego. It was a while before the Lord spoke to me.

'My son, if he is not to call you brother, should he call you sister? Did I not give you your new life? Lay everything down!'

The Lord showed me my own arrogance and told me to learn with humility. That day, I was born again.

In the second week of classes at the King's Finances School, I confessed to the lecturer and small group members before we began, "I was arrogant. From now on, I will receive the training with a willing heart." It seemed like they had only placed people with severe issues in my small group, Group 4. The superintendent of the school, Sister Kim MiJin, said to us:

"Because we don't yet know each one of you, our leaders and lecturers spend a lot of time in prayer before dividing you into groups."

She said that they rely on the guidance of the Lord before

making the groups but are always impressed with the results. "It is often the case that people in the same small group are very much alike. Look for yourself in the members of your small group and train accordingly."
This was absurd.
'How could they think that I belong in a group of such arrogant and ego-centric people?'
But after one or two weeks, I remembered the Apostle Paul's confession, "I am the worst of sinners." It really was true. The Lord got to work on my arrogance by showing me reflections of myself in the members of my small group. When I opened my heart and began to truly take in the lectures, I was deeply moved. I rediscovered the hope of God's kingdom that I had lost.
The school was dynamic; it was an incredible place where the works of the Holy Spirit in these very times were being recorded. I worked together with Lecturer Cho to bring our small group members together. As a result of our efforts, the group previously referred to as the "group of death" came to be known as the "group that never dies." The Holy Spirit transformed the "group of arrogance" into the "group of humility." God was reshaping me for the second ministry of my life.
The King's Finances School was a turning point of my ministry. After the program, I learned what true leadership is through the Changer Leadership School, and I gained a fresh perspective on the Word of God through the Shema Bible School. I quenched my thirst with NCMN's schools

and seminars, and I was able to lay down my pursuit of mere quantitative growth and revival in my church. With the training I received, I was able to see my congregation through the eyes of a loving father, and this brought healing in my church as well.

And for the first time ever, we held a King's Finances Revival in Daegu. After the revival conference, the bound-up finances of both our church and our members were let loose, enabling us to repay all of the church's huge debts.

This meant a new life for me, as well. Now that the church was completely free of debt, I felt as though I could fly. After our entire church staff enrolled in NCMN's training, we were able to create and work towards a unified vision. We adopted the 5K Movement Headquarters' well-devised revival strategy for our church and, as a result, experienced multiple revivals in our church, starting with our Sunday school. Currently, our entire congregation is praying for a new building as our current one is no longer able to seat everyone ever since our church began to multiply. I praise the Lord, who gave us this second chance in our lives.

Hundreds of pastors give their amazing testimonies while attending NCMN's schools. A passion for God and the joy and grace of salvation fills the hearts of the leaders and students of the NCMN who witness the unfolding acts of the Holy Spirit. I was deeply challenged by people who engrain the Word of God deep within their hearts. NCMN's mission statement is, "Lead the Christian Civilization Reform Movement!" It is my hope that our church serves as a partner network church in realizing this mission.

Do Not Limit the Power of God

God executes His power today just as He did in the past. Do not limit or doubt His power, which is the same yesterday, today, and forever. Expand the horizons of your faith. God's amazing works are taking place in NCMN ministries both at home and abroad.

The 500 plus students and leaders who partook in each session of the school are our witnesses, of which around ten percent are pastors and ministers.

- My deaf ears can now hear.
- My crippled legs can now walk.
- Vision has been restored to my blind eyes.
- My chronic fever has suddenly vanished.
- The eczema covering my entire body is healed..
- My leukemia has been completely cured.
- I have conceived a baby after ten years trying unsuccessfully.
- I was planning on receiving surgery for the lump on my forehead, but it disappeared on its own.
- A few large ovarian tumors disappeared overnight.
- I was healed from various cancers.
- The bleeding that lasted for several years stopped.
- I was healed from alcohol addiction.
- I was healed from sex addiction.
- I began to speak in tongues during worship.

It is practically impossible to account for all the works of God that took place over the course of our ministry. Did you know that the miracles recorded in the Word are being continued through people of faith even to this day?

"A man with leprosy came and knelt before him and said, 'Lord, if you are willing, you can make me clean.'... 'I am willing,' he said. 'Be clean!' Immediately he was cleansed of his leprosy" (Matt. 8:2-3).

"A centurion came to him, asking for help. 'Lord,' he said, 'my servant lies at home paralyzed, suffering terribly.'... Then Jesus said to the centurion, 'Go! Let it be done just as you believed it would.' And his servant was healed at that moment" (Matt. 8:5-13).

"Just then a woman who had been subject to bleeding for twelve years came up behind him and touched the edge of his cloak... 'Take heart, daughter,' he said, 'your faith has healed you.' And the woman was healed at that moment" (Matt. 9:20-22).

"As Jesus went on from there, two blind men followed him, calling out, 'Have mercy on us, Son of David!'... Then he touched their eyes and said, 'According to your faith let it be done to you'; and their sight was restored" (Matt. 9:27-30).

"While Jesus was still speaking, some people came from the house of Jairus, the synagogue leader. 'Your daughter is dead,' they said... Overhearing what they said, Jesus told him, 'Don't be afraid; just believe.'... He took her by the hand and said to her, 'Talitha koum!' Immediately the girl stood up and began to walk around. At this they were completely astonished" (Mark 5:35-42).

God's power raised synagogue leaders from the dead, and brought the putrefying corpse of Lazarus back to life.

"This is the disciple who testifies to these things and who wrote them down. We know that his testimony is true" (John 21:24).

"Jesus did many other things as well. If every one of them were written down, I suppose that even the whole world would not have room for the books that would be written" (John 21:25).

"The people were amazed when they saw the mute speaking, the crippled made well, the lame walking and the blind seeing. And they praised the God of Israel" (Matt. 15:31).

We witness firsthand, the healing of the broken, the freeing of the captured, and the loosing of the trapped when the kingdom of God arrives. There is a tendency to focus on the people who prayed when we witness a miracle of healing. Never do this. They have no power; it is God who has done the healing.

The people who prayed were only used as a channel for His power at that moment in time. Though we can be thankful for their goodwill and hard work, we must give all the glory to God. Only the Lord is worthy of praise.

Carried in on the Back of Another, Walked out on One's Own Feet

When I was leading a King's Finances revival conference at the New Canaan Church at the end of 2017, the Lord spoke to me:

'Daughter, I will cure an incurable disease. Spend time in prayer.'

I felt a deep sense of burden from the Lord's words. After struggling with them, I consulted the senior pastor of the church. Thankfully, he believed me and invited Rev. Hong to the end of the revival conference to hold a healing worship service. I did not know who the Lord would heal on that day; all I knew was that he would cure the incurable.

The senior pastor told us that many were healed after the service. Among those healed was his brother-in-law (also a pastor)'s daughter. I was told that she had suddenly lost the ability to walk while attending college. And despite going to all the best hospitals, none of the doctors could name the disease or give a reason why. She had taken some time off from school was resting at home when she was carried into the healing worship service on someone's back. But after the service, she was healed enough to jump rope, and is now able to walk without any problems.

God is a God who works. Faith is all we need to carry out His power on this earth.

After Elijah was taken up to heaven, Elisha asked the Lord this question (see 2 Kgs. 2:14):

PART I Experience God's Supernatural Provision

"Where now is the Lord, the God of Elijah?"

Do not ask such questions. God still is and continues to be with us. To the contrary, we might find that He asks us this question:

"The God of Elijah is always here. But where are all my Elijahs?"

The God Who Brought Me Back to Life Jung YeonSoon

I was attending a theological seminary after leaving my parents, who were nonbelievers when I met my husband through a friend. My husband was born into a family of third-generation Christians. I was very hopeful and excited to be starting a family with someone who I thought would be supportive of my faith and ministry. But my expectations were soon met with the reality of suffering and distress. Unable to afford hospital bills, I spent my days in physical pain from migraines, vertigo, and stomach cramps.

My husband, who had belatedly finished seminary, could not let go of certain things before the Lord even while he served as a pastor. As a result, the responsibility of my family's livelihood rested solely on my shoulders. For 15 years, I endured suffering no woman should have to endure; though a minister, I lived a miserable life. Our piling debts, bad credit, and bankruptcy completely eliminated any hope I had left in life. My marriage was ailing with all the pain my husband had inflicted on our relationship. Yet as a pastor's family, I could not even confide in others.

I was on the subway watching YouTube videos when I came across a King's Finances lecture by chance. The lecture made its way into my mind, and I thought about it constantly. Starting on that day, I began studying the online lectures and realized that I was a worldly poor person (a poor person who is of this world). In tears, I repented for all the wrongs I had done before the Lord. I was determined to escape from a life of debt starting at that very moment.

Although these were the coldest times of my life, I resolved to meet God on a deeper level and registered for the fourth session of the NCMN King's Finances School. It was a time of inner reconstruction, and God used this period to lead me into a new life.

"Forget the former things; do not dwell on the past. See, I am doing a new thing! Now it springs up; do you not perceive it? I am making a way in the wilderness and streams in the wasteland" (Isa. 43:18-19).

My life began changing little by little after I completed the King's Finances School. I rejected all kinds of debt and started to pay off my debts with the "best 1" I had. Most of my debt was money I had borrowed from friends. I trained to live a life completely free of debt while at the King's Finances School. Some of my debt was even forgiven during this time.

I confessed and proclaimed, "God, You are Lord of all! You are the provider of all things! My sense of stability is in You only, Lord!" I trained and trained again. I was simply amazed by the speed at which my debts were being paid off. I experienced big and small supernatural provisions and miraculous events. Through it all, I was able to trust in the Lord again and get back on my feet; it dissolved the fears I harbored about living a life of faith.

I dedicated all my time to God so as to turn back from the life of a miserable worldly poor minister and instead grow closer to Him. When I did that, I received the strength to implement what I had learned through training. My life was completely transformed as I challenged myself to live by faith. Then one day, in the midst of my prayers, the Lord called me to a ministry I had never been involved in before. I was to minister to the disabled and homeless. The Lord told me, From now on, this will be your place of ministry. Although I lacked understanding about the homeless and disabled, the Lord gave me a new heart of compassion for them. He called me and put me in charge of His ministry.

The Lord saved me from a life of subsistence as a miserable minister and restored me. He guided me to a life of the true holy poor; my heart was filled with thanks, joy, and hope. Currently, I am serving in the NCMN 5K Movement's relief ministry, learning more about God's heart while serving 500 homeless and disabled people in Seoul Station, seniors who collect paper and trash to survive, as well as others that are forgotten in the blind spots of society by making them food, giving them haircuts, cutting their nails and toenails, washing their feet, and attending to their wounds. I am faithfully serving the three dozen people the Lord has entrusted to me.

I was healed from my chronic diseases—the migraines, vertigo, and stomach cramp—when I began my new ministry. I also grew a heart for North Korea through the NCMN 5K Movement and began praying for them. Currently, we are diligently preparing to become the first relief team to enter North Korea after unification and devising detailed strategies to serve the orphans, the widows, and foreigners of North Korea.

"The one who sent me is with me; he has not left me alone, for I always do what pleases him" (John 8:29).

— I remember distinctly the first time I met Sister YeonSoon. From the days back when she looked like a walking corpse to today where she serves as a respected minister, her transformation has taken place at a stunning speed. She is a woman who obeys the Lord. She has been reborn an outstanding minister.

> ## The "Let us live it out! Live it out! Live it Out Project" Pre-Implementation Guidelines

1. Stay away from credit card cash advance services, payday loans, and rent-to-own agreements (interest rates of 19-30 percent).
   - It is challenging for low-income people to recover after using one of these systems. These schemes are a way to legally exploit the poor and are made purely for the lender's profit.
   - With the exception of home equity loans for which monthly payments (interest or interest + principal payments) do not surpass 20 to 30 percent of monthly income, debt must be avoided at all costs.

2. Beware of refundable insurance schemes. They are not a sound investment product.
   - Non-refundable insurance and health insurance policies are a sound safety net for the future. The less money you have, the more important it is that you have insurance.

3. I strongly advise against declaring personal bankruptcy. It is a life-shattering and ruinous experience.

4. Take sure steps, one at a time, as though you are learning to walk.

5. Quickly create "starter money (emergency funds)" before you begin. If you have used up that money, store the funds before going on to the next step.

6. Wedding gifts, holiday preparations, sales are never emergencies.

7. All successful people have goals that they have written down on paper.
   – The *Forbes* 400 ranks the wealthiest businesspeople in America. Seventy-five percent of the companies owned by people on the list acquired their wealth without any debt (Royal Greens, Cisco, Microsoft, and Harley Davidson are among the companies that are run with zero debt).

8. Draw up a budget of faith and begin implementing it as a family.

9. When there is an unexpected expense, hold a family meeting to reach a decision on the matter and deduct it from your budget the following month.

10. Do not possess any overdue payments. If you do have overdue payments, set aside the most significant portion of your budget to the repayment of these amounts. Do everything it takes to pay off your debts.

Ex. A family of four with combined monthly earnings of 7 million won

Expenses	Amount
Monthly payment on home equity loan	1,500,000 won
Car installments (inc. gas and vehicle taxes)	1,000,000 won
installments and two phone lines	200,000 won
Monthly credit card expenses (inc. cash services)	2,000,000 won
Living expenses (inc. utilities)	2,000,000 won
Education	500,000 won
Monthly allowances for four family members	700,000 won
Total Expenses	7,900,000 won

From the get-go, this family is bound to be in debt. If left unchanged, a difficult and tiresome life awaits this family even in their retirement 10, 20, 30 years from now. Using one credit card to pay off the next, and drawing from lines of credit, it is obvious what will happen in this family's future. Just by getting rid of their credit cards and car, they could be saving three million won per month. Depositing this money into a compound interest savings account for 30 years, the family would have approximately 1.65 billion won in their hands after taxes.

Ex. Calculation of compound interest with monthly contributions of 3 million won for 30 years at a 3 percent rate of return.

Principal	1,080,000,000 won
Compound interest	672,581,180 won
Total	1,752,581,180 won
Amount received after the 15.4% tax is paid	1,649,003,679 won

Choose to live a life set apart from others. Without debt, ten years is more than enough time to become rich. Being rich will no longer be a mere dream, it will become your reality. Do not lend money to friends and family, and do not be a guarantor for someone else's debt. Lending to them and guaranteeing their debts, you become their master, and they become your slave. This is a sure way to ruin the relationship you have with someone.

11. Remember the following instructions if you want to start accumulating wealth.
   – Do not worry about what others think or about saving face. If you worry about these things, you will end up overspending on wedding gifts, funeral donations, clothing, and eating out. Ninety percent of people spend money on such items without actually having the means to do so.
   – Implement everything you have learned through the King's Finances in full, no matter what.

- If you try to live according to God's will with your budget of faith, the Lord will provide.
- Plan for when you will be completely debt-free
  Save for your children's education and your own retirement. Consistently make diversified investments in mutual funds for 10-15 years. Be on the lookout for financial products with tax benefits.

12. How the truly wealthy use their wealth
    - Do good and be rich in good deeds. Giving and sharing not only brings immense joy to life, but it also brings with it real rewards.
    - Spend happily for themselves and their family.
    - Invest in traveling.
    - Make wise investment choices and increase income with sound investments, investment funds, rental income, and so forth.

My 4(5)-Week Live It Out Project

What are some current challenges that I need to overcome?
(Write down what comes to your mind)

1. Think of the challenges you are facing

   What are some challenges that must be addressed in working toward your life's vision (purpose)?
   (pick one or two challenges; these must not be overly ambitious)

2. Set a strategy for these challenges

   What are the specific goals that I must achieve in 4(5) weeks?

3. Set a detailed action plan for your strategy

4. Self-evaluate your action plan

   Have I done my utmost to achieve my goals?
   Evaluate yourself every day and give yourself a score (out of ten) at the end of 4(5) weeks.

Ex. 1) If you have debt

: Your monthly goals and challenges may change within the six months of training.

What are some current challenges that I need to overcome? (Write down what comes to your mind)

Ex. Repay debt ǀ save ǀ Heavenly Bank account ǀ implementation of the Word and sufficient spiritual food (Reading the Bible, prayer, devotions) ǀ learn something new ǀ keep in touch with family and friends

1. Think of the challenges you are facing

   What are some challenges that must be addressed in working toward your life's vision (purpose)? (pick one or two challenges; these must not be overly ambitious)

   −Repayment of debt (determine the amount you will repay in 4(5) weeks)

2. Set a strategy for these challenges

   What are the specific goals that I must achieve in 4(5) weeks?

   −Groceries; dine out once a month; get a part-time job

3. Set a detailed action plan for your strategy

   −Groceries (50,000 won/week) ǀ dining out (once/month) ǀ spend humbly on family events ǀ Heavenly Bank account

4. Self-evaluate your action plan

   Have I done my utmost to achieve my goals? Evaluate yourself every day and give yourself a score (out of ten) at the end of 4(5) weeks.

THE KING'S FINANCES II

If you have debt – Weekly/ Monthly Evaluation Sheet

* Evaluate yourself based on your stage of implementation: out of ten points (guideline for scoring expenses/service: was it the best way to spend/serve?)

Have I done my best in the following areas?			Week 1	Week 2	Week 3	Week 4	Week 5	Monthly Evaluation
Debt Repayment	Groceries (50,000 won/week)		10	10	10	10	10	50
	Dining Out (once/month)		10	10	10	10	10	50
	Family event expenses (humility)	Amount	×	100,000	50,000	×	×	150,000
		Score	10	10	10	10	10	50
	Additional earned income	Amount	5,000	100,000	30,000	3,000	20,000	158,000
		Score	10	10	10	10	10	50
	Listening to the King's Finances lectures		10	10	10	10	10	50
	Reading *The King's Finances*		10	10	10	10	10	50
Savings	Saving in the best way I can	Amount	500,000	3,000	5,000	100,000	7,500	615,500
		Score	10	10	10	10	10	50
Heavenly Bank Account	Sowing on good soil in the best way I can	Amount	5,500	30,000	120,000	12,000	10,000	177,500
		Score	10	10	10	10	10	50
Spiritual Food	Scripture reading (15 chapters)		10	10	10	10	10	50
	Prayer (1 hour)		10	10	10	10	10	50
	Devotions		10	10	10	10	10	50
	Morning prayer		10	10	10	10	10	50
Spiritual Training for Children	Reading the entire Bible together		10	10	10	10	10	50
Fellowship with the Family	Fellowship during meals		10	10	10	10	10	50
Fellowship Outside the Family	Greetings, words of encouragement, condolence		10	10	10	10	10	50

Ex. 2) If you do not have debt
: Your monthly goals and challenges may change within the six months of training.

What are some current challenges that I need to overcome?
(Write down what comes to your mind)

Ex. Become a holy rich person | save | check the status of my faith | healthy lifestyle | read | study a language | spiritual education for children | keep in touch with family and friends

1. Think of the challenges you are facing

   What are some challenges that must be addressed in working toward your life's vision (purpose)? (pick one or two challenges; these must not be overly ambitious)
   —Become a holy rich person | healthy lifestyle

2. Set a strategy for these challenges

   What are the specific goals that I must achieve in 4(5) weeks?
   —Become a holy rich person | save | make deposits into my Heavenly Bank account

3. Set a detailed action plan for your strategy

   Groceries | dining out (make a plan based on humility) | serve the holy poor as is the purpose of the holy rich
   Continue to train through King's Finances lectures | read *The King's Finances* and take on the challenge of training to be a holy rich person

4. Self-evaluate your action plan

Have I done my utmost to achieve my goals? Evaluate yourself every day and give yourself a score (out of ten) at the end of 4(5) weeks.

If you do not have debt – Weekly/ Monthly Evaluation Sheet

* Evaluate yourself based on your stage of implementation: out of ten points (guideline for scoring expenses/service: was it the best way to spend/serve?)

Have I done my best in the following areas?			Week 1	Week 2	Week 3	Week 4	Week 5	Monthly Evaluation
Becoming a Holy Rich Person	Groceries (80,000 won/week)		10	10	10	10	10	50
	Dining Out (in humility)		10	10	10	10	10	50
	Serving the holy poor	Amount	200,000	100,000	0	50,000	0	350,000
		Score	10	10	10	10	10	50
	Listening to the King's Finances lectures		10	10	10	10	10	50
	Reading *The King's Finances*		10	10	10	10	10	50
	Wisdom for business (always consult the Lord before proceeding)		10	10	10	10	10	50
Savings	Saving in the best way I can	Amount	200,000	500,000	900,000	10,000	30,000	1,640,000
		Score	10	10	10	10	10	50
Heavenly Bank Account	Sowing on good soil in the best way I can	Amount	80,000	100,000	110,000	7,000	13,000	310,000
		Score	10	10	10	10	10	50

PART I Experience God's Supernatural Provision

Spiritual Food	Scripture Reading (15 chapters)	10	10	10	10	10	50
	Prayer (1 hour)	10	10	10	10	10	50
	Devotions	10	10	10	10	10	50
	Morning prayer	10	10	10	10	10	50
Healthy Lifestyle	1-hour workouts everyday	10	10	10	10	10	50
Language Studies	1 hour/day	10	10	10	10	10	50
Reading	1 book/week	10	10	10	10	10	50
Spiritual Training for Children	Reading the entire Bible together	10	10	10	10	10	50
Fellowship with the Family	Fellowship during meals	10	10	10	10	10	50
Fellowship Outside the Family	Greetings, words of encouragement, condolence	10	10	10	10	10	50

Part II
Restore a Life of the Altar and the Tent

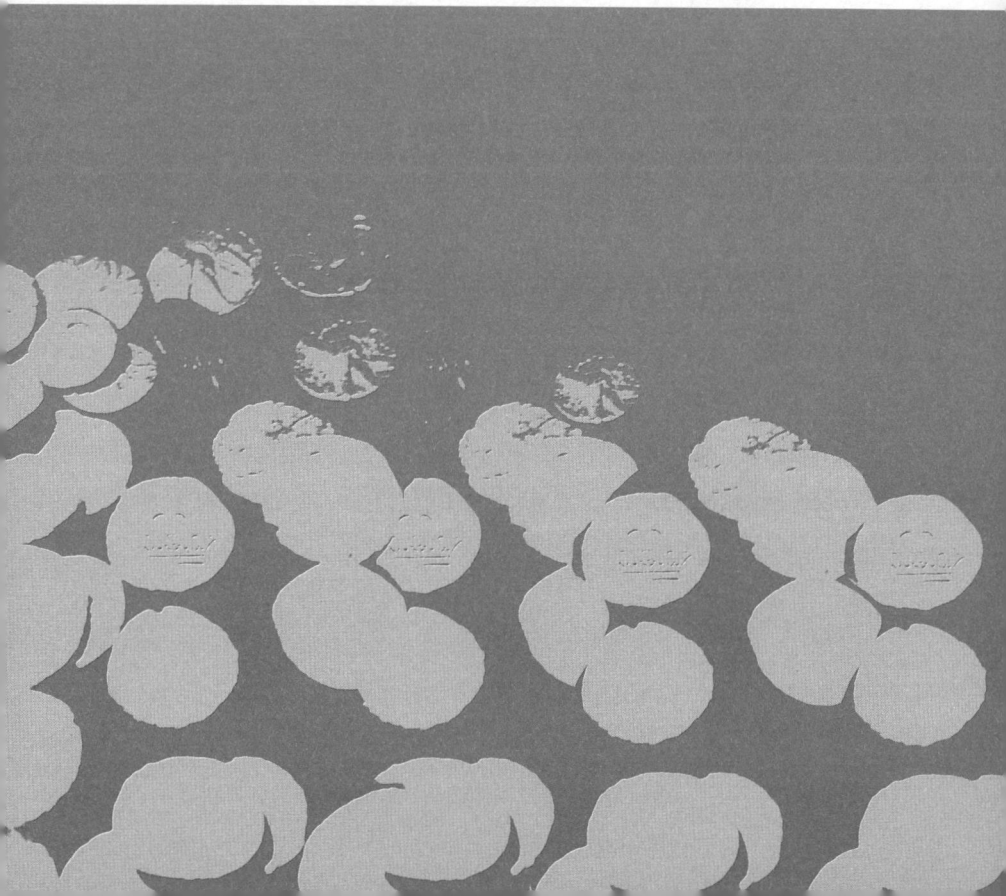

CHATPER 1

There Are Three Seasons to God's Provision

The Season for Supernatural Provision

The manna and quail that were provided for the Israelites in the wilderness was God's supernatural provision. Providing ravens for Elijah to eat, the Widow of Zarephath's unending jar of flour and jug of oil were also God's supernatural provisions.

I also had a season in which I experienced such supernatural provisions. There was a long period in the wilderness during which I could do nothing. My husband would pick edible shoots and leaves from the mountains, catch fish and clams from the sea, and my son and I would dig for edible plants and roots in the fields. We had done nothing to grow them. The Lord let us eat food from the mountains, seas, and fields that He had grown. Sometimes, He provided things through people whose names we did not know.

I wrote down everything the Lord provided for us in a ledger.

"One ice-cream, one chocolate pie, one banana, a plate of seasoned greens, ten sample-sized bottles of Sulwhasoo."

Then I converted the Korean won value of the goods in the ledger. Each month, the Lord, without fail, provided us with 2.5 to 3.5 million won worth of food and other necessities. His spectacular provision, the greatness and attention to detail of His love never ceased to amaze me.

During my first training in the wilderness, I decided to change my master from mammon to God and to make truth the foundation of all the words that come from my mouth. I first changed the way I spoke. I began to speak faith based on the Word.

"Because the Lord God Almighty is my father, my future will be prosperous. My future will be bright. My future is full of hope."

This was the first step in my faith. At the King's Finances School, as well, the first course of training is "Speaking Words of Faith."

Even now, God is answering even the most insignificant of our prayers. Wanting to hear God's voice, one student at the King's Finances School asked the Lord this question:

'Father, what can I flow from the things that I own?'

'Give your power strip to Kim MiJin who travels from country to country to spread the Word.'

Every time the student prayed, she would remember the power strip. I definitely needed a power strip at the time, but I did not do anything to receive it. All I did was work tirelessly for the kingdom of God with all my strength.

Another time, I thought that it would be nice to have a new handkerchief as the one I had was quite worn out. But in between revival conferences, I was not able to find the time to go and buy a new one. Then, someone at the revival conference came to my side and handed me a handkerchief.

"Sister MiJin, don't use rough tissues to wipe your tears. Here, use this handkerchief."

Then, something happened while I was on my way to Sydney, Australia, to lecture at the King's Finances School there. I went into the duty-free store, thinking it would be good to get some sheet face masks as the cabin tends to get very dry during long-distance flights. But after some hesitation, I decided not to buy any as they were a little too expensive. Rev. Hong, who was on the trip with me, saw that I had walked out with my hands empty and asked, "Why didn't you get anything?"

"They were too expensive. I wish I had a hundred of them so I could put one on my face every single day," I replied half-jokingly.

The next week I was back giving lectures at the King's Finances School in Korea. I received a flowing: a flowing of 100 sheet face masks! A student told me that she had gotten them as payment-in-kind for working a part-time job. She was so upset with the payment; she cried out the Lord, 'God, I don't want these!' The Lord replied, 'Give them to MiJin.'

I could not hold back my tears as I read the flowing card in front of 500 students. I was left speechless at the greatness of the Lord's tender, caring love. These events were purely the provision of God's grace and love.

The Season in Which He Feeds Me the Work of Others' Hands

When the people of Israel entered the land of Canaan, God allowed them to eat the produce of the seeds the foreigners had planted and farmed.

> While the people of Israel were encamped at Gilgal, they kept the Passover on the fourteenth day of the month in the evening on the plains of Jericho. And the day after the Passover, on that very day, they ate of the produce of the land, unleavened cakes and parched grain. And the manna ceased the day after they ate of the produce of the land. And there was no longer manna for the people of Israel, but they ate of the fruit of the land of Canaan that year.
>
> Josh. 5:10-12, English Standard Version

- Manna – Provision of God's grace
- The old corn of the land – Eating what others have sown
- The fruit of the land – Eating what I have sown

If I were to use farming as a metaphor for my time in the wilderness, I was unable to do anything because I had no land, no seeds, nor any tools with which to farm. It was at this time the Lord allowed me to eat from the work of someone else's hands or eat from the old corn of the land. On Jeju Island, it is customary to leave a few tangerines on every tree for animals and foreigners to eat. Yet this does not just apply to tangerines; no crop is harvested completely. Farmers would always leave some behind. Thus, I was able to fill my needs with what was left in the fields. There is a season when the Lord feeds us what others have sown.

The Season to Harvest and Eat What I Have Sown

In this season, we plant on our own land and harvest what we planted. It is the season in which God provides during our hard work. During this season, we reap as much as we sow. This is the season in which large movements of wealth can take place. It is an opportunity to put our land to work and achieve success.

The Bible tells us that we must obey the following three rules if we are to succeed.

First, we must pray to the Almighty.
Second, our hearts must be clean and honest.
Third, we must be diligent and not lazy.

There was a season in my life where I, too, was an employee on a salary. During that season, I saved up seed money (funds to start a business) and prepared for the next season. Later, the Lord gave me a piece of farmland and told me to put it to use. It is essential not to go into debt when we are handed this opportunity.

First,   make sure to pay your employees on time.
Second, rent and taxes should never be overdue.
Third,   you must pay your vendors on time.
Fourth, you must save a set amount to prepare for equipment depreciation and future business expansion

To succeed in business, a network of trust needs to be formed both with internal customers (employees) and external customers (vendors) alike. I do not support the mindset that "the customer is always right," which insists employees must sacrifice so as to provide good service. On the contrary, if first employees are well taken care of, they will naturally provide good service to their customers. Employees are a huge asset.

Another important asset is building a strong relationship of trust with vendors. And in fact, when I was struggling, my employees volunteered to receive only 50 to 70 percent of their salaries. They said that they thought of it as saving and that I could pay them back when the company's situation improved. They even told me they would not ask for the money back if the company was unable to recover. Thanks to the trust I had built with my vendors, they gave me a variety of products and took back any inventory I had left, replacing them with new products each month. I only had to pay for the products I was able to sell.

It was this trust my employees and vendors had in me that made me work harder and with a profound sense of responsibility. This was only possible because we trusted each other. Now 20 years have passed and a couple that used to work for me at the time will still make food for me and bring it 2-3 times a year.

We never know what challenges we may face in life. If your vendor sells quality products and has not significantly wronged you, do not change vendors frequently in the pursuit of small gains. For example, do not change the vendor who supplies ingredients for your employee cafeteria over the price of potatoes and carrots.

If a competing vendor offers unreasonably low prices, you will likely be tricked in another area unfamiliar to you. Always try to build trust and create a relationship of mutual benefit based on a principle of mutual understanding.

To save means to cut down on unnecessary expenses; it does not mean that you should be ruthless in how you manage vendors. A relationship that only heavily benefits one side is not a healthy one. Both sides should be able to prosper based on mutual understanding and agreement.

A Budget Plan of Faith Yoon WooJo

I completed my training at the King's Finances School with the 7th graduating class. After learning about it in the King's Finances School, I planned out a budget of faith for myself. And for 15 consecutive months after that, I experienced this budget plan of faith replenish itself in unbelievable ways.

I had no choice but to start a new business to pay back the

1.7 billion won of debt I had acquired while liquidating my former company. I desperately needed the "budget plan of faith" I had learned about in the King's Finances School to work. Each month, I had millions of won in interest and debt to pay back in addition to office operational costs, housing rent, and living expenses.

Seeing that I was over ten million won short each month, it felt futile even to draw up a budget. However, the King's Finances School instructed us to draw up not just any budget plan, but a "budget of faith."

Budget Plan – Setting a budget within my income
Budget Plan of Faith – Setting a budget with the Lord regardless of the instability or lack of income

I resolved to try out the "best 1" I had come to learn at the King's Finances School. Although I had started a new flower delivery business, I did not have the funds to advertise and had to make do with placing stickers—that had only cost me a few ten thousand won—on buildings and walls.

However, amazing things began to happen when I began implementing the training I received on the budget of faith in October of that year. A brother in Christ, who had received training with me, ordered two very expensive foliage plants. That became the start of a flood of blessings I so desperately needed. With each passing day, my sales increased. In just one month, sales were up to ten million won, going up another ten million won the month after that. Those were precious months in which God provided 100 percent of the funds in my budget of faith, a budget I had drawn up in prayer and which only included the absolutely necessary.

This experience gave me hope. For the first time, I was able to pay my rent and debt payments before they were due. But a month into the implementation of my budget of faith, something terrible happened. The tax office had placed a provisional seizure on my bank accounts and stopped all incoming credit card sales payments due to unpaid value-added taxes from my previous business. When I felt like there was nothing else left I could do, I remembered the Scripture they had taught us at the King's Finances School.

"So do this, my son, to free yourself, since you have fallen into your neighbor's hands: Go—to the point of exhaustion—and give your neighbor no rest!" (Prov. 6:3).

All I could do at that point was to go to the tax office and ask for mercy. The tax office told me that if I paid 50 percent of the unpaid tax amount, I could pay the rest in installments over ten months. If I paid 25 million of the 51 million won in overdue taxes and signed an installment payment plan, they would lift the provisional seizure of my bank account as well unfreeze the credit card payments.

Although it felt hopeless, I had to put forth my "best 1." So I scraped up all the cash I could find: 910,000 won. Relying on the Scripture from Proverbs, I made my way to the tax office again to explain my situation. To my amazement, the person in charge was a Christian. Thanks be to God; the problem was completely solved with an upfront payment of only 910,000 won and a signature on an installment payment plan for the rest. God extended His amazing grace as I relied on Scripture in faithful obedience.

God provided 100 percent of my budget on that month as well. I have continued to pay the agreed installments on time and now only have 29 million won left to pay in overdue taxes.

I put forth my best effort to execute the budget of faith which required me to rely on God regardless of my circumstances. I prayed diligently and was not greedy. Always upholding my end of the bargain before the Lord, I lived a humble life of the tent and only spent within the bounds of my budget. Whether I had five million or ten million left over at the end of the month, I never used money on myself. Any budget surpluses were used primarily to repay my debts and then to serve the kingdom of God.

God's amazing grace provided me 100 percent of my budget for nine consecutive months. However, crisis hit on June 28. While doing my accounting, I realized that I was four million short on June's budget. I needed to make sales of two million per day for the remaining two days to meet my budget of faith for June. Surely that was just foolish fancy? Not once had I ever made that many sales in one day since I started the company.

I clung to the Lord in desperation and fought against the overwhelming fear that was taking me over from within. It was at that time the Lord whispered into my heart.

'Why do you limit my power? Am I not a generous God? Do you think I am not able to give you daily sales of two million won?'

I snapped back into my senses and prayed, Lord, I repent. 'Forgive me for limiting your power.' And then the next day, I truly witnessed a miracle. Our daily sales hit 2.6 million won.

A Korean company in China had placed a single order of ten funeral wreaths over KakaoTalk[9]. The next day we made sales of 1.6 million won and thus met the budget of faith for the month. The remaining money was flowed elsewhere for a good purpose.

The Lord led me to the edge of a cliff, a cliff I could only hang onto if I was able to secure the budget for each month. Failure to meet the budget of faith would have led to terrifying harassment for payment by my creditors, and I would have let down my family, who was already scraping by on the bare minimum. An inability to pay back the interest on my debts meant that the government could seize the assets of the family who had guaranteed my debt based on their trust in me. Each day and each month, I stood on the edge of a cliff with nowhere to back down.

I held on even more tightly to the Lord. I always tried to put forth my "best 1" and desperately called out His name,

---

[9] KakaoTalk is South Korea's most popular messaging platform.

asking for His grace. The budget of faith I drew up with the Lord, together with my training to live according to that budget, turned my life into a life of the altar and the tent. My business became the altar on which I built my relationship with the Lord. And living with minimal funds, I naturally became a humbler person.

A year into the implementation of the budget of faith, another crisis hit with the enactment of the Improper Solicitation and Graft Act[10]. Although I was unsure how the new Act would affect my business at first, order cancellations came flooding in, and customers placed orders for only the cheapest flowers.

'Is this the end of a 12-month full provision streak of the budget of faith?' I thought to myself. All I could do at that point was pray. I had almost completely given up hope by the last week of the month. Our sales had fallen by 30 percent.

But while doing the accounting for the month, I made an astounding discovery. I found that the total of 1.8 million won that friends had flowed to me, with three flowings of 1,000,000, 500,000, and 300,000 won each, accounted precisely for the net income of the 30 percent I had lost in sales. Chills went up and down my spine. When I relied on Him, God sent me the ravens to provide for 100 percent of my needs. Sales recovered the following November

---

10 The Improper Solicitation and Graft Act (colloquially, Kim Youngran Act) is a 2016 anti-corruption law in South Korea.

and December. Even now, as I write this testimony, God continues to provide my budget of faith. God is providing for all my needs; I lack nothing. What is more, He is providing me with a couple of hundred thousand extra each month that I may flow as seeds to be sown on good soil.

I spend the last day of each month reviewing sales and the budget of faith. I then plan a budget of faith for the coming month with the Lord. The last day of the month is a blessed day, a day in which I receive special encouragement from the Lord. Looking forward to the day when I am no longer a slave to my creditors swiftly arrives, I once again pledge before the Lord to live a life of the tent and altar in each new month. Through the King's Finances training and implementation of the budget of faith, I truly experienced God as the owner and provider of all things.

CHATPER 2

Abraham's Seed, Solomon the Worldly Rich, David the Godly Rich

Transplant Abraham's Spiritual DNA

A seed, by nature, takes after its parent. Our DNA must match Father Abraham's for us to truly be his seeds.

> The Lord had said to Abraham, "Go from your country, your people and your father's household to the land I will show you. I will make you into a great nation, and I will bless you; I will make your name great, and you will be a blessing. I will bless those who bless you, and whoever curses you I will curse; and all peoples on earth will be blessed through you."
> Gen. 12:1-3

God called Abraham and blessed him with a covenant sealed with His name. God wanted Abraham to establish His kingdom on all the earth. He made His blessing a covenant and made this covenant flow not to Ishmael, but Isaac, and then not to Esau but Jacob among the seeds of Isaac (see Gen. 12:1-3, Ch. 7,9). Who will be the "seeds of Abraham" of today that will establish the kingdom of God through this amazing blessings?

> If you belong to Christ, then you are Abraham's seed, and heirs according to the promise. Understand, then, that those who have faith are children of Abraham. So those who rely

on faith are blessed along with Abraham, the man of faith.
Gal. 3:29,7,9

I learned through this Scripture that I am the rightful heir (one who will continue Abraham's inheritance) to God's covenant as a "seed of Abraham." What is characteristic of a seed? It must be in the likeness of the parent. I remember a picture I posted on our family webpage of the hands of my son and husband. Their hands were so similar that I could not tell which hand belonged to whom.

We can only be deemed the seeds of Abraham when our spiritual DNA resembles that of Abraham.

> • Two aspects of our lives that must resemble Abraham
>   – A life of the altar and the tent
>
> • Two aspects of our spiritual lives that must resemble Abraham
>   – Faith and faithfulness

Two Strands of DNA in Abraham's Life (A Life of the Altar and the Tent)

A life of the altar has to do with our relationship with God.

The First Altar

"The Lord appeared to Abram and said, 'To your offspring I will give this land.' So he built an altar there to the Lord, who had appeared to him. From there he went on toward the hills east of Bethel and pitched his tent, with Bethel on the west and Ai on the east. There he built an altar to the Lord and called on the name of the Lord. Then Abram set out and continued toward the Negev" (Gen. 12:7-9).

The Second Altar

"From the Negev he went from place to place until he came to Bethel, to the place between Bethel and Ai where his tent had been earlier and where he had first built an altar. There Abram called on the name of the Lord" (Gen. 13:3-4).

The Third Altar

"So Abram went to live near the great trees of Mamre at Hebron, where he pitched his tents. There he built an altar to the Lord" (Gen. 13:18).

Abraham's first altar was the altar of "the covenant." After receiving God's covenant, "I will bless you and make your name great," he left with faith and built an altar when he arrived in the Promised Land.

The second altar is the altar of "repentance." Although Abraham made it into the land God had promised him, he left for Egypt when famine hit. His unbelief caused him to fear, and he did the unthinkable of marrying his wife,

Sarah, to Pharaoh. But the Lord protected Sarah in her piety. Abraham then left Egypt, returned to the place where he built his first altar, and built the altar of repentance.

After he and Lot had parted ways, Abraham built the third altar following the Lord's promise to him: "Look around to the north and south, the east and west. All the land that you see I will give to you and your offspring forever." Then Abraham moved his tent to Hebron, where he built an altar. It was the altar of vision (read Gen. Chapters 12,13).

What is distinctive about Abraham's lifestyle is that he lived "a life of the altar and the tent." The life of the altar represents our relationship with God; it is a God-centric life, a life marked by worship, prayer, and fellowship. It means to center oneself around the church, the Bible, prayer, and fellowship (with God and fellow believers).

A life of the tent represents the relationship we have with our possessions. In other words, it has to do with how we handle wealth. I will not go over this separately in this chapter (this topic is dealt with extensively throughout the pages of *The King's Finances* I&II); but in brief, a life of the tent means that you handle wealth with the attitude of a steward and live a simple life, accepting that God is master of all wealth.

Two Strands of Abraham's Spiritual DNA (Faith and Faithfulness)

Why Abraham?

You are the Lord God, who chose Abram and brought him out of Ur of the Chaldeans and named him Abraham. You found his heart faithful to you, and you made a covenant with him Neh. 9:7-8

God did not first make the covenant. He first saw that Abraham was faithful. Faithfulness is imperative if we are to be used by God.

And the things you have heard me say in the presence of many witnesses entrust to reliable people who will also be qualified to teach others. 2 Tim. 2:2

Paul instructs Timothy to entrust the Gospel to the faithful because they will go on to teach others. A faithful person is a multiplier.

My eyes will be on the faithful in the land, that they may dwell with me; the one whose walk is blameless will minister to me. Psa. 101:6

Like a snow-cooled drink at harvest time is a trustworthy messenger to the one who sends him; he refreshes the spirit of his master. Prov. 25:13

Faithfulness is very closely related to how much wealth the Lord entrusts with us. We must be acutely aware of this (see *The King's Finances I*, English translation, p. 153-172).

Why Did I Fail?

1) I just found myself aboard the ship headed for Tarshish

"Go to the great city of Nineveh and preach against it, because its wickedness has come up before me." But Jonah ran away from the Lord and headed for Tarshish. He went down to Joppa, where he found a ship bound for that port. After paying the fare, he went aboard and sailed for Tarshish to flee from the Lord. Jon. 1:2-3

Jonah disobeyed God and planned to flee to Tarshish even though the Lord had told him to go to Nineveh. As luck would have it, he found a ship that was headed for Tarshish at just the right time. What if we are fleeing to disobey and find an escape ship just waiting for us to board?

I wanted to become a successful businesswoman and support the ministries of pastors and missionaries. Just when I began seeking a partner with whom I could expand my business, a person who was most qualified to be my partner had recently finished his studies in the States and returned to Korea. Although I prayed, asking to know if this person was from God, I could not discern His voice.

I decided to do a fleece test. I asked my pastor, my husband, and a friend to pray about this man. If all of them receive the same answer, I will know that it is the will of the Lord, and I will obey; this was my decision. But all three of them came back with the answer that the man was not the partner the Lord had planned for me.

"Do not be yoked together with unbelievers" (2 Cor. 6:14).

I was displeased with their answers. Because, in my heart, I had already decided, I was not able to discern God's will. I decided to do another fleece test. 'Lord, I will go to a prayer retreat center, and if the director of the retreat tells me not to partner with him during our consultations, I will know that it is your will,' I prayed. The director of the retreat center told me that I should not.

But I did not want to throw away all the work I had already put in toward the partnership. Although the man was not a believer, he was truthful, good, and honest. He was the best in Korea in his field. I could not so easily give up on the opportunity with such a person. He was the best partner I could have asked for, someone who had come in at just the right time. To me, he felt like a gift from God. We decided to enter into a 50/50 partnership agreement.

Just as Jonah had, I got on the ship to Tarshish. Just as the ship that Jonas was on encountered a sudden great storm, our partnership became a snare that entrapped both my partner and me. Not only did we end up hurting each other, we ultimately lost all our investments (To this day, I am sorry for all the pain our partnership caused him).

I knew that God's will was not for me to partner with a nonbeliever. But my greed kept me from obeying His Word and put me aboard the ship headed for Tarshish. It was a curse that things went well when I was defying God!

2) The collapse of my life at the altar and the tent

I remember how my mother used to always give the first produce from her small garden to the pastor. The second produce she would give to the elders of the church. Growing up under a mother like that, I have always had a deep respect for pastors and elders in my heart since a young age.

I first got into business while still in college after receiving an investment from the father of a friend. The business was a success, and I expanded into trade. Whenever I needed a business partner, I always tried to do business with strong believers and church elders.

I wanted to repay my friend's father for his investment by succeeding. At the time, I was a young college student with neither experience nor any knowledge on how to work together with business partners. Everything I did was a little bit clumsy and awkward. I did not know who to meet, what to invest in, or which contract to sign. Everything felt difficult, daunting, and burdensome. I prayed, but I could not hear God's voice.

Nevertheless, I tried my best. Every day, I took the list of people I would meet as well as the meeting agenda before the Lord. Then, I wrote down the thoughts that came to my mind during prayer. When I prayed about people, some would arouse a sense of anxiety. The word "loss", or colors such as black and grey would come to my mind; I wrote all this down in my prayer journal. Then, there were others whom I prayed about, those who would place words like "joy, peace, multiples, and blessing" in my mind. I would think of yellow or white lights as well. Again, I transferred all these thoughts into my prayer journal. I spent most of my morning prayer time repeating this process.

I took my prayer journal to meetings, and when I met people for whom I had written down words such as "anxiety, loss, grey, black," I approached them with extreme caution. I held off on signing contracts and making investments with them. On the other hand, when I met with people for whom I had written down, "peace, multiples, joy, yellow," I was at ease. It was much easier to decide whether to sign contracts or invest in these people.

Being too young to understand how business worked and unaware of how to hear the voice of God, I spent every morning kneeling in prayer before the Lord. But to my amazement, the decisions I made at the time led to the growth of my business, and none of those decisions ended up in failure. Looking back, I know that God was speaking to me in a way that I, as a young child, could understand.

My business flourished. I had even more people to meet, and I was always short on time. Then one Wednesday, I was in a meeting with a business partner who was a church elder when the time came for me to go to the Wednesday evening service. I wanted to head to church and finish up the meeting the following day. I asked the elder if we could wrap up the meeting.

I was stunned by his answer. "This business is for the Lord, as well. There's no harm in missing one Wednesday service," he replied. My mother, who was just a deacon at the time, had always told me that I should never miss church. But an elder was telling me that it was okay to miss church sometimes. From that moment on, I believed I had gained freedom from church services with the blessing of a church elder (at the time, I was not even aware that this was a false notion stemming from my immaturity).

Then, I began missing Friday night services for the same reason. I was allocating more and more of my time to running my business. The frequent meetings and the ensuing late nights made attending morning prayers a grueling task. I decided to only attend on Mondays, Wednesdays, and Fridays and catch up on sleep every other day. But of course, there was no way Satan would let this plan be: I ended up sleeping in every day of the week.

Do you see how my life at the altar came crumbling down? The main reason behind my bankruptcy was the collapse of my life at the altar. Because I was sleeping in, I was not able to take notes in my prayer journal. Every day, I was facing seasoned businessmen in their 50s and 60s as a young entrepreneur in her twenties. I was too young and naïve to be dealing with them. Taking in all their words without discretion, I invested and signed as a guarantor according to the advice they gave me. Though at the time it seemed like my business was expanding, it completely collapsed when the Asian Financial Crisis hit.

A life of the tent means that we align everything in the realm of wealth and riches with the will of God. A life of the altar and the tent are powerful tools to protect ourselves from mammon. It was an inevitable consequence that the collapse of my life of the altar brought down with it my life of the tent.

Back then, I was immature. The Lord gave me the ability to earn riches, but I mostly used this ability for myself. I also had a strong desire to store riches on this earth. Although I had completely lost my center, I deluded myself into thinking that I was a good Christian because of my religious background.

Restore the collapsed life of the altar and the tent! This must be your priority above all else.

Single Determination Lee JiHyoung

After hearing Sister Kim MiJin speak at a church meeting, I thought, If I can meet her in person, I bet she can help me earn a lot of money and become rich. I approached her and suggested that we keep in touch, perhaps meeting in person. I never heard back from her. At Shema Bible School (NCMN's Bible school), I paced back and forth hovering around Rev. Hong and Sister Kim MiJin in the hope that they would take notice of me.

"Brother JiHyoung, are you acting out a scene? What are you doing hovering about?"

Although Sister Kim MiJin spoke kindly, I felt as though she could see right through me.

"I'm here because God sent me here. I am here to serve NCMN ministries with my life."

What I actually wanted to say was, "I wanted to meet you and become rich," but I could not bring myself to say the words. Sister MiJin replied:

"Well, then. Don't just hover about. Find something you can do."

I became responsible for running all sorts of tedious errands during the initial founding stages of NCMN. Rev. Hong and Sister Kim MiJin must have deemed me faithful because they saw it fit for me to take on a leadership role.

"Brother JiHyoung, how would you like to be an acting leader in the first King's Finances School?"

"King's Finances School? How would I do that?"

"Don't worry, Brother JiHyoung. I'll be helping you out. I would like you to be a part of the administrative staff as acting leader."

I knew that with that any sign of hesitation, Sister Kim MiJin would offer the opportunity to someone else. I replied immediately, "Okay! I'll serve with everything I've got!"

And just like that, I became an acting leader for the 1st session of the King's Finances School. When the world's first King's Finances School was opened, it felt as though we were in David's Cave of Adullam. The school was filled with people in debt and people plagued with trials and bitterness. Looking at them, I saw reflections of myself. I was no different from them: a once-popular actor now fallen from grace and forgotten; a failed businessman who had lost everything after bankruptcy but his one meager life. I worked hard to learn, thinking that I needed it more than anyone else.

With each passing week of lectures, the students began to change. Some students who used to break down in tears and scream during worship began to heal. Students who trained hard with the execution workbook found areas in which to apply their newfound knowledge. Testimonies of God's work, big and small, came flooding out from their lives.

As the students changed their master from mammon to God, the school became a living record of the acts of the Holy Spirit. Based on the principles of giving and taking, the students filled each other's needs; by learning to forgive and accept, they healed their broken relationships. Students changed their master to God and God only by training to pay full tithes. They began dreaming of a breakthrough in their finances.

It was through God's wondrous grace that I was given the opportunity to serve as an acting leader during the first session of the King's Finances School despite my shortcomings. Currently, there are more than 3,000 influential leaders at the school. Even though NCMN never engages in student recruitment activities, as soon as online signups begin two months before classes start, all 400 spots (350 students, 50 waitlisted students) fill up within 80 seconds most of the time. Students who are accepted on their third, fifth, or tenth tries admit that they were happier to have gotten in than if one of their children had been accepted into one of the most prestigious universities in Korea.

The Lord blesses the longing hearts of students who gather together to worship Him with all that they have, who cry out to Him with joy and emotion. He frees them from their depression, heals their diseases, and fills their hearts with joy.

Around three years into my ministry at NCMN, I received a text message on my phone.

"How have you been? We are preparing to make a movie on Rev. Joo KiChul, and I would like to recommend you for the leading role. Are you available?"

Inside, I screamed, You bet I am! But the date of the audition overlapped with the leaders' training that would be held at the King's Finances School in Sydney. Not knowing what to do, I decided to consult my teacher. Sister MiJin's response to such an important decision in my life was strikingly simple.

"Your prior commitments should take priority. You pray and decide."

Her answer discouraged me. But this might be one of the last chances in my acting career that I get to play a leading role again, I thought. But in the end, I prayed about it and decided to honor my prior commitment. I called the director and said, "Director, I won't be able to audition on that date." And when I explained the reason, he told me that I could come audition immediately, before leaving for Sydney.

So, I went to the audition, went to Sydney, and returned to Korea after faithfully completing the leaders' training course. Upon return, I received the good news.

"Dear Lee JiHyoung, you have been chosen for the role of Rev. Joo KiChul in the movie, Single Determination."

I began to learn the importance of letting go and not trying so hard to make things happen.

One day, Sister MiJin told me in passing, "I would like for you to prepare a finance lecture."

Surprised, I replied, "What? Me? Do you have a lesson plan I can use?"

"No, there's no lesson plan. There are plenty of my lectures online; you can organize them and make one yourself!" That was her answer.

Whenever Sister MiJin reaches a decision about a person after spending time alone with the Lord in prayer, she mentions it to the person briefly, abruptly, and concisely. If this person fails to understand her offer the very moment she makes it, the opportunity is handed on to someone else. However, if he or she can grasp it, Sister MiJin guides, fosters, and makes a leader out of the person. So, I answered her immediately.

Starting that day, I listened again to all her online lectures and got to work on the lesson plan. I checked with Sister MiJin and made improvements along the way. The lectures I rewatched for the lesson plan were transformative. As my longing for the Lord grew more profound, I was able to let go of the things of this world more and more.

Sister MiJin is not about theories. She lives it out in her life; she teaches by example. Saying that Jesus, too, tells us to practice before teaching, Sister MiJin will not even mention things she has not lived out in her life.

That was the beginning of the King's Finances lecturers' multiplier course. We have since produced six King's Finances lecturers. The Kings Finances School for Kids also produced another ten lecturers who are all serving in the King's Finances schools and lectures all around the world. How great the grace of God!

The Worldly Rich Solomon's Attitude Toward Riches

> Definition of the worldly poor:
> First, people who are stingy with God but generous to themselves
>
> Second, people who have acquired wealth through unjust means
>
> See *The King's Finances I*, English translation, p. 186-198.

"Meaningless! Meaningless!" says the Teacher. "Utterly meaningless! Everything is meaningless." Ecc.1:2

Why did Solomon declare everything to be meaningless at the end of his life? There may be many reasons, but his attitude toward riches is worth noting.

"I said to myself, 'Come now, I will test you with pleasure to find out what is good.' But that also proved to be meaningless" (Ecc. 2:1).

What pleasures did Solomon enjoy and why is he saying that it is also meaningless?

"I searched with my heart how to cheer my body with wine—my heart still guiding me with wisdom" (Ecc. 2:3, English Standard Version).

He pleasured his flesh with concubines, women, and wine.

"I made great works. I built houses and planted vineyards for myself" (Ecc. 2:4, ESV).

This verse tells us why Solomon made great works; he built houses and planted vineyards for himself.

"I made myself pools from which to water the forest of growing trees" (Ecc. 2:6, ESV).

The large ponds and reservoirs Solomon made were also for himself.

"I bought male and female slaves, and had slaves who were born in my house. I had also great possessions of herds and flocks, more than any who had been before me in Jerusalem" (Ecc. 2:7, ESV).

All his slaves and possessions of herds and flocks, too, were for himself.

"I also gathered for myself silver and gold and the treasure of kings and provinces. I got singers, both men and women, and many concubines" (Ecc. 2:8, ESV).

Again, he received singers and many concubines for himself.

"Then I considered all that my hands had done and the toil I had expended in doing it, and behold, all was vanity and a striving after wind, and there was nothing to be gained under the sun... for apart from me who can eat or who can have enjoyment?" (Ecc. 2:11,25, ESV).

This is Solomon, the wisest, the world record-breaking richest man on earth, in the last days of his life. The collapse of Solomon's life of the altar, his pursuit of pleasure, and his concubines dragged an entire country down into idol worship. When the life of the altar (our relationship with God) collapses, it naturally leads to the collapse of the life of the tent (our relationship with possessions). This is because the power to live a life of the tent stems from a life of the altar.

Solomon was facing the last of his days; soon, he would be meeting God. Do you think he had the courage to meet Him? How remorseful he must have felt! With a heart of penance, Solomon tells us of his life and gives us his last words of advice.

> The end of the matter; all has been heard. Fear God and keep his commandments, for this is the whole duty of man. For God will bring every deed into judgment, with every secret thing, whether good or evil. Ecc. 12:13-14, ESV

Hear the words of the worldly rich man who is screaming in our ears for attention!

The Holy Rich David's Attitude Toward Riches

Definition of the holy rich:
First, a person whose method of making and spending money is biblical
Second, a person who confesses, "God, you are master, and I am a steward"
Third, a person to whom God has given the ability to earn riches
Fourth, a person merciful and generous

I looked for the reason behind God's anointing of David in David's attitude toward riches. Let us take a close look at how David prepared the materials for the construction of the temple.

"With all my resources I have provided for the temple of my God—gold for the gold work, silver for the silver, bronze for the bronze, iron for the iron and wood for the wood, as well as onyx for the settings, turquoise, stones of various colors, and all kinds of fine stone and marble—all of these in large quantities" (1 Chron. 29:2).

David prepared an immense amount of public (national) resources necessary for the construction of the temple. But he also offered up his own personal resources. How and just how much did David offer up to God for the construction of the temple?

First, he offered up his treasure in his devotion to the temple.

Second, he offered up 3,000 talents of gold from his own treasures.

"Besides, in my devotion to the temple of my God I now give my personal treasures of gold and silver for the temple of my God, over and above everything I have provided for this holy temple: three thousand talents of gold (gold of Ophir) and seven thousand talents of refined silver, for the overlaying of the walls of the buildings, for the gold work and the silver work, and for all the work to be done by the craftsmen. Now, who is willing to consecrate themselves to the Lord today?" (1 Chron. 29:3-5)

> How much is one talent worth today? There are differing opinions among theologians because calculations differ according to the times, changes in value, and inflation. A talent was a unit of weight in ancient Judea; each talent was the equivalent of approximately 34 kilograms. In today's market value, one talent would be worth around two billion won. Hong SungGun

So the 3,000 talents David gave as an offering to the Lord was two billion won × 3,000: six trillion won! Why is this of any significance? It is significant because his actions reveal his heart. As a leader, David always showed how to love God by example. Then he challenged others, "Now, who is willing to consecrate themselves to the Lord today?" Leaders, who had seen the payment and return on faith, obedience, and dedication made the following choice:

"Then the leaders of families, the officers of the tribes of Israel, the commanders of thousands and commanders of hundreds, and the officials in charge of the king's work gave willingly. They gave toward the work on the temple of God five thousand talents and ten thousand darics of gold, ten thousand talents of silver, eighteen thousand talents of bronze and a hundred thousand talents of iron" (1 Chron. 29:6-7).

When converted to today's value, the offerings the leaders of families gave is equally jaw-dropping. Now, look at the decision the people made after seeing the faith and dedication of David and the leaders of families and what they received in return.

"The people rejoiced at the willing response of their leaders, for they had given freely and wholeheartedly to the Lord. David the king also rejoiced greatly" (1 Chron. 29:9).

The dedication of the leader flowed into the leaders of the families. Seeing their leaders, the people followed. The entire nation joyfully volunteered to give to the temple, and King David rejoiced at this. I bow my head in awe of the humble confession that David was able to make even after having given an offering so extraordinary.

"But who am I, and who are my people, that we should

be able to give as generously as this? Everything comes from you, and we have given you only what comes from your hand. Lord our God, all this abundance that we have provided for building you a temple for your Holy Name comes from your hand, and all of it belongs to you."
1 Chron. 29:14,16

See the confession of David, a true holy rich man. He confesses that all his possessions are from the Lord and that therefore, he is merely giving back what he has received. David was a holy rich man and steward to the core.

My Life as a Holy Rich Person Finally Begins

This happened a few years back, at a King's Finances revival conference at the San Francisco Full Gospel Church. A middle-aged sister came to see me during a break in the lecture. She told me that she was a dentist but that her practice had gone bankrupt. She said that her bankruptcy had led to the collapse of many other areas in her life, and when she had decided to take her own life a friend of hers in Korea sent her a link to a lecture through an online messenger, saying, "She's in your exact situation. I hope you watch it and find some encouragement and strength."

From that day, she watched the videos over and over again and began her training with the lectures. She told me she had come to meet me after hearing the news that Rev. Hong and I would be visiting for a seminar. She looked like a strong-willed person who would be capable of many good works. Before we parted, she promised me that she would do all in her power to live out the teachings of the King's Finances in her life.

After our initial meeting, I remembered her in all my prayers. My hope and expectations for this sister in Christ grew each day. Then, on February 1, 2017, I received a text message from her.

> "Sister MiJin, it has been a while, hasn't it? I am the dentist from San Francisco. Today, three years after I began running from debt as though my life depended on it, I paid off all my big debts. I listened to your lectures over 100 times, and I lived them out in my life.
>
> Others my age are slowly retiring and stepping off the stage, but at the age of 60, I am just now beginning. I am doing this to challenge myself to live as a holy rich woman, living on 10 percent and flowing the remaining 90 percent to those in need. It still feels like a dream when I think about how good my life is these days.
>
> Your lectures are what gave me the strength and courage to make it to today. I will send you an email detailing all the times I experienced God and His miracles while I was training with your lectures. I am preparing to treat the teeth of 5,000 people living in poverty. Currently, I am serving the homeless, prison inmates, as well as the elderly in nursing homes. I'm also volunteering with an autoharp group that plays the chromaharp for charity.

I am eternally grateful for God's grace which allowed me to be both spiritually and financially restored. Such grace that I could never repay. If it were not for your testimony and the King's Finances lectures, I would still be lost in that long tunnel of darkness. I give all the glory to God. Your loving sister in Christ."

The reason this message brought me such joy was that she "lived it out." Looking at how God had transformed her from a debtor to a minister who works to establish the kingdom of God, I could feel the heart of the father for his prodigal son.

When the prodigal son returned after squandering away his share of the inheritance, the father did not say, "What have you done with the money? Why have you returned a beggar?" He embraced and kissed his smelly prodigal son, who had returned a failure; he danced and welcomed him with a feast. This father is God, our Father!

"Though the mountains be shaken and the hills be removed, yet my unfailing love for you will not be shaken nor my covenant of peace be removed," says the Lord, who has compassion on you. Isa. 54:10

CHATPER 3

The Six Rules
of Life

PART II Restore a Life of the Altar and the Tent

The Correct Relationship with God, People, and Riches

I was in the wilderness for ten years. I did not know where to go; I was cold and hungry. The pain of others' betrayal plagued me. I was sick in spirit and body, surrounded by despair and confusion. That is what the wilderness is like. But for me, the wilderness was also a blessing because it was there that I restored my closeness with God. There in the wilderness, God gave me a set of rules to follow in life. He gave me a total of six rules: two each for our relationship with God, people, and riches.

Two Rules on Our Relationship with God

First, accept God's sovereignty and give thanks in all circumstances.

Every corner of this world was filled with evil during Enoch's time. What could have been the key to life which enabled Enoch to walk by God's side for 300 years during an age rampant with suspicion, doubt, unbelief, and sin?

"By faith Enoch was taken from this life, so that he did not experience death: 'He could not be found, because God had taken him away.' For before he was taken, he was commended as one who pleased God. And without faith it is impossible to please God, because anyone who comes to him must believe that he exists and that he rewards those who earnestly seek him" (Heb. 11:5-6).

During a time in which the world was full of evil, Enoch declared with faith: "God is alive! He rules over all!"

Enoch was able to live by God's methods in a world where evil seemed to reign triumphant because he had his eye set on the One who unfailingly rewards. Today, we need the same key to life that Enoch once held. We are living in an age in which God's laws are being disregarded in every domain, including the economy, society, and culture. We must have the faith to declare "God is alive and rules over all" even in these times.

We must look to God, who unfailingly rewards those who seek him. This is because only those who seek the Lord can make the ultimate decision to live by God's ways and methods. Only those who acknowledge the sovereignty of God can declare, "Father, I thank you in all circumstances," regardless of the situation.

Saying, "Lord, thank you," is the most powerful expression of faith.

David is the quintessential example. Psalm 34 is a poem David authored while in exile running from Saul when he pretended to be insane in front of Abimelek (Achish) who had driven him away.

> I will extol the Lord at all times; his praise will always be on my lips. I will glory in the Lord; let the afflicted hear and rejoice. Glorify the Lord with me; let us exalt his name together. I sought the Lord, and he answered me; he delivered me from all my fears. Psa. 34:1-4

David, a man after God's own heart! If we summarize his poem into a single sentence, it would be, "Father, thank you in all circumstances." David's poem is overflowing with faith. I, too, wish to follow David's faith.

Second, pay the price to obey God's voice.

Jesus paid the highest price of all. The Cross represents both God's righteousness and His love. The Cross was suffering, but it was also the will of the Father. We can understand this through Jesus' prayer.

> Going a little farther, he fell with his face to the ground and prayed, "My Father, if it is possible, may this cup be taken from me. Yet not as I will, but as you will." Matt. 26:39

Jesus became flesh to obey His Father, and He carried all of humanity's sins to the Cross on our behalf. With the price He paid, Jesus gave salvation to all humankind and defeated the devil.

There is one common characteristic among men and women whom the Lord has used for a great purpose. Although Moses could have become quickly enraged when the people disobeyed and challenged the Lord, he decided that managing his anger was the price to pay and so he knelt before the Lord. Moses was very good at one thing, and that was to fall on his knees before the Lord. He knew that kneeling was the only way he could achieve the task which the Lord had assigned him. A leader, who does not learn to sacrifice his emotions as the price to pay causes the breakdown of peace and relationships.

In faith, Moses paid the price in the following three ways.

First, he declined power.

Moses grew up as the son of Pharaoh's daughter. He was a man of tremendous power.

"By faith Moses, when he had grown up, refused to be known as the son of Pharaoh's daughter" (Heb. 11:24).

Second, he declined the pleasures of the world.

"He chose to be mistreated along with the people of God rather than to enjoy the fleeting pleasures of sin" (Heb. 11:25).

Moses, should he have wanted, had the authority to enjoy all the pleasures of the world. But he chose to suffer together with the people of God rather than to enjoy the pleasures of worldly sin.

Third, he declined the treasures of Egypt.

"He regarded disgrace for the sake of Christ as of greater value than the treasures of Egypt, because he was looking ahead to his reward" (Heb. 11:26).

He turned down all the riches of Egypt. With faith, Moses looked to the Lord who would reward him on that day and was able to turn down the treasure of Egypt: worldly riches, bribes, and unjust wealth. However, those who serve both God and riches could never turn down the riches of Egypt.

In faith, I also learned to decline the power, pleasures, and treasures of Egypt as Moses had done. I willingly paid the price, looking ahead to the reward which the Lord has waiting for me. I chose to live a life of sharing and flowing. I decided to wear less, eat less, and live in lesser comfort.

Two Rules on Our Relationship with People

First, only speak words of hope, both to yourself and others.

Words of faith create hope.

"Let your conversation be always full of grace, seasoned with salt, so that you may know how to answer everyone" (Col. 4:6).

"Words of salt" prevent decay and give life to people. We need to learn to discern what words of salt are before we begin to speak. People are brought back to life when we speak the truth with faith.

"'For I know the plans I have for you,' declares the Lord, 'plans to prosper you and not to harm you, plans to give you hope and a future'" (Jer. 29:11).

God has a plan of peace (success) and hope for our future.

"Because it is the Lord God almighty who makes plans for my future, things will turn out for good. My future will be a success."

I believe these words and declare them with my mouth. This is my faith and what gives me hope.

"We have this hope as an anchor for the soul, firm and secure. It enters the inner sanctuary behind the curtain" (Heb. 6:19).

"May the God of hope fill you with all joy and peace as you trust in him, so that you may overflow with hope by the power of the Holy Spirit" (Rom. 15:13).

Hope has clear signs of showing itself. It brings joy and peace. Then, how might we come to be overflowing with hope? It is through the power of the Holy Spirit. The God of hope fills us with overflowing hope with the power of the Holy Spirit.

Second, overcome your anger and approach both your work and others from a place of love.

Do you want a breakthrough? Then overcome your anger. Anger is rooted in pride.

"Whoever winks maliciously causes grief, and a chattering fool comes to ruin. The mouth of the righteous is a fountain of life, but the mouth of the wicked conceals violence. Hatred stirs up conflict, but love covers over all wrongs" (Prov. 10:10-12).

"A quick-tempered person does foolish things, and the one who devises evil schemes is hated" (Prov. 14:17).

"Better a patient person than a warrior, one with self-control than one who takes a city" (Prov. 16:32).

"The lips of fools bring them strife, and their mouths invite a beating. The mouths of fools are their undoing, and their lips are a snare to their very lives… The tongue has the power of life and death, and those who love it will eat its fruit" (Prov. 18:6-7,21).

"A person's wisdom yields patience; it is to one's glory to overlook an offense… A hot-tempered person must pay the penalty; rescue them, and you will have to do it again" (Prov. 19:11,19).

"Like apples of gold in settings of silver is a ruling rightly given" (Prov. 25:11).

"A new command I give you: Love one another. As I have loved you, so you must love one another. By this everyone will know that you are my disciples, if you love one another" (John 13:34-35).

We must know how to have control over our temper and anger. Many students who train at the King's Finances School remain in the wilderness because of a failure, not in other areas, but because they get stuck in their anger and cannot overcome it. It is the meek who will receive God's promise of His land as an inheritance.

My one wish, while I was in the wilderness, was to become a true disciple of the Lord. The Lord gave me a simple strategy, "Overcome your anger and approach both your work and others from a place of love."

When we love each other, the world will know us to be disciples of Jesus Christ. Simeon and Levi had no control over their anger and thus were removed from the line of Abraham's inheritance; all the blessings of the inheritance were handed down to Judah and Joseph (see Gen. 49:3-22).

Two Rules on Our Relationship with Riches

First, ask yourself this question three times before you purchase anything: "Do I really need this?"

Even if I am buying something small, I always ask myself this question three times before making a purchase. This is a sure way to block impulse buying that stems from mammon and stop the leakage of funds. It is the prevailing question we must ask to structure our finances in such a way that our income exceeds our expenses.

Second, share as soon as things begin to collect in your home.

The Lord asked me in the wilderness, "Do you love me? Then feed my sheep." Through this He showed me the miracle of the five loaves and two fishes. We can experience this miracle in our lives today through a life of sharing. If 100 people share a bit of what they have, they can feed 5000 and still have 12 baskets left over.

"Very truly I tell you, whoever believes in me will do the works I have been doing, and they will do even greater things than these, because I am going to the Father" (John 14:12).

Becoming a Multiplier of the King's Finances   Seo MiHwa

I began married life in 2001 with only 40 million won in savings. In 2007, my husband bought our first apartment with 100 percent debt and put the title in his brother's name. Then through sales and purchases of lotting-out rights, we purchased three apartments in total. Although we struggled to pay the interest and principal on our housing loans, we believed that we could buy a big home if we could sell the apartments we owned at a good price. So, we took out a 240 million won loan and moved to a 36 pyeong apartment. That is how we ended up with four apartments.

We lived on lines of credit and waited for the housing prices to rise. We thought that once they did, all our problems would be solved. But their value never rose, and we were not able to sell any of them. There we were, house poor, barely making ends meet by staving off the debt of one credit card with the other.

At the time, my husband was making 2.2 million won a month, 1.6 million of it went just to pay off the interest. After paying tithes, all we had was 300,000 won to cover our living expenses. I was stuck in the middle of an endless tunnel of poverty. I could do nothing for my children who complained about eating the same thing every day. Despite their cries, I shuddered at the thought of having our assets seized and would scream at them, "No! We don't have money!" That was my life.

'God! How did I ever get here? Please get me out of this situation as soon as possible,' I cried out to the Lord in desperation. I was desperate for any sign of hope; I just wanted it to end. We had nowhere and no one else from whom we could borrow. When I spoke with my husband who was powerless to do anything about it, he told me to figure it out using credit cards. My entire side of the family became credit delinquents because I was not able to repay the money that I had borrowed from them.

Given our financial situation, I began to resent tithing. I felt that not having to tithe would solve many of my problems. My faith dwindled in the face of reality; my once strong faith came tumbling down and disappeared without a trace. What was I thinking when all the income we have is the 2.2 million won a month that my husband makes? Life was hell. I began to understand why people fight, run away, and break up families over money. I neither had a place to run nor a desire to meet people.

To get to church, I rode my husband's old bicycle for over an hour because I did not have money to pay for gas. I would tell my church friends that I did it for the exercise. I wore the exact same clothes and shoes every day; I could not even dream about changing my style. The endless poverty took a toll on my children as well; the emotional neglect they endured made rough people out of them.

I had had enough. I was extremely disappointed with God.

I kept the Sabbath; I paid all my tithes; I served the church and volunteered with everything I had, but still, He did not help. I cried and cried every day, demanding the Lord give me money.

'God! Help me now. Give me money. You can start by giving me 100 million won.'

That was the situation I was in when our church held a King's Finances revival conference. The words spoken during that revival conference shook my life to the core. That meeting was the single stream of light that I needed. That light revealed all the worldly greed that had consumed me from within and I learned about mammon, who had taken me over using my finances.

The Lord asked my husband and me to make a life-changing decision. It was not enough just to hear and be moved by the words; we had to live them out. We signed up for the 7th session of the King's Finances School. During the Oh! My Master musical lecture in the fourth week of classes, actors acted out the lives of "the Debtors" and "the Shiners." When the musical ended, the Debtors asked us to step forward and cut up our credit cards.

Although we cut up those cards with complete determination, mammon was not one to let us go so easily. My husband continued to repeat the process of making new credit cards and cutting them up every time he felt anxious about our finances. I, too, thought about quitting the King's Finances School many times. But my fellow small group members and leader did not allow me to give up and instead encouraged me to keep me on track. With their help, I once again resolved not to back down.

Although I did not understand all the lessons, I believed and began my training in earnest. Rev. Hong and Sister Kim MiJin challenged me to live a life of relentless faith.

"Do not be afraid. The Lord will do His work if you have faith. But do not become a religious fanatic. Faith is not having your wishes granted. Faith is only believing in the Lord's words and obeying them."

With each passing day, a determined attitude of "Let's do this!" consumed each member of my small group. These words, spoken in one of the lecturers, stuck with me.

"The Lord will give you extra money. Experience it for yourselves. The Lord will surely lend His helping hand to you, who have given up everything to live by faith."

The training continued, and each day we witnessed more testimonies, large and small. Then, we began sharing our testimonies. In the process of changing to a new job, my husband received a bonus of 25 million won out of the blue (but this was just the beginning). Just as had been taught to us, we first used the money to pay our tithes and then used the rest to pay off our debts. And when graduation day finally came, a lecturer left us with these words.

"I send you to the mission field of your lives. It all starts now. Let us live it out! Live it out! Live it out! Only those who live it out will be smiling at the finish line."

I resolved to train harder and live out what I learned in

school with even higher intensity. I focused on one online lecture per day and took notes of the key message. I was thankful to God, who looks not at our outward appearance but into hearts.

With the encouragement of the message that God will give me a chance as well, I started training my heart. I took control over my mouth through meekness and humility training. By training to speak with faith and training to obey the Word, I grew in knowledge of the Word of God.
Sister MiJin's tearful visit to her creditor with a single 10,000 won bill in her hand as payment toward her 600 million won debt challenged me to take action for myself. The debtor is slave to his creditor! The debtor's life has no influence! I had no choice but to change my master.
Sister MiJin's testimony of how she was forgiven 300 million of her 600 million won debt with God's grace gave me the strength to put forth my "best 1" and live it out in my life. I purchased a new *The King's Finances Workbook* that day and immediately got to work on my debt repayment project.

I began my first month of training with the workbook. The first thing I did was to record all my income and expenses as they were at the time. I wrote down all my assets, current debts, and repayment plans. I did not have much to write in the income section as my husband's salary was all the income we had.
I took to heart the teaching that we should find dormant

funds and create new funds and began looking for "hidden money." I received refunds for two insurance policies that had reached maturity and received 1.76 million won and 2.69 million for each. I used this money to pay off about four million won in debt. I began looking for savings, gold, and silver that I had forgotten about and repaid about 12 million won in 20 days. Seeing my debt balance decrease, I was both fascinated and overjoyed.

I started having money to spare once I began implementing the methods of the workbook. And each time I paid off a portion of my debt, mammon's grip on me loosened a little bit. I could finally breathe, and I was able to find emotional stability again. Getting closer to the light at the end of the tunnel, to my freedom, I found every day to be a joy and I began meeting up with friends again.

During the first month that I began implementing the workbook, my "budget of faith" was not perfect and I was not able to fulfill all the teachings of the King's Finances. But when I refused to give up and continued to put forth my "best 1," God did His work in the most amazing ways. The only income we had was my husband's salary, but the Lord continued to give us additional income over and over again!

I decided to draw up and implement a new "budget of faith." I set a modest spending budget in accordance to our income at the time and boldly asked the Lord for my most crucial needs.

"If you ask me, Lord, I will obey immediately, completely,

and joyfully! I will live only by faith."

And just like that, Sister MiJin's declaration had become my own. Training with the execution workbook had a huge effect. Every deposit we made in the Heavenly Bank and every seed we planted on good soil was returned to us as God's precise provision; although on a minimal budget, our family was living in much greater abundance than before.

I also learned that sowing in the Heavenly Bank means giving to the person and place that the Lord wants, not giving to those that I choose as I please. To make a deposit in the Heavenly Bank means to sow on good soil. Good soil is the poor; Good soil is the holy poor (God's people); it is the projects of the kingdom of God.

I learned that, even in good deeds, I must act within my means. I changed my attitude on giving from a me-centric, give to save face one, to a God-centric way of giving. I planned for family occasions ahead of time and set apart a budget. By training to consult the Lord about even the smallest of expenditures and flowing as the Holy Spirit moved me, I was able to boldly declare, "Lord, you are the owner of everything."

I collected all the extras we had at home and gathered them together. Sometimes, an object would make me think of a person, and sometimes seeing the needs of someone would make me think of one of those objects. It brought me joy to give my possessions away and hear words of gratitude from the people who received them.

There is a "wants envelope" enclosed in the execution workbook where you write down your wants and pray for them. When we wrote down our family's needs and gave God our best, the Lord met all our needs in a short period of time. We experienced exactly what the workbook said we would experience.

At first, we were the ones flowing what we had. But over time, the Lord provided in abundance according to our needs. And when we were planning our offering for our church's new building in the city, we remembered the teachings from the King's Finances lectures.
"Ladies and gentlemen, if you get the chance to contribute to a church construction, know that you have been given one of God's greatest gifts."
Although I wanted to give everything I had, I was still tied up in debt. Still, we decided to do the best that we could and give money for 4 pyeong, 16 million dollars, paid in one million won installments. But since we would not be able to make any additional donations with my husband's salary at the time, we decided to ask the Lord and began praying with a purpose.
'Father God, please give my husband a raise of exactly one million one.'
The training I received had emboldened me. I was undaunted when asking from the Lord; after all, the money I was asking for was not for me but for the construction of a temple. I remembered Sister Kim MiJin's words.

"Your faith is what creates miracles. God does His powerful work through our prayers. If you are praying for something that is in God's will, then pray until your prayers are answered. He will surely answer!"

And it really was true; a miracle did happen. True faith was to seek the "unseekable." Even under the most impossible of circumstances, my husband was promoted and received a raise of 750,000 won. God also provided extra funds, which allowed us to give our offering as a lump sum. My life proved the teachings of the execution workbook, the budget of faith, and the King's Finances training all to be true.

We tightened our belts and cut down on spending as we were taught to prioritize debt repayment with any extra money that God gave us. We were able to pay an additional one million won toward the repayment of the principals. Although the reduction in our living expenses budget worried me, I had the conviction that God would pay back my savings in the Heavenly Bank with interest when I needed it. And the Lord did provide, faithfully. God provided us in abundance with all sorts of things that we needed, including meat, fruit, kimchi, side dishes to go with rice, skincare products, pots, and all kinds of toiletries.

Seeing the debt balance decrease in my account brought me tremendous joy. I began to dream of a life of service to God, freed from a life of servitude to my creditors. I was able to pay off all our family's debt of 57 million won in a year after I began the workbook. What we did was the impossible, with my husband's salary as our sole source of income.

Even the banks were shocked. We decided to repay all 300 million won in debt, and two years and seven months after making that decision, we were able to free ourselves from servitude to our creditors completely!

'I am free! Now my journey to become a holy rich person can finally begin! First, seek His kingdom and His righteousness, and all these things will be added unto you!'

God did keep His promise. Now, we have paid the middle payment on a lovely apartment in a new city without going into any debt. I also witness God's abundant provision for my children. Executing the workbook is not very difficult. Before I started, I mistakenly thought I would need to cut down on everything to execute the book as it was. However, this could not have been farther from the truth. My heart was full of joy and hope as a result of the abundant results.

And when I grew weary, God was there, cheering me on and telling me, Well done, my daughter. You are doing well. He provided for me and allowed me to experience Him on a deeper level. This is a secret of the kingdom of God which only those who live by faith and have experience in God's provision of extra money could know.

In the past, I would look at myself and see no hope; I was depressed and under pressure from all sides. But with the "Live it out! Execution" training, I experienced just how diverse God's methods of provision are.

I was able to completely restore my relationship with God through the King's Finances training. I was transformed into someone who is able to rejoice always and give thanks in all circumstances. I worship our good God, our God of hope, who enables us to experience Him in limitless ways when we look to Him and put forth our "best 1."

I was taught that the faithful are multipliers; so I began multiplying the King's Finances training with fellow church members. The following testimonies are just two of the many testimonies that came from that group.

Living a Life That Has Riches Under Servitude Deaconess

Kim JungSook (Pseudonym)

The companies for which my husband worked either did not pay his salary properly or shut down repeatedly. So, my income working in study rooms and as a janitor was mostly responsible for making ends meet. Yet raising three children in college and high school, our finances deteriorated and we had to move into a rental studio apartment.

My husband and I borrowed money, sometimes telling each other and sometimes not. After struggling to survive for ten years, both our hearts and minds had grown weary. Although we worked hard, we never had enough. Every month, we had to rely on either borrowed money or credit cards just to get by. Then one day, on Sister MiHwa's recommendation, I purchased *The King's Finances Workbook* and began executing it as though my life depended on it. After all, I had nothing to lose. I was able to profoundly experience God's presence and resolve a massive debt by implementing the "budget of faith." But above all, my greatest prayer request was answered through my training; my husband returned to the Lord.

We received some of the pay that had not been paid and were able to move out of the studio apartment into our own 32 pyeong leased apartment. God provided extra money, and we were able to pay the signing fee for the new apartment. Our lives were transformed; we were no longer slaves to debt but the rulers of riches.

A Couple Becomes One to Clear All Debts Deacon

Kwon SookHee (Pseudonym)

Despite having two incomes as a couple and keeping books for our household finances, we always ended up drawing 500,000-700,000 won from our line of credit at the end of each month. Our debts were snowballing. And although my husband and I had attended a King's Finances revival conference which had desperately inspired us to be a holy rich couple, our reality was that we had no escape from being slaves to our debt. That was our situation when we began training with a small group.

We gave our "best 1" to ensure that our income exceeded our expenses. As a result, we were able to stop using our line of credit and began paying 500,000 won towards our debt each month. The training we underwent as a couple allowed us to live a life of faith as a couple united.

The "Let's Live It Out! Debt Repayment Project" completely

changed our household finances. We escaped from debt and are no longer slaves to our creditors.

CHATPER 4

Is My Arm Too Short?

Remove the Foreign Rabble Within Yourselves

Numbers Chapter 11 describes the Israelites in the wilderness, tired of eating manna and complaining to Moses, saying they want to eat meat.

> The rabble with them began to crave other food, and again the Israelites started wailing and said, "If only we had meat to eat! Num. 11:4

The "foreign rabble" who were among the Israelites instigated the situation with their greed and desires. The same was happening to me: the foreign rabble within me was interfering in my relationship with God. I prayed to the Lord that he might show me the foreign rabble and took notes when He did.

"Envy, greed, complaint, discontent, comparison, pride, unbelief."

These were the foreign rabble residing in me. The more the Lord removed my veil to show me myself, the greater the turmoil I felt within me became. I decided that the Lord could not possibly use me as I was.

Now Is Not the Time to Ask for Meat

The lament and pressure from the Israelites eventually became so great that Moses lost his hope for life.

"Did I conceive all these people? Did I give them birth?... Where can I get meat for all these people?... If this is how you are going to treat me, please go ahead and kill me—if I have found favor in your eyes—and do not let me face my own ruin" (Num. 11:12-15).

The Lord heard the Israelites when they cried, "If only we had meat to eat! We were better off in Egypt!" The Lord told them that He would give them meat to eat and Moses delivered God's message to the people.

"Now the Lord will give you meat, and you will eat it. You will not eat it for just one day, or two days, or five, ten or twenty days, 20 but for a whole month—until it comes out of your nostrils and you loathe it—because you have rejected the Lord, who is among you, and have wailed before him, saying, 'Why did we ever leave Egypt?'" (Num. 11:18-20).

The total number of men to be fed alone was 600,000. Including women and children, the number to be fed is estimated to have been around two to three million. But look at Moses' response when the Lord tells him that He will feed meat to that many for an entire month.

"Would they have enough if flocks and herds were slaughtered for them? Would they have enough if all the fish in the sea were caught for them?" (Num. 11:22).

"The Lord answered Moses, 'Is the Lord's arm too short?

Now you will see whether or not what I say will come true for you'" (Num. 11:23).

The Lord counters Moses' question with another question, "Is the Lord's arm too short?" There is nothing that is impossible for the Almighty. See how He provides meat for the people.

"Now a wind went out from the Lord and drove quail in from the sea. It scattered them up to two cubits deep all around the camp, as far as a day's walk in any direction" (Num. 11:31).

Two cubits are around one meter. The Lord surrounded the camp with quail, up to two cubits deep and as far as a day's walk in every direction. If we consider 30 kilometers to be the distance a person can walk in a day, the distance would be from Gangnam Station to Yangpyeong to the east, Incheon City Hall to the West, Suwon Station to the south, and farther than Uijongbu, up to Yangju to the north.

Can you imagine? God had poured quail a meter deep on an area equivalent to that vast expanse of land with Gangnam Station in the center! Did God give this quail with love? No, He did not. He was angered by the complaints, laments, and unbelief of the Israelites. God was telling them that it was not the time for meat; it was the time to train. He was telling them that it was the time for them to engrain God's vision into their hearts.

You Will Eat Meat when He Has Enlarged Your Territory

I was famished in the wilderness. Some days, I only had water to drink. I fantasized about eating meat for an entire week. That was my miserable reality; I could not stop thinking about meat when, as a mother, I did not have enough to feed my young child, YuJin. My hunger became my prayer and fasting.

'My daughter, now is not the time to eat meat.'

There was one verse that I could not get out of my mind.

> When the Lord your God has enlarged your territory as he promised you, and you crave meat and say, "I would like some meat," then you may eat as much of it as you want
> Deut. 12:20

I had immediately found the answer. Now was not the time to eat meat.

'Now is the time to expand your vision,' I thought to myself.

'Lord! Show me Your vision.'

'Enlarge your territory as the Lord your God has promised you.'

How much has God promised me? Rev. Hong's Genesis Chapter 13 lecture opened my eyes.

"The Lord said to Abram after Lot had parted from him, 'Look around from where you are, to the north and south, to the east and west. All the land that you see I will give to you and your offspring forever… Go, walk through the length and breadth of the land, for I am giving it to you'" (Gen. 13:14-15,17).

There was no limit! It was as far as I could see to the north and south, to the east and west; it was the entire length and breadth of the land that I had traveled.

The Lord was telling me, 'My daughter, overcome the limits of your circumstances.'

I needed faith.

When Abraham's and Lot's possessions became great, the quarrels between the herders of Abraham and Lot grew. Abraham made a proposition to Lot.

"Is not the whole land before you? Let's part company. If you go to the left, I'll go to the right; if you go to the right, I'll go to the left" (Gen. 13:9).

Lot chose the well-watered land of Sodom.

"Lot looked around and saw that the whole plain of the Jordan toward Zoar was well watered, like the garden of the Lord, like the land of Egypt. (This was before the Lord destroyed Sodom and Gomorrah.) So Lot chose for himself the whole plain of the Jordan and set out toward the east. The two men parted company: Abram lived in the land of Canaan, while Lot lived among the cities of the plain and pitched his tents near Sodom. Now the people of Sodom were wicked and were sinning greatly against the Lord" (Gen. 13:10-13).

Here, God shows us two different perspectives on Sodom and Gomorrah.

- Lot's perspective – It is like the garden of the Lord, like the land of Egypt (Gen. 13:10).
- God's perspective – The people of Sodom were wicked and are great sinners (Gen. 13:13).
- Lot's conclusion – That land will guarantee my stability and prosperity.
- God's conclusion – That land will perish.

God's and Lot's perspectives were starkly different. I needed to train to remove Lot's worldly eyes and see through the eyes of God. After Lot had left, God told Abraham to look the north, south, east, and west and said that He would give him all that he sees.

I understood the meaning behind the Scripture. I needed to remove the "things of Lot," which chose the desirable and succulent Sodom and Gomorrah as though the seen world is all there is. Instead, I needed spiritual eyes that could see the unseen world; what I needed was God's vision.

It was not the time to eat meat but to expand my vision and look to the limitless blessings that God promised to Abraham's seeds in faith. I decided to put these words into action and went up to the top of the 63 Building in Yeouido so that I could see as far as possible. But even from the very top of the building, I still could not see all of Seoul with my eyes.

So, I worked part-time and saved up money to buy a plane ticket to Africa, the farthest point away from Korea. And each time the plane flew over a different country, I got up from my seat and walked northward, southward, eastward, and westward in the small space that was available in the cabin, declaring:

"Father, we are now passing through Country C, I look to the north, south, east, and west of this country. Please use me to establish Your kingdom and righteousness on these lands!"

I did this all the way to Africa. When I got there, I walked through the length and breadth of the land as far as I could. This was an act of my faith. Nothing happened after that for ten whole years. At the time, I had no idea what God would do through me. In August 2018, I went to Morocco and Mauritania in West Africa to give lectures. God increased my influence to establish His kingdom. He is expanding my influence as far as my eyes had travelled on that plane. I now have the privilege to journey to the ends of the earth, to the north, south, east, and west to spread the Word of God.

Wherever I went, people were saved, and the finances of heaven were set loose. Remarkable testimonies abound in every place the King's Finances are pronounced. And now, I can enjoy the highest quality meat whenever I want and as much as I want.

The Mighty Power of the Execution Workbook Lee EunJoo

I completed the King's Finances School after first learning about the King's Finances through online lectures. It had been a while since I had last taken *The King's Finances* off the shelf. I turned the cover to the first page where I had written myself a note when I gifted myself the book. It brought back such memories. *The King's Finances* was a powerful book.

I watched the online lectures more than 100 times over two years, a period during which I purchased and trained with the workbook and cut up all my credit cards. I then paid off all of my debt and was completely liberated from servitude to my creditors on January 3, 2017. In 2018, I used 80 percent of my income on myself and flowed 20 percent. This year, I am determined to live on 70 percent and flow 30 percent.

I grew up in a home of idol worshippers. I tried hard to acquire riches. This greed for riches and prestige consumed me, and I too ambitiously expanded my business. My utter failure ultimately brought me back to the Lord, but I had lost all hope in the face of my harsh reality. It was at this time that I watched Sister Kim MiJin's lecture video in which she said, "First seek His kingdom and His righteousness in your life. Things to eat, drink, wear, all of these things will be added unto you." She told us to break through our circumstances by first seeking His kingdom. Her words inspired me to make the decision to evangelize others while on the way to work. But every day, I would travel to and from work without speaking a single word to

PART II Restore a Life of the Altar and the Tent

strangers.

When I told a close friend about the Gospel, she replied with words of persecution. "I'm well-off, and I don't even believe in Jesus; why are you so poor and such a failure?" I was filled with remorse. I felt that my life was standing in the way of spreading the Gospel. I needed to restore the honor of God's name.

I took detailed notes on each King's Finances lecture and resolved to live the teachings out in my life. The first teaching I implemented was "full tithes." Understanding tithing was much easier with the farming metaphor used in the King's Finances lectures. I understood that tithes are not a "matter of faith" but that they are a "matter of life."

Before the lectures, paying full tithes had always seemed a burden to me. But learning that tithing is the method through which God blesses us, tithing became a huge source of hope. I began my King's Finances training and started paying full tithes. The workbook training was especially powerful. My life changed in all domains. In the beginning, there were many instances in which I failed at the execution. Problems ensued in the very first month after I decided to pay full tithes.

I can pay all of the rent and daycare fees with 370,000 won. Do I really have to pay full tithes?

But I knew I had to live it out. I brought my full tithes to the Lord, thinking, Here goes nothing. I found it bewildering that I was not impoverished even after paying the tithes.

One day, I received 3.5 million won from my company as a

token of gratitude for using my personal car for work.

So, this is what they call extra money!

First, I dedicated my son as a minister to the lands of North Korea and gave one million won as an offering. I had listened to the online lectures over a hundred times, and as I watched these videos my wealth slowly became God's wealth.

After paying full tithes for five months, God provided us with a new home. These small and large experiences enabled me to give testimonies to my blessings. The monetary amount of the tithes I paid increased as well. But the 30 million won debt I had acted as a shackle that obstructed me from living a life of faith. I put together a group of five people who had failed as I had, and we embarked on an intensive training journey with The King's Finances book, workbook, and online lectures.

The following was our training program:

1) Read ten chapters of Scripture each day: Understand Scripture through The Word, Cover to Cover in 100 Days, read Proverbs 1 and Psalms 5.
2) Watch one King's Finances lecture each day and summarize key takeaways.
3) Keep the ledger and budget of faith as described in the book and implement it.
4) Pray for over an hour a day using the workbook's "My Devotions" and "Prayer Book."
5) Meet once a week for three hours and share the execution

process (all other sharing is prohibited)
6) Allow leaders to check the progress of the program and members to take pictures of their program milestones and post them in the group chat room
7) Be moved and encouraged by the Holy Spirit through the sharing of testimonies which arise during training

Then we embarked on a debt repayment project, belaboring over every single page of the book. I studied the priority list for debt repayment and created a repayment strategy. It was during this process that I truly began to see how dire my family's finances were. When I looked for the root cause of our debt, I saw that it was both our lack of understanding of debt as well as a general lack of will to pay back our debts. Even in debt, we were eating what we wanted and buying what we wanted using our credit cards.

So, the first thing we did was to get rid of our credit cards. My hands trembled as the scissors I held in my hands cut through the plastic money.

Cutting the cards felt as painful and scary: as though I was cutting my own heart out. The first three months without credit cards were living hell. There were so many monthly installments to pay. The first thing our family decided on was to stop dining out. We had to have the determination to cut down to the bare necessities if we were going to pay off our debt. Every time I wanted to give up, I would remember the teachings of the lectures.

'The broken finger of Sister MiJin's son! The 500 won pair of jeans!'

Every time I was on the verge of giving up, I felt as though there was a ringing in my ear, as if Sister MiJin's voice was calling out, Do not give up. Our God is faithful, and He will surely keep His promises!

Although the training was difficult, the reward was big. I received ten million won of extra money in the third month. And despite having needs of my own, I was compelled to see the needs of the holy poor before mine. The owner of our wealth really had changed. Our faith has grown through the small and large experiences we had throughout our finances training, and our love for the church and the holy poor has grown stronger than ever before.

On January 3, 2017, I was finally freed from servitude to my creditors after 25 months of hard work. Our household finances continue to improve. My experience instilled within me a love for God as well as my neighbors. I pray that our church will adopt the King's Finances training, and I dream of the day when I am living the life of the truly holy rich, living on 10 percent and flowing the remaining 90 percent.

Things Just Seem to Work Out for You   Three Sisters on Jeju Island

In February 2017, a King's Finances revival conference was held at the Full Gospel Jeju Central Church. I went to see Rev. Hong and Sister MiJin with two other friends. When I met them, I shared the testimony of how I had watched online lectures every day over the last five years while working in an orange orchard and how we three friends had lived out the teachings of the lectures. I had my first encounter with God near the end of my college career and became a believer. My monthly income ranged from 2-4 million won. Over the past ten years, I had paid 2-5 million won in offerings each year. As someone from an average household of faith with few spiritual experiences, hearing the King's Finances testimonies greatly challenged and perhaps even shocked me.

The testimonies and lectures on King's Finances taught me that I need to change my master from mammon to God, dedicate my finances and give willingly to God, and live an abundant life of sharing with my neighbors. It also taught me that I should not live as the worldly rich do but rather live to expand God's kingdom.

I listened to the lectures on repeat. Yet each time, there was something new I learned from them. I developed the courage to want to be given the miracles that Sister MiJin had experienced as my own. I prayed, declared, gave offerings, and acted in a way to make these experiences happen to me. I did not stop at being shocked or merely being aware after listening to Sister MiJin's testimony; I changed my entire perspective and chose to give to the Lord before considering spending money on anything else.

I also began relying on and obeying the sermons and vision of my church's senior pastor. When the church decided to build a new temple, my heart was filled with joy and thanks. Although I was already in debt with a housing mortgage, I did the best I could and donated 12 million won toward the construction.

Our senior pastor goes overseas for conferences and outreaches with church members roughly twice a year. Previously, I always hesitated to apply because I thought that I could not afford it. Although there were a few times I did obey and joined, there were many more times that I did not. Things are different now; when it comes to matters of the kingdom of God and the church, I obey without a moment of hesitation.

One time, 20 pastors from different countries visited our church. I supported 50 percent of their accommodation fees, feeling that it was my duty to serve the people of the Lord. This year, I have decided to support 100 percent of their accommodation costs.

I lent some support when our pastor was buying a car. I had a neighbor who needed a license, so I served her the best that I could, even paying to register her for driving classes. Then, strange things began to happen. Although I was using all my time and finances for the church, money was coming in, and my wealth was increasing. Even my mother, an unbeliever, said, "Things just seem to work out for you." My mother, who despised that I served the church and only supported my secular, for-profit endeavors, now simply accepts that I should serve the church.

Starting in 2016, I slowly increased my offerings from the yearly 2-5 million won. The total donation amount recorded on the church accounting books is 39 million won. However, if one were to account for all the unrecorded amounts too, I suspect that my actual donation amount was much higher. My income has gone up accordingly. In 2017, God's grace enabled me to tithe 19.3 million won for the month of February alone, and then tithe over 20 million won again in December. I lift the name of our faithful God on high.

− I heard the testimonies of these three sisters with Rev. Hong. The Lord encouraged us with this testimony. The sisters provided the name of their church and their senior pastor for us to verify their testimony with the church's accounting team. This testimony was fact-checked before being recorded in this book.

CHATPER 5

The Heavenly Bank
= Good Soil

The Poor

The subheadings for 2 Corinthians Chapters 8 and 9 are "generous gift" and "the gift that serves poor believers." In short, these chapters talk about offerings. This is the only section in the Bible in which two chapters deal with the issue of offerings back to back. If we take a closer look at each individual verse, we can gain a clear understanding of God's definition of offerings (see *The King's Finances I*, English translation, p. 319-326).

> **2 Corinthians 9:5**
> So I thought it necessary to urge the brothers to visit you in advance and finish the arrangements for the generous gift you had promised. Then it will be ready as a generous gift, not as one grudgingly given.

We must prepare offerings ahead of time. God is not pleased with the offering we scramble to make by reaching into our pockets or wallets for low denomination bills after the collection basket has reached us. Take some offering envelopes home and put money in it by Saturday, whether it is 1,000 won or 10,000 won, and keep it ready in your bag. Only offering prepared in advance can be a real gift. The "gift" in this verse is used to mean "offering" and especially, "a giving life."

2 Corinthians 9:6
Remember this: Whoever sows sparingly will also reap sparingly, and whoever sows generously will also reap generously.

The "this" here refers to the gift in verse 5. God uses the rules of farming to explain gifts to us through Paul.

2 Corinthians 9:7
Each of you should give what you have decided in your heart to give, not reluctantly or under compulsion, for God loves a cheerful giver.

Offerings must come from a cheerful heart. If we do not want to give reluctantly or under compulsion, we must prepare the offering beforehand.

2 Corinthians 9:8
And God is able to bless you abundantly, so that in all things at all times, having all that you need, you will abound in every good work.

In this one verse, the word "all" is used three times, and the word "every" is used once. "To abound in every good work," means to give to the poor. We can interpret this verse as follows:

"God is able to bless you abundantly with riches, so that in all things at all times, having all the riches that you need, you will abound in every good work. In other words, you will be able to live a life that provides for the poor."

2 Corinthians 9:9
As it is written: "They have freely scattered their gifts to the poor; their righteousness endures forever."

"Scattering" is a farming technique. Verse 9 describes that a giving life is a life that scatters seeds.

2 Corinthians 9:10
Now he who supplies seed (to sow) to the sower and bread for food will also supply and increase your store of seed and will enlarge the harvest of your righteousness.

A "seed" is sown, not eaten. God provides for us in two distinct categories, seeds to sow for the next harvest (seeds that must never be eaten) and bread for food.

2 Corinthians 9:11
You will be enriched in every way so that you can be generous on every occasion, and through us your generosity will result in thanksgiving to God.

Our gifts enable them (the poor) to give thanks to God and glorify His name.

2 Corinthians 9:5-11 reveal the secret of the kingdom of God. God explains gifts to us by using the rules of farming. Gifts, or offerings we make, are not money that just disappears. Just as the farmer reaps an abundant harvest with the seeds he sows, the rules of farming also apply to giving offerings. God's work always reaps in multiples. He always gives us an abundant harvest.

Let us put 2 Corinthians 9:5-11 into perspective.

9:5 Offerings (gifts) = a giving life
9:6 Farming
9:7 Offerings (a giving life)
9:8 Farming + offerings (the rules)
9:9 Farming + offerings (a giving life)
9:10 Farming
9:11 Offerings (a giving life)

In verse 5, God tells us to prepare gifts in advance. In verse 6, He tells us that the farming rule of "whoever sows sparingly will also reap sparingly, and whoever sows generously will also reap generously" plays out in the lives of those to give to the poor. Giving to the poor is like making a deposit in the Heavenly Bank. It is like planting on good soil.

The results come back in multiples. In banking terms, these deposits in the Heavenly Bank have high yields. In farming terms, it is a harvest of 30-fold, 60-fold, or 100-fold. God tells us the following about the interest rates derived from giving to the poor.

"Whoever is kind to the poor lends to the Lord, and he will reward them for what they have done" (Prov. 19:17).

"He who has pity on the poor lends to the Lord, And He will pay back what he has given" (Prov. 19:17, New King James Version).

> The Hebrew word for "to pay back," "shalam," means to repay fully or make full restitution. Hong SungGun

In Matthew 25:33-46, Jesus tells the crowd, "What you did to serve the poor, you did to serve me."

"Truly I tell you, whatever you did for one of the least of these brothers and sisters of mine, you did for me" (Matt. 25:40).

Therefore, taking care of the poor is lending to the Lord. When we help the poor, the Lord immediately tells His angels to record however much it is we have deposited into our Heavenly Bank account. By taking care of the poor, we put our savings in God's Heavenly Bank, where the interest rates are 30-fold, 60-fold, or 100-fold.

God's Interest Rates
If you help the poor among you (Deut. 15:4-11):
1) There will be no poor among you.
2) You will lend to many nations but will borrow from none.

3) You will rule over many nations, but none will rule over you.
4) The Lord your God will bless you in all your work and in everything you put your hand to.

If you help the poor among you (Psa. 41:1-3):
5) The Lord delivers you in times of trouble.
6) You are among the blessed in the land.
7) The Lord sustains you on your sickbed and restores you from your bed of illness.

If you help the poor among you (Isa. 58:7-11):
8) Your healing will take place quickly.
9) Your righteousness will go before you, and the glory of the Lord will be your rear guard.
10) You will call and the Lord will answer.
11) You will be like a well-watered garden, like a spring whose waters never fail.

The only hope for our nation lies in the body of Christ, the Church. The Lord has promised us that we, as a nation, will have no debt, will be wealthy, will not be ruled by other nations, will influence other nations, and be prosperous if we help the poor.

Tithes

> Now he who supplies seed to the sower and bread for food will also supply and increase your store of seed and will enlarge the harvest of your righteousness 2 Cor. 9:10

God supplies and increases our store of seed and blesses us. Seeds are always included in our harvests. It is when we plant these seeds that we activate the rules of farming and harvest abundantly.

When God wishes to give us two ears of corn, He only gives us one single kernel of corn as a seed. Although it may seem small and insignificant, out of this single kernel grows one stalk of corn. From one stalk, you get two ears. Now, count the number of kernels in each ear: it is at least 500. Thus, by sowing one corn, you harvest 1,000 corn. That is the blessing of multiples.

> Be sure to set aside a tenth of all that your fields produce each year Deut. 14:22

This verse says "each year" because the harvests only took place once every year in those times. If we convert this into today's wage system, "each year" would be equivalent to our daily, weekly, monthly, or pension earnings. Tithes are ten percent of our net income; our net income being our "total sales – expenses (rent, employee wages, taxes, etc.)." Debt is not taken into consideration when we calculate how much to tithe. Some people think that tithes need to be calculated over sales. However, there are many businesses in which net profit is only 7-8 percent of sales, which means that a tithe of 10 percent will automatically place the company in debt. Scripture in Deuteronomy tells us to set aside a tenth of all that our fields produce. "All that our fields produce" refers to the amount of produce that has actually been harvested (net income).

Leviticus 27:30
A tithe of everything from the land, whether grain from the soil or fruit from the trees, belongs to the Lord; it is holy to the Lord.

Numbers 18:21
I give to the Levites all the tithes in Israel as their inheritance in return for the work they do while serving at the tent of meeting.

We see from this verse that tithes are also used to cover expenses that arise at the tent of meeting.

Numbers 18:24
Instead, I give to the Levites as their inheritance the tithes that the Israelites present as an offering to the Lord. That is why I said concerning them: "They will have no inheritance among the Israelites."

We also see that God gives the tithes to the Levites as their inheritance.

Malachi 3:7
"Ever since the time of your ancestors you have turned away from my decrees and have not kept them. Return to me, and I will return to you," says the Lord Almighty. "But you ask, 'How are we to return?'"

If the Lord is to return to us, we must be the first ones to return to the Lord. And tithes are the method through which we return to God.

Malachi 3:8
"Will a mere mortal rob God? Yet you rob me. But you ask, 'How are we robbing you?' In tithes and offerings."

It is a false notion that you tithe if your faith is strong and do not if your faith is weak. Because tithes are not our possessions to start with; we have no agency over the issue from the beginning. God says that failure to tithe "is to rob Him of what is His."

Malachi 3:9
You are under a curse—your whole nation—because you are robbing me.

The whole nation was put under a curse (of famine and

poverty) for not paying tithes.

> Tithes mark a watershed between blessing and curse.
> Hong SungGun

Recently, I saw a video online titled, "Do Not Tithe." The greed in people's hearts enables them to accept this message; it is reminiscent of the story in Genesis Chapter 3. The Lord warns Adam and Eve that they will surely die if they eat the fruit of knowledge of good and evil. But the devil lies, telling them that they will surely not die.

The online lecture defined tithes as a command stipulated in the Mosaic covenant. However, tithes did not begin with Moses but with Abraham, 430 years before the Mosaic covenant was even established.

"Just think how great he was: Even the patriarch Abraham gave him a tenth of the plunder!... One might even say that Levi, who collects the tenth, paid the tenth through Abraham" (Heb. 7:4,9).

Jesus tells the teachers of the law that they must pay their tithes. Jesus came not to abolish the Mosaic law but to complete it.

"Woe to you, teachers of the law and Pharisees, you hypocrites! You give a tenth of your spices—mint, dill and cumin. But you have neglected the more important matters of the law—justice, mercy and faithfulness. You should have practiced the latter, without neglecting the former"

(Matt. 23:23).

Enemies continue to try to destroy the tithe; but therein lies a conspiracy.

"I also learned that the portions assigned to the Levites had not been given to them, and that all the Levites and musicians responsible for the service had gone back to their own fields. So I rebuked the officials and asked them, "Why is the house of God neglected?" (Neh. 13:10-11).

Do you see the enemy's plot? It is the Lord's servants and worshippers who go hungry when we fail to tithe. When the servants of the Lord leave to look for their own food, the temple falls into neglect. Unfortunately, the Korean church has a lot of debt today. One way to address this issue is by having all church members pay their full tithes.

The people of Israel repented and turned from their ways.

"Then I called them together and stationed them at their posts. All Judah brought the tithes of grain, new wine and olive oil into the storerooms" (Neh. 13:11-12).

Tithes are the "seeds" of promise. When we plant these seeds, we bring blessings on both the church and ourselves. But when we consume them, we bring poverty upon both. Test God with full tithes and experience God's blessings!

3.3 Percent – The Blessing of "the Other Tithes"

Malachi 3:8

"Will a mere mortal rob God? Yet you rob me. But you ask, 'How are we robbing you?' In tithes and offerings."

Tithes and offerings are of equal standing. Offerings are "another type of tithe."

Deuteronomy 14:27-28
And do not neglect the Levites living in your towns, for they have no allotment or inheritance of their own. At the end of every three years, bring all the tithes of that year's produce and store it in your towns.

This is a "type of tithe" that is given once every three years.

Deuteronomy 26:12
When you have finished setting aside a tenth of all your produce in the third year, the year of the tithe, you shall give it to the Levite, the foreigner, the fatherless and the widow, so that they may eat in your towns and be satisfied.

If we calculate this tithe that is given in the third year, the year of the tithe, in today's terms, it will amount to 3.3 percent of our monthly income. God makes the purpose of this "type of tithe" very clear.

Deuteronomy 14:29
So that the Levites (who have no allotment or inheritance of their own) and the foreigners, the fatherless and the widows who live in

your towns may come and eat and be satisfied, and so that the Lord your God may bless you in all the work of your hands.

The 3.3 percent tithes are to be used as "relief offerings." This tithe is used to serve the people of God (Levites) and the poor. The blessing of these other tithes is God's blessing for all the works produced through our hands. The full tithes mentioned in Malachi refer to tithes that include the 3.3 percent tithe. There is a reason for those relief offering envelopes in churches. It is God's command that we look after the poor.

The Two Blessings of Tithes

First, "'I will prevent pests from devouring your crops,' says the Lord Almighty" (Mal. 3:11).

Satan says the following during a conversation with God about Job.

> "Does Job fear God for nothing?" Satan replied. "Have you not put a hedge around him and his household and everything he has? You have blessed the work of his hands, so that his flocks and herds are spread throughout the land." Job 1:9-10

God protected all of Job's possessions by putting a hedge around them. When pests infest a field, they obliterate the crops. Likewise, when pests infiltrate into our lives, they eat away at our savings. Pests, including accidents, hospital fees, failed partnerships, and unreturned money, have devastating effects on our finances. Just as God blessed Job, God prevents pests from getting to the crops in the fields of those who pay their full tithes.

Second, "'And the vines in your fields will not drop their fruit before it is ripe,' says the Lord Almighty" (Mal. 3:11).

When God tells us that the vines in our fields will not drop their fruit before it is ripe, He is telling us that even when storms wash away the fruit on the vines of our neighbors. He will protect our fruit and continue to provide for us during our time of need.

If you find yourself in a position in which you have to quit your job for whatever reason, do not worry. If you have paid your tithes in full, the Lord will provide. You might get a new job, start a new business, or God may decide to provide for you in supernatural ways.

God tells us to test the holiest of names, His name, with our full tithes. "'Test me in this,' says the Lord Almighty, 'and see if I will not throw open the floodgates of heaven and pour out so much blessing that there will not be room enough to store it'" (see Mal. 3:10).

> Tithes are the keys which open up the storehouses of heaven. Hong SungGun

Those who pay their full tithes will be known for the blessing of bountiful fruit they have received, even among foreigners.

"Then all the nations will call you blessed, for yours will be a delightful land," says the Lord Almighty. Mal. 3:12

Part III
Look After the Poor

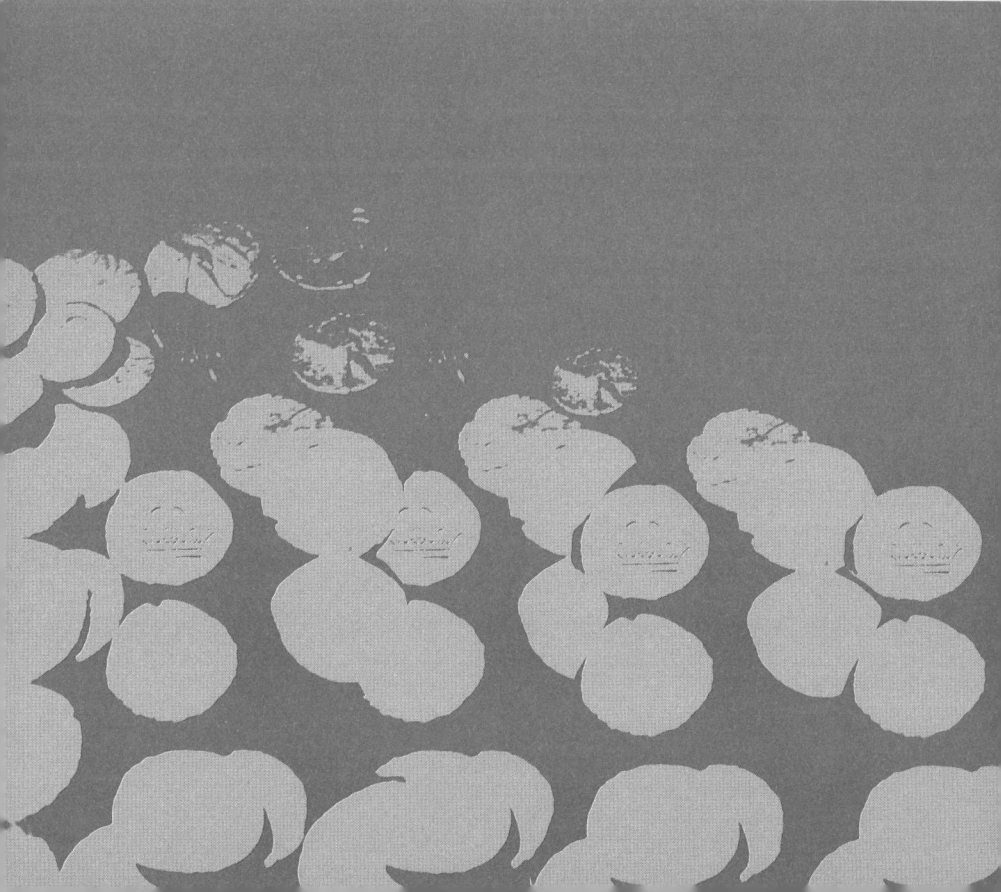

CHATPER 1

The Miracle of the Five Loaves and Two Fishes Continues to This Day

PART III Look After the Poor

Give Them Something to Eat

Jesus replied, "They do not need to go away. You give them something to eat." "We have here only five loaves of bread and two fish," they answered. "Bring them here to me," he said... Looking up to heaven, he gave thanks and broke the loaves. Then he gave them to the disciples, and the disciples gave them to the people. They all ate and were satisfied, and the disciples picked up twelve basketfuls of broken pieces that were left over. The number of those who ate was about five thousand men, besides women and children. Matt. 14:16-21

Jesus called his disciples to him and said, "I have compassion for these people... I do not want to send them away hungry, or they may collapse on the way." His disciples answered, "Where could we get enough bread in this remote place to feed such a crowd?" "How many loaves do you have?" Jesus asked. "Seven," they replied, "and a few small fish."... and when he had given thanks, he broke them and gave them to the disciples, and they in turn to the people. They all ate and were satisfied. Afterward the disciples picked up seven basketfuls of broken pieces that were left over. The number of those who ate was four thousand men, besides women and children. Matt. 15:32-38

The Bible has 214 passages on faith, 218 on salvation, and around 3,000 on riches and wealth. God tells us that those without faith may not be saved while those who are saved must prove their faith through their actions. He tells us that faith, salvation, and wealth are all closely intertwined.

> **Devotional Passages**
>
> Mark 10:17-25: The Rich Young Man
> Luke 16:19-31: The Rich Man and Lazarus
> Matthew 25:33-46: The Sheep and the Goats
> Luke 3:2-14: John the Baptist's Message (the crowds, tax collectors, and soldiers)

Jesus said, "Whoever believes in me will do the works I have been doing, and they will do even greater things than these" (John 14:12). It is now our task to continue the work of Jesus who, after feeding crowds of 5,000 and 4,000, still had food left over. The Lord gave plenty of food, enough to feed the whole world. He has also given us enough food to eat. Pay attention to the Lord's words.

"Give them something to eat."

"How many loaves of bread do you have?"

Sell your possessions and give to the poor. Provide purses for yourselves that will not wear out, a treasure in heaven that will never fail, where no thief comes near and no moth destroys. For where your treasure is, there your heart will be also. Luke 12:33-34

Who does the master put in charge of all those treasures? The one who gives the servants their food at the right time will be put in charge of all his master's possessions.

The Lord answered, "Who then is the faithful and wise manager, whom the master puts in charge of his servants to give them their food allowance at the proper time? It will be good for that servant whom the master finds doing so when he returns. Truly I tell you, he will put him in charge of all his possessions." Luke 12:42-44

Be the maker of the miracle of the five loaves and two fishes through a life of sharing. You will become the manager of all of the Lord's possessions.

The Lord Does Not Take What You Do Not Have

I asked this question to a male student in the 14th session of the King's Finances School in 2018 while teaching about offerings.

"Brother, you have a bull, lamb, deer, pig, duck, and a chicken. What will you bring to the Lord as an offering?"

"I would offer him eggs."

The whole classroom erupted in laughter at his unconventional response. Although it was a frugal answer, it was a truthful one. The training continued. Then at the graduation ceremony after a 6-week outreach training, I called on the same student and repeated the same question.

"Brother, you have a bull, lamb, deer, pig, duck, and a chicken. What will you bring to the Lord as an offering?"

"I would make an offering of the best ram I have!"

The student's voice rang with conviction and joy. God is not one to require of us what we do not have.

"For if the willingness is there, the gift is acceptable according to what one has, not according to what one does not have" (2 Cor. 8:12).

1) The Rich Man's Offering

> Speak to the Israelites and say to them: "When anyone among you brings an offering to the Lord, bring as your offering an animal from either the herd or the flock." Lev. 1:2

Our offerings to the Lord must be from the herd or the flock. If someone has bulls, lamb, deer, pigs, ducks, and chickens, God will take the bulls and the lamb. He requires that those who have the means make an offering of the most expensive livestock they own.

But what about the poor who have neither bulls nor lamb to give? Should they borrow from the rich to make an offering? Do they need to make such an offering even if it means they will go into debt?

2) The Poor Man's Offering

Anyone who cannot afford a lamb is to bring two doves or two young pigeons to the Lord as a penalty for their sin—one for a sin offering and the other for a burnt offering. Lev. 5:7

God is considerate of those that cannot afford to offer a lamb and allows them to bring two doves or two young pigeons. In God's eyes, a poor man's two doves are of equal worth to the rich man's lamb. But what about the even poorer? What about those who do not even have doves to bring as an offering?

3) The Even Poorer Man's Offering

If, however, they cannot afford two doves or two young pigeons, they are to bring as an offering for their sin a tenth of an ephah of the finest flour for a sin offering. Lev. 5:11

The even poorer are to bring a tenth of an ephah (2.2 liter) of the finest flour. God considers this the same as the offering of the lamb. This verse is not saying that we are allowed to bring small, inexpensive offerings before the Lord. What we offer up to the Lord must be holy and set apart, chosen from the most valuable of our possessions. God is not interested in the monetary value of our offerings; He is interested in our hearts.

When Jesus saw the widow put two Leptons in the

collection box, He praised her in front of His disciples. "Truly I tell you, this poor widow has put more into the treasury than all the others. They all gave out of their wealth; but she, out of her poverty, put in everything—all she had to live on" (Mark 12:43-44). Jesus also said, "For where your treasure is, there your heart will be also" (Matt. 6:21).

When I was bankrupt, I was poor. No, I was even poorer than poor. But still, I took out loans, borrowed, and paid off one credit with the other to continue to offer bulls or lambs to God. But when I searched my heart, I realized that such actions came from a desire to save face and receive recognition in front of others.

These Scriptures completely set me free from the pressure of giving offerings. God was newly revealed to me from that day. Although God has freed me of my heavy burden, I had taken on a huge yoke of my own accord. I did not know the path of real faith. Then, a heart that yearned to provide offerings from the herd and the flock without going into debt formed within me. I decided that I would make even greater offerings to the kingdom of God as a holy rich person.

> Christianity is not a religion of strict nomism or asceticism. Christianity transcends such ideologies. God is neither a strict nomist nor a ruthless judge. He is pleased to give us the best. He is our Loving Father; He frees us from the ties and shackles that bind us. Hong SungGun

> Come to me, all you who are weary and burdened, and I will give you rest. Matt. 11:28

Must I Close Shop on Sundays?
1) You will yield enough for three years

"Do I absolutely have to close my shop on Sundays? Can't I open my shop after the Sunday service?"

I find it very difficult whenever people come to me to consult on this issue. They tell me that it is not easy to close their business when Sunday sales are several times higher than sales on a weekday. It is a real concern given that even mid-level church leaders, including elders, deaconesses, and deacons, come to me with these concerns.

Having been through devastating economic hardship myself, I sometimes just smile, unable to provide them a direct answer. In one church meeting, a deaconess asked me this same question, and all I could do was hug her in silence because I knew exactly how she felt. I could not bring myself to say the words, "Live by faith." This is exactly why we must pay ever more attention to the Word of God.

> Observe the Sabbath day by keeping it holy, as the Lord your God has commanded you. Six days you shall labor and do all your work, but the seventh day is a sabbath to the Lord your God. On it you shall not do any work, neither you, nor your son or daughter, nor your male or female servant, nor your ox, your donkey or any of your animals, nor any foreigner

residing in your towns, so that your male and female servants may rest, as you do. Remember that you were slaves in Egypt and that the Lord your God brought you out of there with a mighty hand and an outstretched arm. Therefore the Lord your God has commanded you to observe the Sabbath day.
Deut. 5:12-15

Observing the Sabbath means more than merely closing shop for the day.

People who go golfing immediately after making a quick appearance at the Sunday service
People who have a whole itinerary of shopping plans following their brief appearance at the Sunday service
People who have plans to go out as a family after making a quick appearance at the Sunday service
People who spend all day lazing and sleeping at home after a short appearance at the Sunday service
People who go to academies for self-development after a quick appearance at the Sunday service

Unfortunately, the following people do not understand what it means to observe the Sabbath. What difference is there between such people and someone who opens their shop on Sundays? None of them observe the Sabbath.

To observe the Sabbath means to live a life centered around worship, prayer, and fellowship. It means to be in fellowship with God and fellow believers.

PART III Look After the Poor

The Lord commands us to rest from everything on Sundays. By doing so we receive healing in all areas of our lives, in flesh and in spirit. Those who understand the value of God's work of creation will take a day of true rest. For me, it was a failure that allowed me to reset all these different areas of my life.

> Taking a full day of rest on Sunday does not mean that we must have a sense of religious obligation. In our time of rest, we will receive healing and renewed anointment from the Lord. By taking this day of rest, we are able not merely to survive the week ahead but instead live a life that has influence and brings change, furthering God's kingdom. God always wants to provide us with what is best. Spend your Sundays in joy and happiness. Even if it is volunteer work that you have to do, call on the Holy Spirit's power and take the day of rest. Hong SungGun

You may ask, "What will we eat in the seventh year if we do not plant or harvest our crops?" I will send you such a blessing in the sixth year that the land will yield enough for three years. Lev. 25:20-21

How amazing are these words! People ask, "What will we eat in the seventh year if we do not plant or harvest our crops?" But God blesses us in the sixth year with a year's bonus that is enough to last us three years. The Lord gives us enough to eat on the Sabbath year and plenty to last until planting season in the next year.

2) I will make you reap double

The Lord gave as much as the Israelites needed when He gave them manna as well.

"Everyone is to gather as much as they need" (Exo. 16:16).

"The one who gathered much did not have too much, and the one who gathered little did not have too little. Everyone had gathered just as much as they needed" (Exo. 16:18).

He gave them manna on the following day and on the day after that. He told them not to keep any of it until morning. Nevertheless, some worried that they may not get manna the next day and kept some until morning.

"Then Moses said to them, 'No one is to keep any of it until morning.' However, some of them paid no attention to Moses; they kept part of it until morning, but it was full of maggots and began to smell. So Moses was angry with them" (Exo. 16:19-20).

What was it that angered Moses? It was the greed, fear, and worry of the Israelites. Unbelief leads to disobedience.

On the sixth day, the Lord gave them twice as much manna. He did so in consideration of Sabbath the next day.

"On the sixth day, they gathered twice as much—two omers for each person" (Exo 16:22).

"Nevertheless, some of the people went out on the seventh day to gather it, but they found none" (Exo. 16:27).

Their actions are of unbelief, of disobedience.

> We learn the following through manna:
> First, do not be greedy.
> Second, share if you gather more than you need.
> Third, the wealth of the greedy will dissipate.
> Fourth, the Lord gives twice the blessing to those who obey the Word and rest.

Faith is "spiritual warfare." I earnestly hope that you emerge as the victor.

> Spiritual warfare is not simply crying out, "Be gone, devil." It means doing the right thing at the right time, and in the right place. In other words, spiritual warfare is living in obedience to God's Word. Hong SungGun

King's Finances Training for the Whole Family Seomun JinHee
Paying back my debt of 764 million won

I heard that a King's Finances revival conference would be taking place at my church. Although I had not come across the name before, I found the topic interesting. The amount of debt I had at the time was 764 million won. My brother-in-law's tuition, my husband's living expenses from when he studied abroad, hospital fees, my daughters' private tutoring fees which I paid out of a vain desire to "beat the competition", a church construction offering I had made with loans, losses from the operation of a welfare facility (sanatorium); these were the reasons behind all the debt I had. But up until that point, I was not yet aware of the gravity of the debt that had ballooned and I could not make any sense of it.

God's words, "the debtor is slave to his creditor", spoken during the lectures shook me to my core. I came to know of the existence of mammon, who was tying me down with debt. I resolved and challenged myself to pay back all my debts. As soon as the revival conference came to a close, I purchased *The King's Finances Workbook,* studied it, and lived out the teachings as though my life depended on it for eight months. I was able to pay back 97 million won at remarkable speed.

Seeing my debt balance begin to go down firsthand, I enrolled in the 6th session of the King's Finances School. I wanted to repay my debts even more quickly and be reborn as a servant of the Lord. At the time, I was the pastor of a church, a Ph.D. holder, and a university professor, while my husband was a high ranking senior civil servant. But despite all these fancy titles, the Lord showed me who I was inside; I was "Seomun JinHee, the debtor."

Creating a breakthrough with the budget of faith

I did not feel like a debtor as money was undoubtedly deposited into our accounts each payday and we had enough to live on after paying interest. Nevertheless, I

PART III Look After the Poor

firmly resolved to pay off all my debts after realizing that failure to do so would mean struggling just to stave off interest with our pensions into retirement and ultimately leave nothing but debt as an inheritance for our children. Then, I drafted a training program just as I had been taught at the King's Finances School.

- Read ten chapters from the Bible before a meal each day
- Pray for one hour each day
- Implement the debt repayment project as in the workbook
- Solve the equation of faith through the execution of the "Live It Out Project!"
  0×100 million $= 0$, 1×100 million $= 100$ million
  $5+2=7$, $5+2=5000+12$

I started by putting forth my "best 1" following these equations. I decided to sell my car and use public transportation. The car sold for a mere 1.2 million won as it was a used car. And although buying another car later could cost a lot more, I wanted to put forth my "best 1" before the Lord.

I decided not to eat out or buy new clothes. Before I made the decision, I always thought I had nothing to wear every time the seasons changed, but once I had changed my perspective, I felt like I could dress myself for another ten years just with the clothes that were already in my closet. After I decided not to spend on cosmetics, I began to value even the sample sized products that were lying around the house. I did not even go grocery shopping until I finished all the food in my freezer.

Sister MiJin ate nothing but kimchi until she had paid off all her debt, the least I can do is try. That is how I began living on the food in our fridge. We had kimchi; so, I made fried kimchi, kimchi soup, and even rice wraps from rinsed kimchi leaves. We also had some anchovies, which at times I fried or ate with red pepper paste. But I am a person who enjoys her meat. And eating only the food in our fridge for several months, I desperately craved meat. It was at that time the Lord spoke to me with the words of Deuteronomy 12:20.

'My dear JinHee, you can have as much meat as you want once you are done with your debt repayment training.'

I grew closer each day to the loving God who consoled and encouraged me throughout the process. After 100 days of training and saving money this way, I was able to repay an additional 30 million won toward my debt.

Deciding to receive the King's Finances training as a family

I decided that we should enroll in the King's Finances School as a family so as to receive structured finances training. I had attended the King's Finances revival conference alone, so my husband was not entirely familiar with the program. "Could we sign up for the King's Finances School? This will be the very last thing I ask you to do for me," I pleaded with my husband. It was not an easy decision to make for my husband who was a senior civil servant at the time, but he agreed. I was grateful. But my pleas fell on deaf ears when it came to my two daughters who were in their 20s.

I could not possibly bring myself to tell my daughters to give up their precious Saturdays for 12 weeks to receive the finances training as a family. So instead, I planned a trip to Jeju Island with my most precious treasures, my two daughters. After a week of strategic prayer, I transferred ownership of my two daughters to the Lord. I declared before the Lord and my two daughters:

"Father, my beloved Seo JungWon and Seo MyungJoo are no longer my treasures but Your treasures. I will respect them as individuals and in no way intervene in their lives. I will not worry. I will wholly support them through the Word and prayer."

My two daughters grew solemn after my prayer. I made the same request to them as I had made to my husband. With the Lord's help, my two daughters agreed. And for one year after that my whole family completed NCMN's three schools (the King's Finances School, Changer Leadership School, and Shema Bible School). I began to see an amazing change in my daughters. My two daughters, who barely made it to church on Sundays, were quickly transformed into women of God. They implemented what they learned through the school and experienced immense spiritual growth (My eldest daughter is currently serving in the 5K Movement headquarters).

Standing against mammon and deciding to break my own stinginess

I found the root cause of my stinginess while learning about mammon's influence. Mammon was instilling in me a fear of the future and constant worry about becoming poor. However, the Holy Spirit tells us that we must break down our stinginess if we are to live prosperous lives. Sister MiJin told us of the times when she would change 10,000 won or 1,000 won bills into 10 won coins and practice sharing by giving handfuls of them to people.

The principle of buying and selling may apply in this world, but in the kingdom of God the principle of giving and receiving applies. I engrained these words into my heart. During finances training, I willingly flowed the possessions that I had previously purchased to fill a void in my life. When I began flowing at least one possession a day, I came to realize how selfish and miserly I had been: only educating my daughters and pursuing my own goals of a doctorate degree and becoming a professor while failing to take care of the needs of my siblings.

I asked the Lord for forgiveness. I started sending packages to my siblings from time to time. Once I began doing that, the love and relationship between the siblings on both sides of the family was restored at miraculous speed. When I checked the number of deposits I had made in the Heavenly Bank during my finances training, I counted a total of 106 deposits. I had flowed money and goods worth around 18 million won to my family on both sides and small group members. When I did away with my stinginess, we were able to create family chatrooms on both my side and my husband's side of the family and our broken relationships were healed. The great reward of the "restoration of love among siblings" was given to me as interest for the deposits I had made in the Heavenly Bank.

One day, my husband and I were on our way back home from the King's Finances School. I gladly gave 1,000 won to the disabled brother who was asking for help on the subway. But only a few minutes later, one more person came asking for help. I opened my wallet to give money but saw that I only had 10,000 won bills in my purse. I was torn, and I hesitated for a moment.

'I just gave some money to another person, so I can let it go this time.' I convinced myself and looked the other way. A few days after the incident, I received a gift of health foods worth 1.08 million won from a friend. As she was explaining that had sent me the gift because she wanted to share the joy of something good that had happened to her, the scene in the subway flashed through my mind. My heart was overwhelmed with emotion at the benevolence and generosity of God, who chose not to rebuke me but instruct me through a gift.

In the King's Finances School, you set up an account in the Heavenly Bank. What I have been taught and have learned through experience is that "the kingdom of God is a kingdom of multiples." Some leaders in the King's Finances school decided to collect money to buy new shoes for Sister Kim MiJin who had spent all day lecturing in her uncomfortable shoes. Sister Kim MyoungJa humbly contributed 300 won. We saw her contribution returned to her as a flowing of 300,000 won.

'Wow! God pays back in 1000-fold returns!'

In each of these moments, I was witness to the meticulous teachings of God's love.

Passing the qualification exam

On June 26, about a month after I had begun flowing to family, I checked the balance of my Heavenly Bank account and saw that I had deposited a total of 12,559,100 won.

'What is a 1000-fold return on that? Twelve billion won! Will He really pay me back with that much?'

I thought to myself. It seemed impossible. But because He does not always pay back in riches but sometimes with "the truth," I decided to be thankful for the restoration of love between siblings on both sides of the family. Then, on June 26, Rev. Hong said these words as though he had read exactly what was weighing on my heart.

"Ladies and gentlemen, you might hope that the seeds you have sown in God's kingdom are returned to you in riches. But multiples do not only come back as wealth. God knows what each of you needs the most."

He said that God sees my heart and knows what I treasure the most. I was amazed to learn the principle that while wealth sown can come back as wealth, God can also return the multiples by giving us a fruit of the Holy Spirit to be used for the expansion of God's kingdom, or as a fresh path toward a new ministry. As a university professor and Doctor of Philosophy, what struck me most was finding out that all the teachings of the King's Finances School are grounded in Scripture. This is a common experience among the countless pastors that enter the King's Finances School.

On July 2, Rev. Hong, Sister Kim MiJin and her husband, and my husband and I all met over dinner. With the three leaders of NCMN we discussed important issues as we ate our meals. Although I had looked for ways to revive the South Korean church over the past ten years through a church welfare ministry, I had not been able to achieve much success. In that meeting, I became convinced that NCMN's 5K Movement welfare ministry was the path to achieve revival in the church. Currently, I am serving as an acting leader in the 5K Movement headquarters and making preparations for a unified Korea. Gaining an understanding of God's heart for the salvation of lost souls through the King's Finances School is one of the greatest blessings that God has given me.

− JungWon, Dr. Seomun JinHee's daughter, was using a phone with a broken screen. When I wanted to flow her the cost of getting her screen replaced, JungWon replied, "I cannot accept any gifts exceeding 30,000 won in value, given my parents' jobs as civil servants." Dr. Seomun JinHee also practices resharing whenever she receives a gift. I am a personal witness to the integrity and honesty of the life which this family leads.

About This Time Tomorrow, I Will Turn Around and See You

Ben-Hadad king of Aram mobilized his entire army and marched up and laid an ironclad siege to Samaria, the capital of Israel. His strategy was to block anything from going in or out of the city and starve to death the people inside.

Just as he had planned, a great famine took hold of the city. The people were so hungry that a donkey's head sold for eighty shekels of silver, and a quarter of a cab of seed pods for five shekels (see 2Kgs. 6:24-25). The people were plagued by astronomical prices and unable to get even the lowliest of foods despite their willingness to spend a fortune.

The people were so hungry that a woman finally went to the king of Israel and cried out, "My king, help us!" Let us hear the words of the woman.

"Then he asked her, 'What's the matter?' She answered, 'This woman said to me, "Give up your son so we may eat him today, and tomorrow we'll eat my son." So we cooked my son and ate him. The next day I said to her, "Give up your son so we may eat him," but she had hidden him'" (2Kgs. 6:28-29).

This story is an astounding historical fact. The Lord spoke to Elisha at this time, and Elisha delivered His words to the king of Israel.

"Elisha replied, 'Hear the word of the Lord. This is what the Lord says: About this time tomorrow, a seah of the finest flour will sell for a shekel and two seahs of barley for a shekel at the gate of Samaria'" (2Kgs. 7:1).

The Lord spoke to the Samarians who were suffering from extreme hunger.

"About this time tomorrow, I will take care of you!"

A seah of the finest flour selling for a shekel and two seahs of barley for a shekel in 24 hours meant that there would be a massive increase in the food supply within that time. What if you were inside Samaria right now? How would you respond to the message God delivered through Elisha? An officer who the king of Israel relied on gave the following response.

"The officer on whose arm the king was leaning said to the man of God, 'Look, even if the Lord should open the floodgates of the heavens, could this happen?' 'You will see it with your own eyes,' answered Elisha, 'but you will not eat any of it!'" (2Kgs. 7:2).

The officer's reply was, "Even if the Lord were able to open the floodgates of the heavens, what you say could never happen. It's impossible!" But God had a fantastic solution.

Four men with leprosy, who were at the entrance of the city, said to each other, "If we stay here, we will die, and if we go into the city, we will also die because of the famine. Let us surrender to the Arameans; if they spare us, we live, and if they kill us, then we die" (see 2Kgs. 7:3-4).

How dreadful and tiring that road to the Aramean camp

must have been! Were they even able to walk properly with their hunger and leprosy? I once volunteered with a charity that worked with leprosy patients in the past. Their fingers and toes literally just fell off, and their ears decayed. I personally witnessed them struggle to walk, even with the help of a walking stick.

The Lord made the Arameans hear the sound of chariots and horses and a great army instead of the footsteps of the four men who were on their way to the Aramean camp to surrender.

"For the Lord had caused the Arameans to hear the sound of chariots and horses and a great army, so that they said to one another, 'Look, the king of Israel has hired the Hittite and Egyptian kings to attack us!' So they got up and fled in the dusk and abandoned their tents and their horses and donkeys. They left the camp as it was and ran for their lives" (2Kgs. 7:6-7).

When the men with leprosy arrived at the camp, there was not a single soul remaining at the site.

"The men who had leprosy reached the edge of the camp, entered one of the tents and ate and drank. Then they took silver, gold and clothes, and went off and hid them. They returned and entered another tent and took some things from it and hid them also. Then they said to each other, 'What we're doing is not right. This is a day of good news and we are keeping it to ourselves. If we wait until daylight, punishment will overtake us. Let's go at once and report this to the royal palace'" (2Kgs. 7:8-9).

These events had taken place by "about this time tomorrow," or within 24 hours, just as the Lord had made known through Elisha. The faithless officer saw this take place but was trampled to death before he could eat any of the food.

"Then the people went out and plundered the camp of the Arameans. So a seah of the finest flour sold for a shekel, and two seahs of barley sold for a shekel, as the Lord had said… And that is exactly what happened to him, for the people trampled him in the gateway, and he died" (2Kgs. 7:16,20).

Do not limit God's power. The officer did not believe in God's promise because he was looking at the circumstances. This is unbelief. We must learn to respond with faith, as faith transcends circumstances. It overcomes the bounds of our limited abilities. Our God is an almighty God who does the amazing through the least and smallest of us.

> The least of you will become a thousand, the smallest a mighty nation. I am the Lord; in its time I will do this swiftly.
> Isa. 60:22

The more we train and gain spiritual muscle, the more God's covenants are fulfilled within us.

Taking Ownership of God's Promise in Faith

"About this time tomorrow (within 24 hours), I will take care of you."

These words were a huge source of encouragement while I was in the wilderness. God told me not to limit His power and He revealed the results of my obedience when I trained to live a life of faith.

On the last day of the NCMN Youth Hero Camp in August 2018, Sister Oh JinSook, who was a staff member at the camp, came to me with a prayer request.

"Sister MiJin, could you pray that my surgery goes well tomorrow?"

"What surgery?"

"I was feeling unwell, so I went to the hospital a day before the camp started. They found six or so fist-sized tumors in my uterus. The doctor said that they're in a tricky place and need to be removed immediately with surgery."

God's promise to those who take care of the poor (see Psa. 41:1-3) flashed through my mind.

'First, the Lord will deliver them in times of trouble. Second, they will be blessed in the land. Third, He will sustain them on their sickbed and restore them from their bed of illness.'

I had seen how diligently Sister JinSook had served the poor. Now is the time to experience God's promise, I thought.

"Sister JinSook, you've served the poor with greater dedication than anyone else I know. Why don't you think that God could remove your tumors today just as He promised?"

Then I read her the Scripture of Psalms 41:1-3.

"I'm sorry. I forgot about God's promise when the doctor explained the size and location of my tumors on images. I believe in God's promise and in His power."

Illnesses can be healed with medication or surgery, but God can also choose to cure them directly. No matter how, I believe that it is the goodness of God that heals.

Other staff members gathered around and lay hands on Sister JinSook to pray for her. I placed my hand on her stomach and prayed. My prayer was not long as I was neither her healer nor did I have the power to heal. I prayed a prayer of faith, firmly believing in God's promise. I prayed that His promise would be fulfilled through our faith and that He would be glorified as everyone experienced Him through the healing of Sister JinSook. When we had finished praying, Sister JinSook declared, "I believe that my tumors are gone!"

"You should go now to the hospital and get them checked," we told her.

One day passed. With her voice overflowing with joy, Sister JinSook cried, "Hallelujah! The doctors told me that the tumors have disappeared without a trace!" The students and staff of NCMN do not consider such miracles that happen on a weekly basis to be anything out of the ordinary. We have witnessed people with extremely poor eyesight regain vision, hearing in deaf ears restored, the complete healing of legs that otherwise required surgery. We also have seen the birth of a child under medically impossible circumstances. It is faith that enables us to experience the power of God.

"I am a useless servant. You did it, Lord! God, you are Almighty and faithful!" This should be the confession coming out of our mouths.

Treating My Leprous Spirit by Restoring the Love I First Had

The abundance of riches takes away our longing for the Lord while poverty in its extremes steals away our hope in the Lord. I was spiritually diseased, just like Naaman, the leprous commander of the army of Aram in the days of Elisha. People with leprosy cannot feel anything, even if their fingers or toes fall from their bodies. Similarly, I had lost my spiritual sensations.

My heart was cold even after hearing the Sunday sermon and attending revival conferences. I was not moved or awakened when I read the Word of God. I worshipped God and served the church out of a sense of obligation and with no anticipation for the Lord in my heart. I was a woman of religion, going through the motions out of habit. Leprosy, if left untreated, causes the entire body to decay, and in extreme cases even leads to death. It is a disease that cannot be left untreated.

That was me when the Lord exiled me into the wilderness. The wilderness was a blessing for me because it was there that I saw my spiritual state in its rawest form. The wilderness of dire famine brought me back to the

Lord in utter desperation. I was in critical need of spiritual healing. I was grasping at straws, but I did not know where or how to even begin.

Then, Rev. Hong's sermon titled, "Restore the Love You Had at First," based on Revelation 2:1-7, showed me where my spiritual restoration should begin.

> "We find the path to healing for our spiritual leprosy by restoring the love we had at first!"

> The church of Ephesus was awe-inspiring. Its members endured and persevered through anything for the Lord. They never grew weary and served the Lord with utmost diligence, so much so that the Lord said, "I know your deeds, your hard work, and your perseverance".
>
> "I know your deeds, your hard work and your perseverance… You have persevered and have endured hardships for my name, and have not grown weary. Yet I hold this against you: You have forsaken the love you had at first" (Rev. 2:2-4).
>
> Yet still, the Lord rebuked the Ephesians because they had abandoned the love that they had at first. Surprisingly, losing the love we had at first can be the cause of our lampstand being removed from its place. But the Lord gives us a path to restoration.
>
> "Consider how far you have fallen! Repent and do the things you did at first" (Rev. 2:5).
>
> The road to recovery begins when we do the things that we did at first.

> The love we had at first is not about the feelings we had but the actions we took. Hong SungGun

Jeremiah 2:2 depicts a clear picture of what the things we did at first are.

"Go and proclaim in the hearing of Jerusalem: 'This is what the Lord says: "I remember the devotion of your youth, how as a bride you loved me and followed me through the wilderness, through a land not sown.""

"You followed me through the wilderness;" this is an action that truly exemplifies the love we had at first. The wilderness is where we prove the extent of our love for the Lord.

"The barren wilderness, through a land of deserts and ravines, a land of drought and utter darkness, a land where no one travels and no one lives" (Jer. 2:6).

The Characteristics of the Wilderness

- A land of deserts and ravines
  - It is where our lives are threatened. A land of anxiety and fear.
- A land of drought and utter darkness
  - It is an arid land shaped by the shadow of death.

> - A land where no one travels and no one lives
>   - It is a land without roads or inhabitable environment. There is only turmoil and loneliness.

Even in such a wilderness, Israel did not complain or feel fear. Israel walked on, relying only on the Lord all because of the love they had for the Lord. This kind of love is the love we had at first. Jeremiah 2:2 gives us the secret to restoring this love we had at first.

First, remember the devotion of your youth.

The devotion of our youth refers to our acts of dedication. It is referring to our burning love for the Lord and the dedication of our youth when we willingly and joyfully walked through anything if it was with God, even the wilderness. These are the things that we did at first. Restoring our actions is the path to recovering our first love.

Second, remember your love as a bride.

No hardship in the world can shake the love newlyweds have for each other. Their love overcomes everything. They are happy even if they are uncomfortable and lacking in everything.

Third, follow the Lord through the wilderness, through the land not sown.

The dedication of youth and the love of a new bride, these enable us to follow the Lord no matter how difficult it gets in the wilderness.

> The dedication of youth, the love of a new bride, the passion and commitment to follow the Lord, even into the wilderness, is the love we had at first. When we restore the things we did back then, we can restore the love we had at first. Hong SungGun

I, who was a spiritual leper, needed to restore the "things I did at first" when I began following Him. That was the path to restoring the love I had at first. I first quit the habit of acting according to my emotions and circumstances.

I stopped saying, "I just wish I were dead."

I stopped saying, "I'm not in the mood to pray right now" and immediately began crying out to the Lord.

I stopped saying, "I'm not in the mood to worship right now" and went to the place of worship no matter what.

I stopped saying, "I don't feel like going to church to serve others" and immediately went to the place of service.

The restoration of the things I did at first was indeed the restoration of the love I had at first! The prayers that came out of my mouth when I first met the Lord in person were revived. Once again, the emotions of the times during which I was thankful for everything came back to me. I was once again able to declare with my mouth that the Lord is sufficient. The days of overflowing joy, even as I participated in every single church outreach, had once again come back to me.

CHATPER 2

Solicit a Visit from God

PART III Look After the Poor

A Cry of Desperation

The only way to get God to visit our lives is to cry out His name in desperation. The Lord heard the cries of the seeds of Abraham and remembered His covenant with them.

> During that long period, the king of Egypt died. The Israelites groaned in their slavery and cried out, and their cry for help because of their slavery went up to God. God heard their groaning and he remembered his covenant with Abraham, with Isaac and with Jacob. Exo. 2:23-24

God sees, hears, and is concerned about the suffering of Abraham's seeds. He comes down, rescues them, and brings them up to the Promised Land.

> The Lord said, "I have indeed seen the misery of my people in Egypt. I have heard them crying out because of their slave drivers, and I am concerned about their suffering. So I have come down to rescue them from the hand of the Egyptians and to bring them up out of that land into a good and spacious land, a land flowing with milk and honey—the home of the Canaanites, Hittites, Amorites, Perizzites, Hivites and Jebusites." Exo. 3:7-8

When the seeds of Abraham cry out to Him, the Lord comes down to visit them. Without doubt, He delivers us from the hand of the Egyptians and leads us to the Promised Land. The hand of the Egyptians is the suffering caused by the breakdown of our finances, health, and relationships.

I groaned and cried out to the Lord. He heard my cries and came down into the center of my life. That is when my life became a series of testimonies. As He promised, the Lord delivered me from the hands of my oppressor. There were no strings attached. Faith in His covenant and faith that I am Abraham's seed were sufficient. Start now and cry out to the Lord to live!

The Way God Works: He Sends the Hornets

I am Abraham's seed, but why can I not see God's promise being fulfilled in my life? Why is His covenant taking so long to unfold in my life?

These were the questions to which I most wanted answers. We must have biblical answers to these questions.

> To learn about the way God works:
> - Is My Arm Too Short? (see Part 2 Chapter 4)
> - About This Time Tomorrow, I Will Turn Around to See You (see Part 3 Chapter 1)

I saw the Almighty, the faithful God, who can solve the impossible. God's arm is never too short, even under my current situation and circumstances. So, I needed to find out why God's covenant was not being fulfilled for me.

> I will send the hornet ahead of you to drive the Hivites, Canaanites and Hittites out of your way. Exo. 23:28

> But I will not drive them out in a single year, because the land would become desolate and the wild animals too numerous for you. Little by little I will drive them out before you, until you have increased enough to take possession of the land.
> Exo. 23:29-30

God promised the land of Canaan to Abraham and his descendants. However, the land was already occupied by powerful nations. God tells the Israelites that He will send the hornets ahead of them to drive out the Hivites, Canaanites, and Hittites. He said that the hornets would drive out these powerful peoples.

The hornets in these verses represent God's power. Our Lord works ahead of His people. This was true in this story, as well. As previously mentioned, Jericho was an impenetrable fortress, built so strong that the top of the wall of Jericho was thick enough for two trains to pass side-by-side.

But even that fortress came tumbling down after the Israelites marched around the city once for six days and seven times on the seventh day, priests sounding the trumpet blast and all men shouting loud (see. Josh. 6:1-21). God's power brought the heavily fortified walls of Jericho to ruins. God fulfills His promises through people of faith.

But why are we not experiencing the fulfillment of God's covenant when we are the seeds of Abraham and the Lord's covenant people? I found the answer in the "but" between verses 28 and 29 of Exodus 23. Verse 29 explains why God said that He would send His power (the hornets) ahead of the people but not rush to do so.

He tells us that He is worried "because the land would become desolate and the wild animals too numerous for you." What does this mean? Would mammon ever leave us alone if all our problems were solved at once and we gained possession of an enormous amount of riches without proper training? Too quickly would we abandon being a holy rich person to become a worldly rich person, and our lives would degenerate into a life that chases after money rather than faith.

Take a second look at the way that God does His work. The hornets drive out the powerful people of the land. But He does not do this in a rush for fear that the land will become desolate and the wild animals harm us. He does it little by little until we have increased enough in faith to receive the land as an inheritance.

Here, we can gain an understanding of how God works. It is up to us to first become spiritually strong by implementing God's principles in our lives. After that,

God drives out the powerful and gives us the land as an inheritance. He gives us more and more of the land as we make progress in training through His methods.

If we want God's covenant to become our own, we must implement God's principles in our lives and train. To become a holy rich person, we must cut all ties we have with mammon and the worldly rich and rule over our riches with God's financial principles. When we undergo the training, we build the spiritual muscle necessary to manage our wealth. When we become stewards, God allows our wealth to become ours, piece by piece. Only a religious fanatic does not train and waits for God's promise without taking any action.

Train! Train! And Train Again! Lee MyoungSook

In June 2014, both my real estate business and my husband's business had to stop all operations due to unpaid rent expenses. We defaulted on our credit card payments, and both our home and offices had their gas cut off. The constant harassment I received from debt collectors over small and large overdue credit card payments suffocated me. We received many notices of seizure, containing the details of fees that were past due, as well as information on seized property auctions. And on July 6, our car was stripped of its license plate as a result of unpaid vehicle taxes.

While working in real estate, I got into foreclosure auctions and bought as many properties as I could, ending up with more than 20 houses with 80 percent loan financing. I lived under the misconception that I had become extremely rich. It was only after my bankruptcy that I finally realized my actual situation. I was a worldly rich woman, filled with the things of mammon.

After I was introduced to the King's Finances, I sold off the houses that were not selling at meager prices. But even after that, I still had 1.2 billion won of debt remaining. The testimony of Sister Kim MiJin's breakthrough served as hope during this time. Determined to train with everything I had, I enrolled in the King's Finances School.

The school taught us how to create a breakthrough by making use of the workbook and the budget of faith. I was unconvinced by the content of the lectures and implementation methods that were taught at the school, 'Are they making this up? Will God really send extra money?' But I had no other options. They told us to train, train, and train again to build spiritual muscle. Had I been alone in the process, I would most likely have given up. However, my small group's support and the watchful eyes of my small group leader kept me training, albeit reluctantly.

I was surprised to see my sense of stability gradually move from money to the Lord through the training. Training for faithfulness was excruciating, but it changed me into a person who cherishes even the littlest things and does not waste even the most minor things in life. Training, such as "not wasting toilet paper, parking within the lines, not being wasteful with others' money," reestablished the boundaries that had been broken down in my life. I also slowly began to regain the closeness I once had with God. And when these things happened, my dulled sensitivity to sin was sharpened again.

If the real estate business brutally trained me in relationships through the disappointment of repeated last-minute change of minds by property buyers and the hurt that was given to and received from others, the King's Finances School trained my lips.

"Give thanks in all circumstances! Thanksgiving is the best expression of faith. Train the words that come from your lips."

Repeating this training created amazing changes in everyone. My emotions became more and more grounded, and I was able to restore the broken relationships I had with those around me. But the change I was in most desperate need of was in the area of finances. I drew up a budget of faith and cried out to the Lord.

"For the eyes of the Lord range throughout the earth to strengthen those whose hearts are fully committed to him. You have done a foolish thing, and from now on you will be at war" (2 Chron. 16:9).

I prayed fervently, holding tightly on to this verse. I was as desperate as the Canaanite woman who confessed that even though she had caused her own misery, she could not survive without at least the crumbs of grace that fell from the table (see Matt. 15:21-28). Because without God's help, I was not ever getting out of that swamp.

Day and night, I executed the King's Finances training and cried out to the Lord; I went before Him with everything I had. Then, on a day I felt so close to giving up, God sent me a client. That client signed a contract for the sale of a 10.5 billion won factory. It was the first time I had seen a buyer sign such a massive contract for a factory entirely in cash with no debt financing.

All the income that I had lost due to buyers' changes of heart at the final stage of the contract came in all at once. It sent chills up and down my spine. I had been the problem all along. I could do nothing but cry thinking of the gentle touch of the Father that reached out to me every time I was in trouble, His touch that was making a woman of faith, faithfulness, and meekness out of me.

"No temptation has overtaken you except what is common to mankind. And God is faithful; he will not let you be tempted beyond what you can bear. But when you are tempted, he will also provide a way out so that you can endure it" (1 Cor. 10:13).

Although I had nothing to say for myself as my test was not from God but a yoke that mammon had placed upon me using my greed, these verses were a source of encouragement to me.

I was also grateful that NCMN is a church-centered entity rather than an organization-centered entity. NCMN sent all of its students back to their home churches and taught us to be involved in church-centered ministries. I, too, was sent back to my church after completing the course at the King's Finances School.

Although I am still growing, and despite the setbacks I have experienced along the way, I have matured a great deal in comparison to the past. And trusting in the authority of my senior pastor, I am now involved in a 5K relief ministry together with my church. In 2018, we went on a homeless outreach all the way to Israel along with our senior pastor and fellow church members. I had also been praying for a King's Finances revival conference to be held at our church so that I could share the amazing financial principles that I had been taught with my church. After only 19 months of prayer, a King's Finances revival conference took place in our church!

I am slowly changing from a self-centered person to a church and God-centered person. I pray that I might be used to give 30,000-50,000 pyeong of land toward the evangelization of North Korea. I lift high the name of the Lord who enabled me to settle my debt of 1.2 billion completely in just two years.

Characteristics of God-Given Riches

1) Beware of easily acquired riches

Youth these days are very interested in amassing wealth the easy way.

"Dishonest money dwindles away, but whoever gathers

money little by little makes it grow" (Prov. 13:11).

"An inheritance claimed too soon will not be blessed at the end" (Prov. 20:21).

"A fortune made by a lying tongue is a fleeting vapor and a deadly snare" (Prov. 21:6).

"Those who work their land will have abundant food, but those who chase fantasies will have their fill of poverty. A faithful person will be richly blessed, but one eager to get rich will not go unpunished" (Prov. 28:19-20).

The worldly rich have a tendency to try to get rich the easy way. Such people include those who place their hopes in the lottery, those who seek to get rich quickly by gambling, those who invest in stocks with borrowed money, people who trade in cryptocurrency, and many others alike. They are lured into traps such as "If you invest 100 million won into this financial pyramid scheme, you will receive several times your investment in just 2-3 years" or "We will give you a 20 percent commission if you bring in investors." This wreaks havoc on their churches and brings significant financial losses upon their families and friends.

Financial pyramid schemes copy the business plans of business ideas that are hotly discussed in the media at the time and promote them as good investments for the future to raise funds as though they are raising money as a genuine company would. However, most of these companies are paper companies (a company with no physical operations and that exists only on paper).

They often trick people with the words, "The CEO has selected only a handful of close friends to share his stake in the company." But why would the CEO want to divide up his shares if they would indeed be worth several times more in a few years? Do they not see the trickery? Many fall for this trick and invest all the money they and those around them have, only to take their own lives when they can no longer bear the suffering they have caused. Mammon drives us into death. Beware the get-rich-quick schemes! They will take away your discretion.

To receive riches from the Lord, we must be diligent and work by the sweat of our brows. That is faith (see *The King's Finances I*, English translation, p. 232).

"Lazy hands make for poverty, but diligent hands bring wealth" (Prov. 10:4).

"Diligent hands will rule, but laziness ends in forced labor" (Prov. 12:24).

"The plans of the diligent lead to profit as surely as haste leads to poverty" (Prov. 21:5).

2) Beware of bribes

Do not give or take bribes. God prohibits us from doing so. The difference between a bribe and a gift is not in the amount. It is the motivation and purpose behind them that distinguishes the two.

> Gift: No quid pro quo
> The motivation of the heart is love, gratefulness, and respect.
>
> Bribe: Quid pro quo
> The motivation of the heart lies in the expectation of a particular outcome.

"A bribe is like a magic stone in the eyes of the one who gives it; wherever he turns he prospers" (Prov. 17:8, ESV).

If you consider this translation as shedding a positive light on bribery, that is a false interpretation of these words. The New International Version and the Good News Translation portray the meaning of this verse very well.

"A bribe is seen as a charm by the one who gives it; they think success will come at every turn" (Prov. 17:8).

"Some people think a bribe works like magic; they believe it can do anything" (Prov. 17:8, GNT).

God speaks even more lucidly about bribes in Exodus 23:8.

"Do not accept a bribe, for a bribe blinds those who see and twists the words of the innocent."

Bribes are not money from God. Christians! Do not give or take bribes.

Keywords for Moving the Riches of Heaven – Uprightness

When I attend the opening ceremony of a fellow believer's business, I often see a framed sign with the following words:

> Your beginnings will seem humble, so prosperous will your future be. Job 8:7

But I went into complete bankruptcy with the same frame hanging on the wall. It was because I had not fully understood God's words of promise. God gives us success. He does this so we may expand His kingdom. But there are conditions to these wonderful words of promise. I had failed to take notice of the prerequisites that must be met before God's promise is fulfilled. Take a look at the verses preceding God's words of promise.

> But if you will seek God earnestly and plead with the Almighty, if you are pure and upright, even now he will rouse himself on your behalf and restore you to your prosperous state. Job 8:5-6

First, seek God and plead with the Almighty.

Second, be pure and upright.

"He holds success in store for the upright, he is a shield to those whose walk is blameless" (Prov. 2:7).

"The Lord detests dishonest scales, but accurate weights find favor with him" (Prov. 11:1).

"The righteousness of the upright delivers them, but the unfaithful are trapped by evil desires" (Prov. 11:6).

"The way of the sluggard is blocked with thorns, but the path of the upright is a highway" (Prov. 15:19).

"Better a little with righteousness than much gain with injustice" (Prov. 16:8).

"It is better to have a little, honestly earned, than to have a large income, dishonestly gained" (Prov. 16:8, GNT).

"Honest scales and balances belong to the Lord; all the weights in the bag are of his making" (Prov. 16:11).

"Differing weights and differing measures—the Lord detests them both" (Prov. 20:10).

"A fortune made by a lying tongue is a fleeting vapor and a deadly snare" (Prov. 21:6).

When we seek His kingdom and His righteousness on this earth, He adds unto us what we need to eat, drink, and wear.

> So do not worry, saying, "What shall we eat?" or "What shall we drink?" or "What shall we wear?" For the pagans run after all these things, and your heavenly Father knows that you need them. But seek first his kingdom and his righteousness, and all these things will be given to you as well. Matt. 6:31-33

God's righteousness is uprightness. God provides a protective shield to the lives of those who bring out God's righteousness in the realm of economics through the upright management of their businesses. It is then that God unleashes His wisdom and riches. The path of the upright is a highway.

For example, someone who advertises the benefits of deer velvet extracts but, in fact, sells a watered-down solution of deer velvet extract is running a dishonest business. Being upright means that a company's products contain the exact amount of ingredients as advertised.

Falsely marketing imported beef as Hanwoo beef[11] and using dishonest scales are all the same. Do not say, "I'm selling at a loss," but say, "I'm selling at a low profit margin." Upright management stems from honest words and a pure heart. When we can do this, the promise in the words of the frame will be fulfilled.

Keywords for Moving the Riches of Heaven – Diligence

The lazy find excuses to skip work and lay on the couch at home. They are not diligent with the work that has been assigned to them. We must never forget that God fulfills His promises when we live in accordance with His ways.

---

11 A premium Korean beef from cattle indigenous to Korea.

"Go to the ant, you sluggard; consider its ways and be wise... it stores its provisions in summer and gathers its food at harvest" (Prov. 6:6,8).

"Lazy hands make for poverty, but diligent hands bring wealth" (Prov. 10:4).

"Diligent hands will rule, but laziness ends in forced labor" (Prov. 12:24).

"The lazy do not roast any game, but the diligent feed on the riches of the hunt" (Prov. 12:27).

"Sluggards do not plow in season; so at harvest time they look but find nothing... Do not love sleep or you will grow poor; stay awake and you will have food to spare" (Prov. 20:4,13).

"The plans of the diligent lead to profit as surely as haste leads to poverty... The craving of a sluggard will be the death of him, because his hands refuse to work" (Prov. 21:5,25).

"A little sleep, a little slumber, a little folding of the hands to rest—and poverty will come on you like a thief and scarcity like an armed man" (Prov. 24:33-34).

"A sluggard says, 'There's a lion in the road, a fierce lion roaming the streets!' As a door turns on its hinges, so a sluggard turns on his bed" (Prov. 26:13-14).

"Why don't lazy people ever get out of the house? What are they afraid of Lions? Lazy people turn over in bed. They get no farther than a door swinging on its hinges." (Prov. 26:13-14, GNT).

> **Economic Keywords that Move Riches**
> - Uprightness
> - Diligence
> - A pure heart
> - Pleading with the Almighty

God Rebukes My Dishonesty

Back when I was not yet aware of biblical financial principles, I thought that those in business giving and receiving bribes were a necessary evil, as many others around me did as well. Friends who were more experienced in business would provide me with advice such as these:

"You work like a dog for money and spend that money like a king."

"Is it even possible to run a business by paying all your taxes?"

"You need to keep two sets of books and stay on top of them."

The reason for my bankruptcy was the collapse of my life at the altar and my failure to keep the Bible as my absolute standard. I ran my businesses with a compound belief that came from good management textbooks and advice from friends.

One Sunday, the pastor gave a sermon titled, "The blessings He gives to the upright." However, during his sermon, the pastor stretched his hand in my direction, looked straight into my eyes and said, "God blesses the upright. You need to repent today and turn back from your ways."

He did this three times throughout the sermon, which I found to be rather upsetting. I wondered if my accountant, who was a member of the same church, had told the pastor about all my dishonesty and called her to confront her about it.

"Were you the one that told the pastor about everything?"

"Of course not. I'd be too embarrassed even to mention it. It's a blessing and opportunity that the pastor addressed you specifically like that today. Be an upright person."

I was not happy to hear what she had to say. When I came home after church and opened up the Bible, all I could see was the word "upright." This bothered me even more.

'Lord, send me one clear message.'

Then I opened up the Bible to a random page in the middle.

"The riches you get by dishonesty soon disappear, but not before they lead you into the jaws of death" (Prov. 21:6, GNT).

His message secretly shocked me. But still, I did not turn from my ways. I consoled myself with the thought, 'I donate more to missions than anybody else I know!' That was a chance of repentance I did not take.

I only realized after going completely bankrupt that the Lord had given me several chances to turn back. I experienced firsthand what God meant when He said that

PART III Look After the Poor

the children of the worldly rich will never have enough to eat and that He would move their wealth to the righteous. Not a single piece of the money I earned during that time was passed on to my son, and all the wealth I had gained through dishonest means simply vanished.

> "Cast but a glance at riches, and they are gone, for they will surely sprout wings and fly off to the sky like an eagle."
> Prov. 23:5

> "Don't wear yourself out trying to get rich; restrain yourself! Riches disappear in the blink of an eye; wealth sprouts wings and flies off into the wild blue yonder" Prov. 23:5, The Message

CHATPER 3

Those Under Mammon's Captivity

Judas Iscariot

"Then Satan entered Judas, called Iscariot, one of the Twelve" (Luke 22:3).

"The evening meal was in progress, and the devil had already prompted Judas, the son of Simon Iscariot, to betray Jesus" (John 13:2).

"Then one of the Twelve—the one called Judas Iscariot—went to the chief priests and asked, 'What are you willing to give me if I deliver him over to you?' So they counted out for him thirty pieces of silver. From then on Judas watched for an opportunity to hand him over" (Matt. 26:14-16).

"So Judas threw the money into the temple and left. Then he went away and hanged himself" (Matt. 27:5).

Satan causes people to either kill themselves or kill someone else. When money is involved, parents and their children fight each other to the death. We often hear news about families—married couples and siblings—who fight war amongst themselves for money.

Achan

The Lord commanded the Israelites to devote all of Jericho—the first city they took—because He wanted to give to them the entire land of Canaan. He told them to put the devoted items into the Lord's treasury.

"All the silver and gold and the articles of bronze and iron are sacred to the Lord and must go into his treasury" (Josh. 6:19).

But they faced a problem. The Israelites tried to use the momentum of their victory in Jericho and take the city of Ai, a city seemingly much easier to conquer than Jericho. They failed miserably. When Joshua went before the Lord lamenting over their defeat, the Lord said to him:

"Stand up! What are you doing down on your face? Israel has sinned; they have violated my covenant, which I commanded them to keep. They have taken some of the devoted things; they have stolen, they have lied, they have put them with their own possessions" (Josh. 7:10-11).

"That is why the Israelites cannot stand against their enemies; they turn their backs and run because they have been made liable to destruction. I will not be with you anymore unless you destroy whatever among you is devoted to destruction. Go, consecrate the people. Tell them, 'Consecrate yourselves in preparation for tomorrow; for this is what the Lord, the God of Israel, says: There are devoted things among you, Israel. You cannot stand against your enemies until you remove them'" (Josh. 7:12-13).

Israel suffered an unlikely defeat at Ai because someone, who mammon had taken captive, decided to steal what belonged to the Lord. When they drew names to find the culprit, Achan of the tribe of Judah was singled out. Achan confessed his sin before everyone.

"When I saw in the plunder a beautiful robe from Babylonia (Shinar), two hundred shekels of silver and a bar of gold weighing fifty shekels, I coveted them and took them" (Josh. 7:21).

The moment Achan set eyes on the Babylonian robe, silver, and gold, mammon planted greed in Achan's thoughts. Out of his avarice, Achan stole the devoted things.

"Then Joshua, together with all Israel, took Achan son of Zerah, the silver, the robe, the gold bar, his sons and daughters, his cattle, donkeys and sheep, his tent and all that he had, to the Valley of Achor… Then all Israel stoned him, and after they had stoned the rest, they burned them. Over Achan they heaped up a large pile of rocks… Therefore that place has been called the Valley of Achor ever since" (Josh. 7:24-26).

The Israelites buried not only Achan and everything he had stolen in the Valley of Achor, but also his sons and daughters, his cattle, donkeys and sheep, his tent, and all that he had. How tragic is this? Because of a single person who was taken captive by mammon, all his possessions, including his family, had to suffer the consequences. The Lord commanded Joshua settle the matter harshly. He taught the entire nation of Israel a brutal lesson.

> Why was it so important? Did God have to do this? Do you think that it was overly cruel? If it were a cancer cell, we would be willing to sacrifice anything and everything until those cells were utterly destroyed. Because if left untreated, the cancer cells would metastasize throughout our entire body. Likewise, if we leave the acts of Achan untreated, we drive entire nations into ruin. Hong SungGun

The Israelites were able to devote their first city, Jericho, only after they had buried Achan under a pile of rocks. After that, God gave them another ten cities. The Lord asked the Israelites to devote the first city in its entirety because He wanted to provide them with everything. The same applies to tithes. If we are to defeat the powerful tribes of Canaan and conquer the Promised Land, we must definitively remove the things of Achan; we must not allow greed and avarice to cause us to hold back in the things that are devoted to the Lord.

Gehazi: The Servant of Elisha

When Naaman, the commander of the army of Aram, had leprosy and came to Elisha asking for help, Elisha said to him:

"Go, wash yourself seven times in the Jordan, and your flesh will be restored and you will be cleansed" (2Kgs. 5:10).

PART III Look After the Poor

Naaman dipped himself in the River Jordan seven times and his flesh became clean like that of a young boy. Although Naaman wanted to give gifts to Elisha, Elisha refused.

"As surely as the Lord lives, whom I serve, I will not accept a thing." And even though Naaman urged him, he refused (2Kgs. 5:16).

Naaman lowered himself even more and thanked Elisha before he went on his way back home. Soon after, Gehazi, the servant of Elisha, caught after Naaman and lied.

"My master sent me to say, 'Two young men from the company of the prophets have just come to me from the hill country of Ephraim. Please give them a talent of silver and two sets of clothing'" (2Kgs. 5:22).

Thrilled to hear this, Namaan gave the servant not one, but two talents of silver. When mammon takes us captive, no lie and no betrayal of conscience are ever off-limits for money.

> One talent is equivalent to approximately 34 kilograms in weight. Both gold and silver talents were used as currency. One silver talent was worth 3,000 shekels. If the value of one shekel is converted to 400,000 won in today's exchange, one silver talent would be valued at a tremendous 1.2 billion won. Naaman gave double the silver that Gehazi requested, worth about 2.4 billion won. Hong SungGun

THE KING'S FINANCES II

Naaman put the two heavy talents of silver in two bags and made two of Gehazi's servants carry them. Gehazi later took the bags from the servants and hid them in his house. Then, he sent the men away and when to meet Elisha (see 2Kgs. 5:23-25).

"Gehazi, where were you?" Elisha asked him.

"I was here," answered Gehazi.

Elisha said to Gehazi:

"Is this the time to take money or to accept clothes—or olive groves and vineyards, or flocks and herds, or male and female slaves? Naaman's leprosy will cling to you and to your descendants forever." Then Gehazi went from Elisha's presence and his skin was leprous—it had become as white as snow (2Kgs. 5:26-27).

Leprosy not only remained with Gehazi, it was also passed down to his descendants. Elisha said to Gehazi, "Is this the time to take money or to accept clothes?" The time was one of alarm as Aram was preparing for war against Israel. Therefore, the time was a time to pray and kneel before the Lord.

Elisha refused Naaman's gifts because the gifts were the riches of this world, not of God. Yet Gehazi failed to understand why Elisha had not taken the gifts; he was not awake, and he was unable to discern the correct course of action. It was because mammon had taken his heart captive. As a result, generations of Gehazi's descendants were left to pay the bitter price of Gehazi's actions.

Ananias and Sapphira

Ananias and Sapphira sold a piece of their property to dedicate to the Lord. But, with their hearts taken captive by mammon, the couple was not able to display complete obedience. They lied.

With his wife's full knowledge, he kept back part of the money for himself but brought the rest and put it at the apostles' feet. Then "Peter said, 'Ananias, how is it that Satan has so filled your heart that you have lied to the Holy Spirit and have kept for yourself some of the money you received for the land?... What made you think of doing such a thing? You have not lied just to human beings but to God.' When Ananias heard this, he fell down and died. And great fear seized all who heard what had happened" (Act. 5:2-5).

About three hours later, his wife came in and told the same lie, clueless about everything that had happened.

"Peter asked her, 'Tell me, is this the price you and Ananias got for the land?' 'Yes,' she said, 'that is the price.' Peter said to her, 'How could you conspire to test the Spirit of the Lord? Listen! The feet of the men who buried your husband are at the door, and they will carry you out also.' At that moment she fell down at his feet and died" (Act. 5:8-10).

This is typical behavior of those who have been taken captive by mammon.

Give Me Back My Donations

A friend who was in charge of church finances called

me to tell me that something astounding had happened at church. A member had called and asked my friend to refund all the donations he had ever made to the church as he would be moving away. She also told me about another time when a person of important standing in the church asked for the land back that he had donated for a new church construction because his business was in trouble. Although I had heard of such incidents, I did not want to believe that they actually happened.

But similar things took place in NCMN a few times. I was distraught seeing these people who would argue, "Why are you not giving back the money that I donated?" despite Rev. Hong's attempts to help them understand.

From a church or organization's perspective, the money can be given back; it bears no negative effect on the part of the church or organization. It is the individual that will have to bear the consequences because mammon's hold is what causes them to act in this manner. It is by mammon's design that people believe God's sacred offerings belong to them. We call offerings "sacred" because the moment we dedicate them to the Lord, they become of the Lord. We must never ask back what we have given to the Lord.

Rev. Hong regretted that their response was so aggressive when his only intention was to save them from mammon. Giving offerings to the church is not the same as putting money in a savings account. Those who asked for their money back said that they needed the money for something urgent, or that they wanted to send the money to another mission field which was in a greater need for the money (The money was given back to them as they wished).

Do not fall prey to Satan's deception! These actions are the result of unbelief in God's sovereignty and mammon-planted thoughts that say, 'I am the owner of my money.' The end is certain destruction. Mammon's strategy is to not only ruin the person himself but to bring his children into ruin as well.

The Worldly Rich 2

I recommend studying "The Worldly Rich 2" after reading the chapters "Eliminate the Worldly Rich Within" and "The Mammon-Made Rich—The Worldly Rich" in *The King's Finances I*.

- Definition of the worldly rich
  - They are generous to themselves but are miserly when it comes to God and others.
  - They live deceitful and dishonest lives.

- How to eradicate the ways of the worldly rich
  - Train to share and be upright.
  - The Bible warns strictly against living a life of the worldly rich.

1) The Story of the Rich Young Man

A rich young man asked Jesus a question.

"What must I do to inherit eternal life?" (Mark 10:17).

"Go, sell everything you have and give to the poor, and you will have treasure in heaven. Then come, follow me" (Mark 10:21).

Jesus gave the answer "wealth" to the young man who wanted to know how to inherit eternal life. The young man did not heed Jesus' words and went on his way. Faith is obedience to the Lord's words. It is as if this young rich man was placed right in the middle of the events that took place in Genesis Chapter 3.

God said to Adam:

"But you must not eat from the tree of the knowledge of good and evil, for when you eat from it you will certainly die" (Gen. 2:17).

The serpent (Satan) said to the woman:

"You will not certainly die. For God knows that when you eat from it your eyes will be opened, and you will be like God" (Gen. 3:4-5).

The tree of the knowledge of good and evil incident in Genesis Chapter 3 asks the following question of faith, "Who is your master?" By obeying the words of Satan, Adam and Eve became Satan's slaves.

"Don't you know that when you offer yourselves to someone as obedient slaves, you are slaves of the one you obey" (Rom. 6:16).

The rich young man was asked the same question.

"Whose words do you obey? Who is your master? Is it Jesus Christ, or is it wealth?"

Jesus said: "Sell everything you have and give it to the poor."
Mammon said: "No, all your money is yours to keep."

"At this the man's face fell. He went away sad, because he had great wealth" (Mark 10:22).

"Jesus looked around and said to his disciples, 'How hard it is for the rich to enter the kingdom of God!... It is easier for a camel to go through the eye of a needle than for someone who is rich to enter the kingdom of God'" (Mark 10:23,25).

The "someone who is rich" here refers to the worldly rich, not the holy rich. The holy rich will surely inherit the kingdom of God as an inheritance. David enjoyed wealth and honor into old age (see 1 Chron. 29:28). Isaac reaped a hundredfold of the crops he planted, and his wealth continued to grow until he became very rich (see Gen. 26:12-13).

The focal point of the rich young man's story is not money, but rather the following two questions: "Who is your master?" and "Who can enter the kingdom of God?"

2) The Story of the Rich Man and Lazarus

Jesus drew a comparison between heaven and hell through the story of the rich man and the beggar named

Lazarus. After both had died, the beggar named Lazarus was in the bosom of Abraham while the rich man suffered torment in hell. In his agony in the fire of hell, the rich man called out to Abraham for help.

"I have five brothers; please send Lazarus to them to testify so that they will not also come to this place of torment." But Abraham told the rich man that his brothers already have Moses and the Prophets to listen to and that if they do not listen to Moses and the Prophets, even Lazarus will not be able to convince them (see Luke 16:19-31).

This story also deals with the question of "Who is your master?" The story of the rich man, the man who did not look after the destitute Lazarus and went to hell after he died, should awaken a sense of vigilance within us.

3) The Parable of the Sheep and the Goats

Jesus used the metaphor of the sheep and the goats to explain heaven and hell (see Matt. 25:31-46). When that day comes, people will be separated and will either be granted eternal punishment or eternal life. The standard for this separation is whether or not one has taken care of those in absolute need. Jesus speaks to those who have gone into eternal life:

"For I was hungry and you gave me something to eat, I was thirsty and you gave me something to drink, I was a stranger and you invited me in, I needed clothes and you clothed me, I was sick and you looked after me, I was in prison and you came to visit me"

And then He turns to those who have gone into eternal punishment and says:

"For I was hungry and you gave me nothing to eat, I was thirsty and you gave me nothing to drink, I was a stranger and you did not invite me in, I needed clothes and you did not clothe me, I was sick and in prison and you did not look after me"

Then, He reveals an amazing secret.

"Whatever you did for one of the least of these brothers and sisters of mine, you did for me" (Matt. 25:40).

The question is not just about whether or not we have served the poor, the question He is asking us, as He calls us to a life of faith, is "In what have you placed your faith?"

4) Flee from the Coming Wrath

"John said to the crowds coming out to be baptized by him, 'You brood of vipers! Who warned you to flee from the coming wrath? Produce fruit in keeping with repentance.'" (Luke 3:7-8). How do we flee from the coming wrath? And what fruit should we produce in keeping with repentance? The crowd, which had heard John the Baptist's words, gathered around him to ask questions.

"What should we do then?" (Luke 3:10).

"Anyone who has two shirts should share with the one who has none, and anyone who has food should do the same" (Luke 3:11).

In other words, he told them to look after the poor and needy. The tax collectors also asked.

"What should we do?" (Luke 3:12).

"Don't collect any more than you are required to" (Luke 3:13).

Shortly put, he told them to eradicate the dishonest ways of the rich. Then some soldiers came and asked.

"And what should we do?" (Luke 3:14).

"Don't extort money and don't accuse people falsely—be content with your pay" (Luke 3:14).

Through John the Baptist, God explains all the different ways of fleeing from the coming wrath using only "money" as an example. This also has to do with the question of "Who is your master?" God demands that we eradicate the ways of the worldly rich with His Word.

The Life of the Worldly Rich Who Have Been Captured by Mammon

What are some characteristics of the worldly rich are under the influence of mammon?

1) They live for the wrong master

"No one can serve two masters. Either you will hate the one and love the other, or you will be devoted to the one and despise the other. You cannot serve both God and money (mammon)" (Matt. 6:24).

PART III Look After the Poor

- Mammon's goal – changing your master
  (Matt. 6:24; Luke 16:13)
- Mammon's strategy – make you love money (1 Tim. 6:10)
- Mammon's desired goal – make you abandon your faith (1 Tim. 6:10)

"For the love of money is a root of all kinds of evil. Some people, eager for money, have wandered from the faith and pierced themselves with many griefs" (1 Tim. 6:10). Mammon plants the love of money in our hearts, and that love for money becomes the "root of all evil." Everything evil stems from this. The roots determine the quality of the fruit harvested. Evil roots produce evil fruit, and good roots produce good fruit.

Mammon's strategy is to make people love money so much that they abandon their faith and, ultimately, bring about their demise. He makes people spend all their lives' energy on money, because of money, and to chase after money. Such people can still say that they are living for the kingdom of God, but their words only make them hypocrites. This is because they are living a life that is void of faith.

To resolve this issue, we must first change the object of our love from "love for money" to "love for God." The master of our lives must be God and God only, not mammon.

"I love those who love me, and those who seek me find me. With me are riches and honor, enduring wealth and prosperity... bestowing a rich inheritance on those who love me and making their treasuries full. (Prov. 8:17,18,21).

Everything belongs to God (see Lev. 25:23; Deut. 10:14; 1 Chron. 29:11-12; Psa. 24:1, 50:10-12; Hag. 2:8; 1 Cor. 10:26).

2) They live a life without influence because they are tied to mammon with debt

I refer to department stores and home shopping channels as "the temple of mammon." People lose their minds once they set foot in them. To empty your pockets, department stores' strategy and planning departments provide immediate discount offers when you sign-up for a credit card with their store and spare no effort in helping you make impulse purchases and drag you deep into debt. Do not make a habit of buying from home shopping channels. They will lead you to debt. It is now time to understand what mammon really is and stop using one credit card to stave off the debt of another credit card. If credit cards cause you to go into debt, cut them up!

3) They are miserly

When people are under the influence of mammon, they become misers. They use their wealth only for themselves instead of sharing with others or giving to others. They buy goods not based on their utility but based on their greed and avarice. They buy things that they do not need, such as a better car, a bigger house, nicer furniture, and other such things. Their closets are filled with clothes they barely wear once a year.

4) They have no problem being dishonest when it is about money

We've already read about the consequences of dishonesty and the promise given to the upright. The worldly rich use any means necessary to get money.

5) Their happiness hinges on money

Mammon whispers into the ears of the worldly rich incessantly.

"Money will make you happy."

This is a lie. Money can never make us happy. Happiness can only be achieved in Jesus Christ our Lord. Stand against mammon and eliminate the worldly rich within!

Part IV
Awaken the Next Generation of Faith

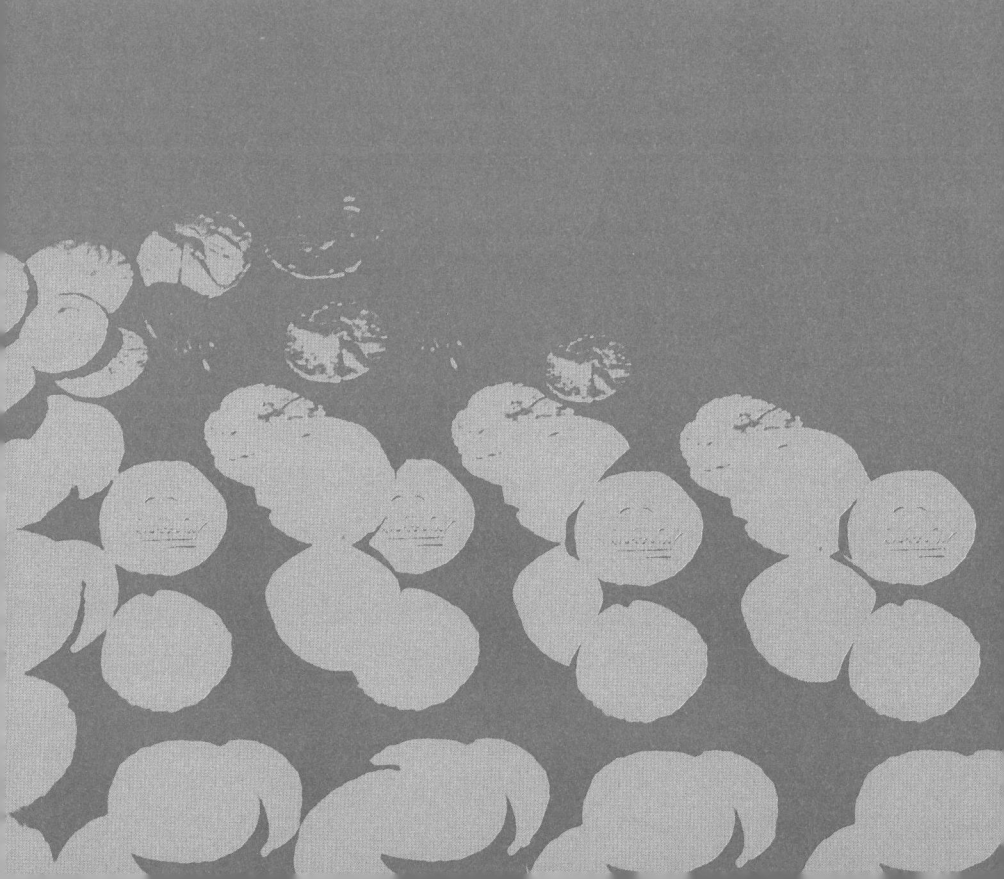

CHATPER 1

The Secret to a Life of Contentment

PART IV Awaken the Next Generation of Faith

Be Content

One area in which the Lord continually taught me was learning how to be content. I am still learning. When we are self-content, we can break free from mammon's influence and the ways of the worldly rich. It took me some time to understand that self-contentment is the most fundamental spiritual muscle which allows us to live as the holy rich.

Being content has brought me tremendous prosperity, both spiritually and materially. A content life begins with sharing with others and giving abundantly to others.

Hebrews 13:5 tells us the secrets to being content.

"Keep your lives free from the love of money and be content with what you have, because God has said, 'Never will I leave you; never will I forsake you.'"

First, it is keeping free from the love of money.

This fulfilled, we can save ourselves from falling into mammon's traps of greed and avarice.

Second, it is knowing how to be content with what you have.

"But godliness with contentment is great gain. For we brought nothing into the world, and we can take nothing out of it. But if we have food and clothing, we will be content with that. Those who want to get rich fall into temptation and a trap and into many foolish and harmful desires that plunge people into ruin and destruction. For the love of money is a root of all kinds of evil. Some people, eager for money, have wandered from the faith and pierced themselves with many griefs" (1 Tim. 6:6-10).

The standard for being content is laid out in this verse "But if we have food and clothing, we will be content with that" (1 Tim. 6:8). The standard which the Lord gave us is straightforward. Having enough to eat and wear should be the standard for being content in our lives.

Being content helps us achieve godliness. What is godliness? In the past, I misunderstood what a godly life and godly person really meant. I thought that a godly man was a quiet person who walks around slowly with a Bible tucked under his arm. But I finally understood the meaning of godliness through one of Rev. Hong's sermons.

1 Timothy 3:16 explains what godliness looks like in our lives.

"Beyond all question, the mystery from which true godliness springs is great: He appeared in the flesh, was vindicated by the Spirit, was seen by angels, was preached among the nations, was believed on in the world, was taken up in glory."

Jesus Christ, who appeared in the flesh, is the mystery of godliness. A godly person is a person who reflects Christ with his or her life. Traits of Jesus, such as love, sharing, acceptance, humility, meekness, are also reflected in the lives of the godly. This is how I grew to understand the words, being content helps us achieve godliness.

Third, it is placing our sense of security only in Jesus.

Jesus' words, "Never will I leave you; never will I forsake you" (Heb. 13:5), bring peace to my heart. I cannot help but mouth the words, "Thank you." My faith in the Lord brings me a sense of stability whether I live in abundance or need because the Lord has promised, "Never will I leave you; never will I forsake you."

The power of the Apostle Paul's ministry also lies in contentment.

"I am not saying this because I am in need, for I have learned to be content whatever the circumstances. I know what it is to be in need, and I know what it is to have plenty. I have learned the secret of being content in any and every situation, whether well fed or hungry, whether living in plenty or in want" (Phil. 4:11-12).

I learned that contentment comes not from money, honor, or the things of this world, but from God alone. This is what gives me the strength to be more than content in life.

And we have such trust through Christ toward God. Not that we are sufficient of ourselves to think of anything as being from ourselves, but our sufficiency is from God

2Cor 3:4-5, New King James Version

This is the secret to living a life of contentment.

Stop Practicing Usury

Two sisters at the King's Finances School asked to consult with me on the same issue.

"Does the Bible allow personal bankruptcy?"

They had borrowed 100 million won from a deaconess at their church with the promise of paying back two million won per month as interest. Their business did okay, so they continued to pay the interest for five years. But when one of their husbands' companies suddenly started struggling, their business also suffered. So they went to see their creditor, the deaconess. "Could you count the money we give you from now as payment on the principal and not the interest?" they asked.

They had already paid more than 100 million won, the amount of the principal, in interest payments alone. But the deaconess rejected their offer and demanded that they continue to pay the interest or immediately repay the entire amount of the principal. She did not discount a single won from their interest payments.

This sister did not want this issue to cause problems within the church, so she continued to pay the interest by taking out another loan. And when she did that, her debt began to swell. She did not have anyone else to whom to turn for a loan, nor did she have the means to pay back her existing loans. Her entire family suffered as a consequence, and had it not been for the fear of hell, she would have made the decision to take her own life. At last, she decided to file for bankruptcy.

I could understand the positions of both the creditor and the debtor. Much of the debt I had incurred was due to others' loans for which I had signed as a guarantor. Many had also borrowed money from me.

"Whoever increases wealth by taking interest or profit from the poor amasses it for another, who will be kind to the poor" (Prov. 28:8).

"Get as rich as you want through cheating and extortion, but eventually some friend of the poor is going to give it all back to them" (Prov. 28:8, The Message).

God moves the wealth of the worldly rich to the righteous.

"He oppresses the poor and needy. He commits robbery. He does not return what he took in pledge. He looks to the idols. He does detestable things. He lends at interest and takes a profit. Will such a man live? He will not! Because he has done all these detestable things, he is to be put to death; his blood will be on his own head" (Ezek. 18:12-13).

The Bible warns us time and time again to stay away from usury and cancel the debts of our debtors if they have become poor. If we have received more in interest payments than the amount of the principle, it is the law of the kingdom of God that we reduce our debtor's principal (see Deut. 15:1; Neh.5:1-13).

"The wicked borrow and do not repay, but the righteous give generously (Psa. 37:21).

"May a creditor seize all he has; may strangers plunder the fruits of his labor. May no one extend kindness to him or take pity on his fatherless children. May his descendants be cut off, their names blotted out from the next generation" (Psa. 109:11-13).

The Creditor's Attitude

The creditor must be aware of the debtor's financial situation. If a creditor charges high-interest rates to the poor, he ends up harming himself. Be gracious and have a generous heart.

The Debtor's Attitude

Borrowed money must be paid back. The Bible says, "You will store up but save nothing, because what you save I will give to the sword" (Mic. 6:14), about debtors who hide their wealth to avoid repaying their debts.

The wicked characteristically borrow and do not repay.

"Therefore, the kingdom of heaven is like a king who wanted to settle accounts with his servants. As he began the settlement, a man who owed him ten thousand talents of gold was brought to him. Since he was not able to pay... The servant's master took pity on him, canceled the debt and let him go. But when that servant went out, he found one of his fellow servants who owed him a hundred denarii. He grabbed him and began to choke him. 'Pay back what you owe me!' he demanded. "His fellow servant fell to his knees and begged him, 'Be patient with me, and I will pay it back.' But he refused. Instead, he went off and had the man thrown into prison until he could pay the debt. When the other servants saw what had happened, they were outraged and went and told their master everything that had happened. Then the master called the servant in. 'You wicked servant,' he said, 'I canceled all that debt of yours because you begged me to. Shouldn't you have had mercy on your fellow servant just as I had on you?' In anger his master handed him over to the jailers to be tortured, until he should pay back all he owed" (Matt. 18:23-34).

One talent is worth about 1.8-2 billion won today. As such, the cancellation of a debt of 10,000 talents is an astounding, unthinkable incident. On the other hand, one denarius is worth about what a worker would be paid for a day's labor today. One hundred denarii are worth about three months' wages.

I meditated on this metaphor of heaven. I was the debtor who was forgiven his debt of 10,000 talents! All my sins have been canceled and forgiven. Therefore, the only logical conclusion is that I should also forgive others.

Be Faithful with Others' Wealth

I have an embarrassing confession to make. When I used to serve as a Sunday school teacher, I used the church copier to photocopy some personal documents while copying scores for the Sunday school choir. The time I spent in the wilderness cleansed me. I remembered what I did back then and sought penance; I gave back many times the amount of what I took.

I learned about biblical financial principles from Rev. Hong after my bankruptcy. What captivated my heart the most was that there exists a Heavenly Bank. As a bankrupt woman, I was very interested to hear about the high-interest rates in that bank. So, I decided to begin saving in one of the three possible savings accounts that Rev. Hong had talked about in his sermons.

> The poor, those in absolute need
> The people of God (workers: the holy poor)
> Projects of the kingdom of God

Putting my finances to use in these areas was to sow in the Heavenly Bank. When I worked part-time, I set aside 300,000 won by saving the lunch money that my work gave me for six months. Then I invited a pastor couple who were a strong support during my bankruptcy to the finest Hanwoo barbeque restaurant in town.

But to my dismay, they had brought their five children with them! A single portion of Hanwoo at that restaurant cost 60,000-70,000 won. The children began eating the side dishes on the table before we ordered our food. I was extremely flustered. The pastor's wife put in the first order.

"Excuse me, could we have five portions of the Hanwoo ribeye steak?"

I did a quick calculation in my head and almost lost my

PART IV Awaken the Next Generation of Faith

breath.

"Should we order rice and soup too?" I asked the pastor's wife, hoping we could fill our stomachs with cheaper options.

"No, we're at a barbeque restaurant; we should eat our meat first and then move on to the rice."

We were a table of eight. Five portions were nowhere near enough for the couple's growing children.

"Ma'am, could you give us five more portions?" the pastor's wife said to the waitress.

And like that, ten portions of Hanwoo ribeye steak just vanished. I had not eaten a single piece.

"Ma'am, another five portions, please."

I despaired. When the pastor couple's seven-year-old boy spat out a piece of meat because he had just had too much meat, the pastor's wife picked up a new piece of meat for her son.

Placing that new piece of meat into her son's mouth, she said, "Eat up as much as you can now. When do you think we'll ever be able to eat such expensive beef again?"

After the meal, I sent the family on their way but had to remain at the restaurant because I did not have the money to pay for the bill. I called my friends to ask for help, but none of them answered their phones. In the end, I was barely able to make it out of there thanks to the manager of my optician shop before I was bankrupt who came and paid for it with his credit card to be billed in ten-month installments. Even to this day, I can only force a bitter smile when I think back to that time.

Another friend always ordered the cheapest coffee when she was buying but ordered the most expensive drink when it was someone else who was paying. I did not wish to maintain a close relationship with her. I do not wish to partner in ministry or business with such people. God entrusts us with much when we are faithful with the very little. He allows us to handle true riches when we prove that we are faithful with worldly wealth. We receive our own when we are faithful with the property of others (see Luke 16:10-12).

The wilderness ended up being a blessing for me. The principles I learned during my time there made me a more respected person. How can we be faithful with others' property? By not being wasteful and treating it as if it were our own. The wilderness taught me how to appreciate what belongs to others just as much as I appreciate what is mine.

The Equity of God's Kingdom

For if the willingness is there, the gift is acceptable according to what one has, not according to what one does not have. Our desire is not that others might be relieved while you are hard pressed, but that there might be equality. At the present time your plenty will supply what they need, so that in turn their plenty will supply what you need. The goal is equality, as it is written: "The one who gathered much did not have too

much, and the one who gathered little did not have too little"
2Cor. 8:12-15

The focus of this scripture is to have enough for everyone through equality. The Lord wants wealth to flow like water. Water in a stream first fills its immediate area before flowing down into a lower altitude. When the lower area is completely filled, then the water flows into an even lower place. The principle of the flow of water is that it fills every space, leaving no surface or area uncovered.

God wishes for us to use our wealth in a way that resembles the flow of water. The haves and have nots stand on different altitudes. The Lord tells those with plenty to let their wealth flow so as to fill the needs of those who lack so that there might be equality and everyone might have all that they need.

The Lord tells us first to fill the needs of our believers in Christ, then our neighbors (people within a 5km radius), then even more people beyond that. He tells us to fill the needs of South Korea, then North Korea, and then to fill the needs of frontline mission fields across the world. He supplies us with plenty so that we might fill the needs of others with what is ours.

The Lord gave manna to the Israelites so that all of them might have enough. What is remarkable is that neither the one who gathered much had too much nor the one who gathered little had too little. This does not mean that it just happened to be so after everyone had gathered their manna;

some may have been sick and unable to collect manna for themselves. It means that they shared what they gathered with each other. If someone was greedy and decided to collect more than their need, and then had leftovers, the manna would smell and be full of maggots.

Very rarely, I am genuinely puzzled by the issues on which people consult me. They tell me, as if to complain, that they served the church and ministers by using loans, lines of credit, and credit card cash services, but that they find themselves are always lacking.

God never told us to go into debt to serve others. The Bible tells us that the Lord does not take what we do not have. The Lord takes what we willingly give within our means. When we give what we do not have, even going into debt to do so, we ultimately create discontent and unbalance. God wants us to be at peace (see 2 Cor. 8:12-13).

True disciples of Jesus Christ consider one another and practice sharing in their lives. Sharing is the solution to the age-old problem of "the gap between the haves and have nots." The only answer to this problem is the Christian spirit. The world may operate on "the principle of buying and selling," but the kingdom of God operates on "the principle of giving and receiving."

When we live out the Word, God pours His overflowing blessing into our business so that we, in turn, may flow our prosperity to where there is a lack and share in the burden of the poor.

"Equality" does not mean an equal distribution to

everyone (1/n) but rather that everyone is distributed to just as much as their needs. This is the most fundamental of Christian financial principles. For example, when collecting funds for a particular purpose, everyone should be asked to contribute according to their means. This means that those who have plenty can pay a little more, and those who have little can pay a little less.

This is equity in God's kingdom. Even when receiving, those with much receive a little less and those with little a little more.

⟨Equality in the world⟩   ⟨Equity in the kingdom of God⟩

This happened while I was attending a revival conference in Japan. The church in which the revival conference was held was a small one operating on a tight budget. I will never forget the testimony which the assistant pastor of that church gave during the meeting.

"Our senior pastor's salary is lower than mine. He tells me, 'My children have now all grown up. You have three young children; you need the money much more than I do.'"

We can also see the Christian spirit in the life of the wealthy merchant Im SangOk in the late Joseon Dynasty. It is said that he had quoted, "Wealth is as flat as water, people are fair like scales," written on the inside of his favorite glass.

Because wealth is like water, it flows down from high to low. Through NCMN's 5K Movement, the sharing life is spreading rapidly throughout Korea and to all corners of the world. There are already NCMN 5K offices in all eight provinces of South Korea, and other offices are being set up abroad at immense speed. Trying to monopolize such wealth, which flows like water, will most certainly bring destruction by that very wealth. An unfair and dishonest business inevitably ends up in ruins.

Out of Debt and Into the Light Shin HeeJae

I got acquainted with the King's Finances lectures through online videos. At the time, I was running two different businesses. Profits were excellent, and I used the money I made from those businesses to start another healthy bakery franchise (Papamain) business. But despite my initial high expectations, the new bakery business continued to make losses. When I funneled all the money from my successful companies to make up for the losses in the bakery, my employees lost their motivation to work. I needed a breakthrough. I enrolled in the King's Finances School and asked Sister Kim MiJin for a consultation. I hoped that she would be able to lead me to a business breakthrough from God.

But after hearing what I had to say, she said, "I wouldn't be in that bakery business if I were you." In short, she was telling me to cut my losses and pull out of the bakery business. Although I replied, "Yes," for the lack of a better answer, I had many concerns; I had already invested too much and was running four franchise bakeries. What is more, I was upset that she sought to end a consultation so important to me so lightly and tell me to just shut down the business as if it were so simple.

And every time I saw Sister MiJin after that, she would repeat, "Shut them down as soon as you can." Her words were on my mind, but I could not bring myself to close down the business. I was convinced that success was just around the corner with a little more effort. Over two years, the bakery business accumulated losses of 2 billion won, and my total debt increased to 2.8 billion won. I went to Sister Kim MiJin for another consultation.

"Why are you being so stubborn? I've been bankrupt before; I can see when something is not a good idea!"

In the end, I closed down the bakery business and resolved to live out the biblical financial principles to perfection.

Paying back my debts became my first priority.

One day during my prayers, I felt a lingering urge to give something to the Lord. I wanted to give a 3-floor, 1 basement, 4-story building in Yeongdeungpo as an offering to the Lord. When I consulted Sister Kim MiJin about it, her answer was as concise as always, "Give it to the place the Lord directs."

"A realtor reached out to me a few days ago; he wants to buy the property from me for 4.8 billion won. What should I do?"

"You just said that you want to give it to the Lord. Do what the Lord tells you or you might regret it later."

My family was thrilled when they heard about my plans at a family meeting.

"Darling, let's give it to the Lord."

"Father, I have joy in my heart! Give it to the Lord."

I felt like the only faithless person in town. During prayer, I felt compelled to donate my building to be used as the HQ offices for NCMN, an organization that will lead the Christian Civilization Reform Movement. And after receiving my family's cheerful blessing, I told Sister Kim MiJin about my decision.

"Lord, Thank you. Thank the Lord, as it is He who has given you a good heart, and He who has given you the strength to do this good deed. Just give thanks."

Although some others may have been offended by her reaction, I was simply thankful that Rev. Hong and Sister MiJin had even accepted the building, having observed them up close for a long time. A few years ago, the two turned down someone's offer to donate a building worth 12 billion won; they also turned down a donation of good land. Rev. Hong and Sister Kim MiJin told the donors that the building and land were not in the location they had been praying for and that they should donate them to their respective churches.

Now, I have repaid all 2.8 billion won of my debt and am debt-free. I give endless thanks to the Lord.

Having Certainty with Faith Shin YongSun

My wife and I are newlyweds in our second month of marriage. Financially speaking, we were quite desperate. We had zero income as I had quit my job and enrolled in the theological seminary to continue life as a holy poor man. I was determined to live by the budget of faith; I would take detailed notes on 2-hour online lectures while watching them at 0.3x speed.

While I was trying to draw up the budget of faith according to the principles taught in the online videos, I had no one from whom I could seek guidance. So my wife and I began drafting our budget based on the online lectures. We separated some of the little savings we had as starter money and emergency funds. We decided to use one million a month from our savings, of which 200,000 won were set for living expenses and 20,000 won for pocket money.

Although our monthly budget was 1 million won, our

monthly "budget of faith" was 1.75 million won. And even though we could have used more money than we set aside for ourselves, we set apart a budget for sowing and reaping (the Heavenly Bank) in faith. On the day we were drafting up our budget of faith, we received news – to our amazement – that I had received a scholarship. We had not included the scholarship in our budget of faith because we could not determine the exact amount of the scholarship despite having already submitted the application documents and them being processed.

This happened when my wife and I went to Hongik University Station to prepare for a MY 5K event. There were some street vendors selling ddeokboggi[12] around the station. I really craved some, but I forced myself to turn away because I had made the decision to live by a budget. Spending 2000-3000 won was nothing when I was working, I thought. It saddened me that 2000-3000 won was too much for me to spend on some snacks.

The most difficult part of it was that I was putting my wife through the same experience. But still, we resolved to live it out and pressed on. We prepared for the event to the best of our abilities, and this filled us with hope. During the preparations, Sister Kim MyungJa bought ddeokboggi for everyone who was involved in getting ready for the event. Words cannot express how grateful I was on that day.

---

12 A rice cake dish in a spicy red sauce popular among Koreans as a snack.

It was some time after deciding to live by a budget of faith when the sole of my shoe fell off. I had no way of fixing it. Had it been before, I would have just bought new shoes. However, I had decided to live on a budget of faith. I usually tried to be well-dressed, but in this case, all I could do was survive on the single pair of good shoes that I had left. Luckily, I had some old shoes back at home, and I wore those after my family had them sent to me. My hair also grew long, but I did not have the budget for it so I just let it grow out.

When a friend gave me a tangerine, I could not possibly eat it on my own and took it home to my wife. She immediately wrote in a withdrawal of 500 won in the Heavenly Bank budget. She did the same even for a 1,900 won cup of coffee; we were determined to record and keep track of every penny we received.

We also recorded the deposits we made as well. And even though the amounts felt minuscule and insignificant at times, we never gave up. We gave toward church construction and helping those in need. We also donated goods to our church's 5K Share Love box.

We also received many unexpected donations: 300,000 won as pocket money, 200,000 won from a younger church friend who I met in the 1st King's Finances School in Malaysia, as well as 850,000 won for rent. One preacher even sent us 50,000 won to cover living expenses.

From the beginning, we saw our needs met at an astounding speed. When I prayed to the Lord about our extra money, He told me to get a haircut. So I found a good cheap place and got that done. I thought that we would not be able to tithe for a while due to our lack of money, but in some miraculous way we were given the funds to pay our tithes.

Although our will began to falter three weeks in, we were able to get back on track with prayer. We recorded the missed entries in our Heavenly Bank account and completed our daily bookkeeping entries. When we were done entering everything, we saw that we had withdrawn a total of 2.19 million won from our Heavenly Bank account.

I was moved seeing how God had met our material and monetary needs. I was also happy to see that our deposits into the Heavenly Bank account exceeded our initial target of 50,000 won and stood at 73,000 won. And when I divided our total withdrawals of 2.19 million won by 30 days just out of curiosity, the daily average was 73,000 won! We were amazed that God gave back exactly 30-fold on our deposits. Looking back, the key to achieving a breakthrough was "having certainty with faith." I learned that it is by having this certainty that our faith becomes our reality. I experienced firsthand that our God is a faithful God who let us bear fruit, 30, 60, 100 times what was sown. The one month of living on a budget of faith that began in tears turned out to be an opportunity for us to experience God as never before.

Awaken the Goodness in Korea's Heart

I began feeling a sense of responsibility to awaken the goodness in the hearts of Koreans when I started praying for reunification two years ago.

'How can we awaken the dormant goodness in the hearts of both believers and nonbelievers?'

Rev. Hong and I prayed for the Lord to give us a strategy. The strategy the Lord gave us was quite simple: He told us to march around the fortified walls of Jericho seven times to have it come tumbling down.

'Lord, what should we march around seven times?'

The Lord answered, 'The Seoul Plaza.'

We needed an acting leader to realize this seemingly simple strategy. We prayed for the Lord to send us someone. And when we prayed, the Lord showed me Brother Shin HeeJae the businessman. But when I got to know him, I found out that he was Brother Shin Hee-Jae the debtor. He was knee-deep in debt from his bakery business, and though we told him to wrap it up as soon as possible, he continued to run his bakery business. Intrigued by this stubbornness of his, I continued to watch him closely.

'Lord, are you sure that he is the person best suited for this job?'

During his consultations with me, I realized that Brother Shin HeeJae did not have a sense of the severity of his debts. I continued to watch him and keep him in my prayers.

I prayed, 'Lord, if you wish to use him to do this important work, please give him the desire to repay his debts and live a life of diligent faith.'

I observed him like that for two whole years. I saw the amazing ways in which God touched him and led his entire family to a life of faith. We believed with conviction that he was the right person and decided to place him in the position of acting leader.

When I wanted to check just one more time that he indeed was the right person and asked him, "Brother Shin, let's take a walk for the Lord," he replied the very next day, "If we are going to walk for the Lord, we should do it in the middle of Seoul." God never failed to send us the right people to do His work.

Let's Walk Together – MY 5K Shin HeeJae

I was assigned a project by NCMN.

"Awaken the dormant goodness in Korea's heart!"

I immediately became a part of the team. I was filled with motivation and confidence in this new project that had been assigned to me. During a meeting for the leaders of the project, Sister MiJin said to me. "Brother HeeJae, let go a little bit. You're running this project as if it were a business."

I had no idea what she was talking about when she first said that to me.

Let's Walk Together – MY 5K Walking Campaign
Host: NCMN
Organizer: 5K Movement Headquarters

Purpose: Awaken the good conscience of Korea to put loving our neighbors into practice
Route: 5km – from Seoul Plaza to the Peace Plaza in front of the War Memorial of Korea
Keywords: Love, Togetherness, Transformation, Miracles
Number of Participants: 5000 (max. number of persons allowed to gather at the Peace Plaza)
Date: April 20, 2019 (Disabled Persons' Day)
Patrons of the Event: NCMN King's Business Group, NC Group, Oregin, Far East Broadcasting Company, Kukmin Ilbo, Kyujang Publishing House, Korea Broadcasting Association for the Disabled Actors (KBADA), Seoul Sports Association for the Differently Abled (SSAD)
Sponsor: Changam Elrin Welfare Foundation

We received the authorization to use Seoul Plaza. We checked and double-checked all the events that would be taking place at the start and finish points of the walk. We recruited 500 volunteers, and each of them carried out their responsibilities exceptionally well. The only thing left was to receive road usage authorization from the Seoul Police Department. However, it was denied. The police department said that they had never granted permission to a civic organization to block a road and host a march in the heart of Seoul.

We went many times, but each time our request was denied. We were stuck, unable to receive authorization for the most integral piece of the event, the road. I called in all the favors

I could using my connections, but they were of no use. Having reached my wit's end, I went to Sister MiJin to brief her truthfully on the issue.

"Let go a little bit. You can't expect to do the Lord's work with your own power and strength."

Her words sucked the last bit of energy I had left from me. I asked, unable to understand why no paths were being opened if God was the one who had told us to host this event.

"Are you sure God asked us to host this event?"

Sister Kim MiJin chuckled.

"I say, let go, and you let go of your faith! God will make a way. All we have to do is obey. Just continue doing what you're doing and engage in prayer and fasting."

'Is she serious? How can she be so calm? The whole event will go down the drain if we can't get permission for the road usage...'

My mouth dried up. I called up my connections again to push for authorization but failed yet again. With only 45 days left until the event, this posed a huge problem. We had already recruited a significant percentage of the people who would be participating in the walk. I had placed an order for 5,000 t-shirts for the event, and we had already made the usage fee payment for the Peace Plaza. Over 80 percent of all the event preparations had already been completed.

When I went to Sister MiJin again with my concerns, all she told me was that business and ministry are two different things and that I should pray earnestly for God to open up

PART IV Awaken the Next Generation of Faith

a path.

'I tell her we don't have permission to use the road, and yet she tells me to just pray... what difference could there possibly be between business and ministry?'

On March 19, our team had an appointment with the Changam Elrin Welfare Foundation on Jeju Island to film our volunteers serving and walking with the disabled. The weather forecast predicted a 90 percent chance of heavy rain. And when we arrived on the island on the evening of the 18th, the downpour had already begun. Sister MiJin took us to a Jeju Black Pork restaurant to provide us with a meal there. Everyone enjoyed the meal, but I could not bring myself to have even a single piece of meat. The entire camera crew was already there, but the director said that we would not be able to film if there were rain.

"Sister MiJin, there's a 90 percent chance of heavy rain tomorrow."

"Brother HeeJae, as soon as you let go a little, I'm sure the rain will go away. You know how much we've prayed to the Lord about the weather. Just enjoy the food now."

I was burning with anxiety. When we got back to the hotel, I tossed and turned in bed until I finally went outside at 4 am. It was still raining. I went to a nearby park and prayed a desperate prayer, my arms stretched toward the sky.

"Lord, is the weather not strictly under your control? Father, help us."

When I got back to the hotel, Sister MiJin asked to go to breakfast together.

"Brother HeeJae don't worry. When we get to the Changam Elrin Welfare Foundation, God will give us the best possible weather so we can serve them in the best way that we can."

And it really turned out that way! Even Pastor Lim SangPil, the chairman of the board of the foundation, said that it was one of the nicest, sunniest, and most windless days he had seen in Jeju over the past year. Little by little, I understood what Sister MiJin meant when she told me to let go.

I received a phone call while I was serving my disabled brothers. It was a call from someone at the police department telling me to make my way quickly to the police department. When we got back to Seoul, I visited the department with a handful of NCMN leaders. There, we met with an officer in a senior position who asked us:

"With whom and with what words did you put in the request for road usage permission for the Let's Walk Together – MY 5K Walking Campaign?"

I told him the truth; I said that I did not know anyone high up and that I had exhausted all the means and connections I had at my disposal to no avail. I told him that all I had left to do was pray, which was what I was doing. He looked surprised.

"Well, then God must have opened up your path."

Tears streamed down my face. A man who was not a believer of Christ was glorifying God with his lips. God had opened up a path for us and even sent the military bands of the Capital Defense Command and the Korea Military Academy to join us on Disabled Persons' Day and

PART IV Awaken the Next Generation of Faith

encourage the little ones with their performances.
On the Disabled Persons' Day of April 20, 2019, we walked alongside the disabled under the watch of the entire nation. Our walk itself was a message sent out to the rest of the world.

Love – our love makes us walk.
Togetherness – to love is to share, and to share is to be together.
Transformation – walks taken together transform the world.
Miracles – you who walk together are the agent of miracles.

⟨Let's Walk Together – MY 5K Walking Campaign Poster⟩

Our disabled brothers, the homeless, people from all walks of life, everyone from young to old; together, we formed an impressive group. Korean churches and various organizations from all parts of society participated in the MY 5K project to awaken the goodness in Korea's heart. I give God all the glory. I thank all the leaders and over 500 volunteers who worked tirelessly on the project.

The NCMN 5K HQ is in network with churches all around the country; wearing their red vests, our volunteers serve the poor in around 300 different zones. Our goal is to expand into 400 zones by the end of 2019 and 1,159 zones by 2023.

When we divided North Korea into 5km radius areas, we ended up with 1,159 zones. Each 5K relief ministry team in the South is tied with a corresponding zone in North Korea. Every quarter (4 times a year), we host a "5K Distribution Ceremony for the Network of Churches and Businesses."

When North Korea opens its doors, 5K teams will be the first to enter. One thousand one hundred and fifty-nine relief ministry teams will be prepared for immediate entry into North Korea with a rice ball (bread) in one hand and the Gospel in the other.

Likewise, local churches and businesses are preparing the finances for the North Korean zone that has been distributed to them. 5K relief ministry teams, local churches, and businesses will join hands to serve their respective zones (Churches, businesses, and relief ministry teams can apply to have a North Korea 5K zone distributed to them through NCMN's website).

Fruit of the 5K Sharing Love Movement Shin HeeJae

The leaders of the NCMN Movement team in Paju visit

PART IV Awaken the Next Generation of Faith

the elderly once a week to bring them food and clean their houses. Grandpa Lee BaeGeun is one such elderly recipient. He could not stand up, let alone walk after suffering a stroke (Now, thanks to the care of our volunteers, he is able to walk and move about slowly).

But in his home, Grandpa Lee BaeGeun had a framed Daesoon Jinrihoe[13] sign and prayer statue. One day, as we were installing a gas stove in his kitchen, we carefully asked if we could remove them from his house. Thankfully, he gave us permission, and we hung a cross in their place. Seeing Grandpa BaeGeun never fail to say "Thank you," I realized how the hard work of love was creating miracles.

On that day, we planned to install six gas stoves for families who had lived without one until then. And although the day on which we planned to do this was a replacement national holiday, the owner of the installation company himself came to set up the LPG pipes. The owner was there with us for approximately two hours to install the pipelines and LPG tank.

Even though some houses were in quite remote areas, the owner went from house to house carrying the heavy gas tanks without a word. But when we wanted to pay him after the final installation, he was already gone. We called him about the payment. He answered: "I don't know much

---

[13] Daesoon Jinrihoe (meaning "the Fellowship of Daesoon Truth") is the largest movement among around one hundred groups that originated in Korea from the activities of Kang IlSun.

about who you are, but seeing the work you do, I wanted to do something to serve as well. I won't take the payment for the gas today."

I asked him how he had reached the decision. He replied: "I'm happy that I was there with you today. I, too, will receive blessings from God in return for my sharing and service today." God is performing the miracle of the five loaves and two fishes with our little displays of love and sharing.

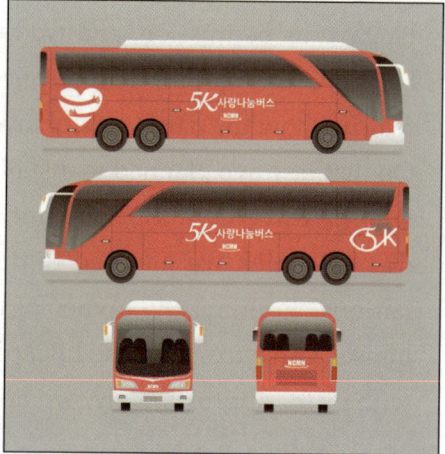

⟨5K Sharing Love Bus⟩

CHATPER 2

The Kingdom of God vs. The Kingdom of the World

There is No Middle Ground for the Believer

Do not be yoked together with unbelievers. For what do righteousness and wickedness have in common? Or what fellowship can light have with darkness? What harmony is there between Christ and Belial? Or what does a believer have in common with an unbeliever? What agreement is there between the temple of God and idols? For we are the temple of the living God. 2Cor. 6:14-16

The Kingdom of God	The Kingdom of the World
The Kingdom of Believers	The Kingdom of Unbelievers
Righteousness	Wickedness
Light	Darkness
Christ	Belial
The Temple of God	Idols

The kingdom of God and the kingdom of the world are exact opposites. There is no middle ground for the believer. Will you live by faith according to the Word of the Lord, or will you live as the worldly according to your circumstances and money even as you attend church?

	The Kingdom of God	The Kingdom of the World
View on finances	Honest A Life that Gives and Receives	Dishonest A Life that Sells and Buys
Attitude on Life	Diligent, Faithful, Generous	Lazy, Unfaithful, Miserly
Center of Attitude	Humility, Hope, Patience, Endurance	Arrogance Discouragement, Anxiety, Rashness
Future	Faith, Peace, Success	Fear
Mathematical Equation	5+2=5000+12 1x100 Million= 100 Million The Power of God	5+2=7 0x100 Million=0 My Power, My Strength

Pass on the Inheritance of Holy Riches to Your Children

The Bible warns that the wealth of the wicked will never be enough to satisfy the hunger of his children. The Lord makes it clear that He will give the wealth of the worldly rich to the righteous. (See Job 27:13-17; Mic. 6:10-16, and many other Scriptures explain this).

"A good person leaves an inheritance for their children's children, but a sinner's wealth is stored up for the righteous" (Prov. 13:22).

"Houses and wealth are inherited from parents, but a prudent wife is from the Lord" (Prov. 19:14).

But the Lord tells the holy rich to pass on their wealth as

an inheritance. How will we pass it on? Devise a plan. Only passing on wealth will lead to the demise of your children.

> - First, instruct them on the biblical principles of finance.
> - Teach them to set up and implement the budget of faith.
> - Teach them not to be in debt.
> - Teach them to share and have mercy for the poor.
> - Teach them how to serve others and God with their wealth.
> - Do not pass on your inheritance until they have learned to handle money.
> - If possible, do not pass on significant amounts of wealth before the age of 45.

Awaken the Next and Not a Different Generation

Do you truly love your children? Do not pass on money to your children who are not yet prepared, or you will bring them to ruin. If we cannot pass on our faith to the next generation, they will fall into idol worship and serve Baal (mammon), and God's wrath will descend upon them.

After Joshua had dismissed the Israelites, they went to take possession of the land, each to their own inheritance. The people served the Lord throughout the lifetime of Joshua and of the elders who outlived him and who had seen all the great things the Lord had done for Israel. Judg. 2:6-7

- Two characteristics of Joshua and the elders' generations:
  First, they knew God.
  Second, they experienced the power of God.
  As a result, they served the Lord.

After they had lived for many years, they all went back to be with their ancestors.

"After that whole generation had been gathered to their ancestors, another generation grew up who knew neither the Lord nor what he had done for Israel" (Judg. 2:10).

After a generation of faith has passed, the next generation of faith is supposed to rise. But here, we see not the next generation of faith, but a different generation.

- The characteristics of a different generation:
  First, they do not know God.
  Second, they have not experienced the power of God.
  As a result, they were wicked and worshipped idols.

They did not live a life of influence but instead were influenced by others.

"Then the Israelites did evil in the eyes of the Lord and

served the Baals... They followed and worshiped various gods of the peoples around them. They aroused the Lord's anger because they forsook him and served Baal and the Ashtoreths" (Judg. 2:11-13).

See how God makes the different generation of Israelites who had sinned against the Lord and fell into idol worship return to Him.

"In his anger against Israel the Lord gave them into the hands of raiders who plundered them. He sold them into the hands of their enemies all around, whom they were no longer able to resist. Whenever Israel went out to fight, the hand of the Lord was against them to defeat them... They were in great distress" (Judg. 2:14-15).

God has never once changed in the way He deals with us humans. Even to this day, He sends illnesses upon the bodies and famine upon the wealth of the hardened to break them. This is God's love. He embraces, restores, heals and blesses those who repent and return to Him.

If you love your children, pass on to them, not your wealth but your faith. Teach them inside the family so that you may rescue them from the world outside!

The Obedience of Sacrificing Isaac

On May 13, 2019, a sister came to see me after a meeting at the Eunchong Church in Daejeon. The sister told me she repaid her entire debt of 2.3 billion won after living out the budget of faith she had learned through *The King's Finances*

I and workbook. A deacon from the church and her son and daughter came as her witnesses. Sister Oh JinSook, a fellow minister, was there with me when I met her.

The sister cried incessantly as she gave her testimony. She said she overcame and broke through her panic disorder and insomnia after she was introduced to the King's Finances. Then, she gave us the deed of a property that she had been saving as an inheritance for her children; she asked us to use it for our ministry. She was apologetic, saying that her donation was as the widow's small jar of oil when compared to the greatness of God's love.

As I looked over her deed, the hard work the sister had put into earning that deed felt almost tangible. The obedience and heart of Abraham as he gave Isaac up to the Lord! That was what I saw. I took the deed, blessed it, and returned it to her immediately.

"My sister, I've received your gift, and now, I am flowing it back to you. You can use it for the Lord's ministry together with your church. Our God accepted Abraham's obedience when he gave Isaac and returned his son to him."

The sister cried without words, and her children watched in amazement as the building was returned to them. I have no interest in the value or size of the building. I was deeply moved to see a YouTube student who had never met me before be so obedient to the Lord.

That evening, the sister attended the revival conference. I testified about her sacrifice to the congregation, showing them the pictures of her handing her property deed over to me. May the Lord, who creates new testimonies and miracles through the obedience of believers, be raised on high.

The Heroes of the Hero Camps

NCMN hosts camps named Hero 300 Camps. The Young Adult Hero 300 Camp, geared toward young adults and college students, is held in January each year. The Youth Hero 300 Camp for adolescents and teenagers is organized around the end of July or the beginning of August every year. Rev. Hong and NCMN leaders felt a great sense of responsibility toward the next generation and prayed to the Lord for a specific strategy. The Lord gave us a clear plan.

First, remove the excesses of worship and only worship the Lord.

Second, over 3 nights and 4 days, read the entire New Testament aloud in small groups

Third, simplify the program (early morning spiritual training, morning finances training, afternoon identity and calling training, and evening Hero worship).

Regardless of the age group, each camp operates under the same schedule. The camp makes full use of all 24 hours in a day with eight hours of lectures, five hours of worship including meal times, six hours of Scripture reading, and five hours of sleep. Given the tight schedule, participants are not allowed access to their cellphones; these are collected at the beginning of the camp and returned to their owners at the end.

There are 300-350 participants in every camp, and participants are divided into small groups of 5,6 members. Each group is assigned two small group leaders, meaning the leader to student ratio is about 2:3. In total, there are about 500 people in each camp. Leaders and students eat, sleep, and take turns reading verses from the Bible aloud together with their respective small groups. At the end of the 3 nights and 4 days camp, everyone reads the complete New Testament from cover to cover.

Can such a camp succeed? I needed to spend many hours in prayer to believe and be sure that this itinerary was from the Lord. Looking at the kids these days, I knew that the power of the Holy Spirit was the only way we could deliver what the Lord had commanded. Our purpose was to mold heroes of faith through our camps.

We were determined to make a breakthrough with prayer and recruited 1,000 people to engage in intercessory prayer 6 months before the camp began. Thousands of volunteers supported the camp through their intercessory prayers. During the camp, a special forces comprised of dozens guarded the campgrounds through prayer and fasting. Despite all our prayers and preparations, chaos broke out in the 1st Hero Camp. Many of the students were children of pastors and church ministers. The majority were from Christian families, and most were "conscripted" rather than "Voluntary" campers. Children who had been forcibly entered into the camp by their parents revolted against having their phones taken away. Some even went back home after finding out they could complete the camp only if they finished reading the entire New Testament over the four days.

The Light of the Word Looses Bound Children

More young adults had never read the Bible from cover to cover than we could have ever imagined. Some did not even know where Genesis was. Some had no clue whether the Gospel of Matthew was in the New or Old Testament. Rev. Hong and the camp lecturers began to fast. We were all desperate because we knew that only the power of the Holy Spirit could lead them to the Cross.

Some of the students really were a handful. Even though everyone could tell that I was a lecturer at the camp by looking at the camp posters and banners, there was a student who dismissively said, "Who is this woman anyway? This camp is so annoying." Then, there was another student who had eight earrings in just one ear. I was just blankly staring at him when the Lord gave me a Scripture verse of promise.

"Your troops will be willing on your day of battle. Arrayed in holy splendor, your young men will come to you like dew from the morning's womb" (Psa. 110:3).

I doubted my ears when I heard the Lord said, I will use

that child.' I needed my eyes to emblepo[14] (Just as the Lord saw the rock inside Peter instead of the weak-willed person that he appeared to be on the inside). I went up to that child and said, "Hey, you! The Lord has called you to be a leader of the future. He tells me that you're going to be someone great." I saw him again during the camp.

"You! The Lord says that He will use you. You need more training. Come to our school after the camp is over."

This student who used to smirk and belittle my words began to change throughout the camp. So much so, in fact, that the change was visible to the eye. He began taking off his earrings one by one, saying that they were heavy and got in the way. He eventually took all of them off and is now preparing to enroll in a seminary to minister to adolescents and teenagers.

As stated previously, one of the conditions for completing the camp is reading the New Testament from cover to cover. The students need to read the Bible aloud quickly to finish reading in the given time. Many students who were reading the Bible quickly broke out in tongues and began confessing their sins. Their gaming, pornographic, and sex addictions were broken when they received the Holy Spirit. They were healed from their psychological and physical illnesses as they prayed and read the Bible. Countless students who have completed the camps can attest to this.

---

14 Metaphorically to look at with the mind; to consider.

One student came to the camp on the brink of suicide. He said that he had planned on taking his final breath at the camp as he no longer had any reason to live. His parents were completely unaware of their son's condition. Even we only found out through the young man's testimony. This young man found his identity and calling through the Word and was freed from his depression; the spirit of darkness could no longer sustain its grip on him. He has since dedicated himself to Jesus and spends his time serving Him.

I Have Been Transformed by the King's Finances School for Kids
Jung Ahln

I am an elementary school student in the sixth grade. Before I came to the King's Finances School for Kids, I always thought that I was faithful in the eyes of the Lord because I went to church every Sunday without pressure from anyone. But after listening to the lectures, I found out that I was not as faithful as I had first thought.

Whenever my parents gave me pocket money, I spent it on the things that I wanted to buy and gave what remained as an offering on Sundays. When I did not have any money, I would borrow some from my friends and pay it back later. I expected the Lord to give me great things when I myself was not faithful with even the least (chores, cleaning my room, homework, etc.). I never once thought of giving my parents money or felt that I should give to the poor.

Then one day, I began speaking in tongues during an intense worship service at the King's Finances School for Kids. Until then, I had always given 1,000 won as my Sunday offering. However, after my training at the school, I began giving 2,000 won each week and paying all my tithes. After that, the Lord blessed me by increasing my allowance from 20,000 won to 30,000 won each week. I became a person who can give with joy, even flowing the things that I hold most dear.

In the fourth week of the King's Finances School for Kids, I heard the voice of the Lord.

'My daughter, I am pleased with you. I love you. I have chosen you to speak of Me, the Lord, across the entire globe. Do not fear; I will be with you.'

But I wanted to make sure that the words were spoken to me by the Lord and that I had not just made them up.

So, I prayed.

'Lord, if you really have put these words in my heart, please send me a designated flowing today.'

I could not believe it; I received the designated flow on that very day just as I had prayed. This proved to me that God really is alive.

I first learned about debt through my finances training. And I prayed that my family's debt would be repaid as well. I prayed for my father who had the means but was refusing to repay his debts. The Lord promised me that our debt would be repaid, and I received a flowing of 100,000 won that very week.

I gave 10,000 won to the Lord as my tithe and the remaining 90,000 won to my dad so he could use it to pay his debts. My dad was touched by my gesture and paid back a debt of four million won. The Lord had touched my father's heart.

When I completed my finances training, I resolved to spend a portion of my allowance on paying back our family debts. My father told me that he would double the amount I paid and put it toward the repayment of our debts. Sometimes it is really challenging to use money as we are taught during training. But as someone who has received this training, I wish to continue to consult the Lord about planning my finances and be a person who is faithful with her wealth.

Children Who Come as Unbelievers and Return as Devotees

After hearing how the Lord had blessed the first Hero Camp, parents rushed to get their children in the second camp. On the first day of the second camp, every one of these young adults was a mere bystander, not even participating in worship. None of them had an interest in getting to know Jesus. That was until they came across a lecture that thoroughly shocked them, the lectures on finances that went on for hours every morning.

Standing before the Lord, the students shared their possessions with others in need and flowed their possession to other unknown students at the camp with a little hand-written note. A young man from a poor family who was working his way through college saw his tuition paid in full with God's gracious provision. Witnessing students break apart their possessions to flow to each other felt like being inside a scene directly out of the Book of Acts.

Over the duration of the camp which lasted 3 nights and 4 days, a total of 100 million won was flowed among the students. Students, who were previously too stingy to buy each other even a cup of coffee became fully immersed in God's world. A world in which a completely new set of rules applied. It was one miracle after the other. Although there was not a separate time for offerings, youth, filled with the Word of God, provided for each other's needs, following after God's heart.

We neither collected nor received a single won from students at the camp. I witnessed how the Holy Spirit healed and broke the stubbornness in the students' hearts through Scripture, worship, and prayer. Many of them accepted Jesus as their Lord and Savior through lectures on identity and calling. Every camp, dozens of the youth resolve to lead lives that are set apart from their previous ones.

I had the opportunity to speak with and hear the concerns of many young adults during these camps. After hearing their stories, I believe that it is the parents that are the most clueless about their children. One student said that when she was a senior in high school her parents told her to focus on her studies and pause church until college when she was a senior in high school. She left the church and was no longer interested when she became a college student. She told me that she could not get the thought, 'Why do I have to go to church if it's less important than college?' out of her mind. Parents can either make or break their children's faiths

The children of a close missionary family and a pastor's family came to the camp. The families' two children were young adults who served and volunteered diligently in the church. But on the last day of camp, they both came on the stage in tears and accepted Jesus into their hearts! Shocked, I called the two to my side later.

They both confessed that they served the church out of habit despite not actually believing in Jesus. They said that they began speaking in tongues during prayer and could not stop their tears. They both can now proudly confess, "Jesus is my Lord and Savior!"

Heroes Come to Camp Prepared

Unlike the first camp, more and more students who came to camp in the following years came from their homes as prepared heroes. A successful faith is rooted in the family because it is the parents who are the best equipped to serve as examples of faith. These prepared children were completely reborn as heroes at the "Hero! Hero! Hero!" worship on the third night.

On the first night, we ask the question: Who is my true hero? It is only Jesus!

On the second night, Who will follow Jesus, our hero, with their life? This is the night when heroes are born.

On the third night, Who will multiply other heroes? The heroes who transform the worldly culture of these lands into God's culture! Who will live as a reformer and revolutionary? This is the night young men and women are reborn as heroes who will create the Christian Civilization Reform Movement in the world's culture.

Each night Rev. Hong calls on the students to dedicate themselves as foreigners in this world. Foreigners are distinguished from ordinary people by their language, culture, principles of life, sense of purpose, values, worldview, and standards of decision making.

God used foreigners to bring judgment upon Babylon (see Jer. 51:1-3). Rev. Hong captures the hearts of young adults and leads them to the Cross, before which they surrender as heroes. And on their camp completion certificates, each student's name and last name are written down next to the word "foreigner."

> I will live as a foreigner in this world!
> I will use a different language than that of this world!
> I will create a different culture than that of this world!
> I will make decisions based on different principles than that of this world!

PART IV Awaken the Next Generation of Faith

> I will live with a different sense of purpose than that of this world!
> Wherever I may be, I will establish the kingdom of God!

'I will awaken the next generation of faith. Let those who fear be gone! I will raise Gideon's army of 300 warriors. Arm the next generation and prepare for Korea to serve the whole world.'

These are the words our Lord promised during the Hero camps. But I was always overwhelmed with worry when the Youth Hero Camp's starting day neared. Collecting the cellphones of middle and high school students who are in the most rebellious stage of their lives and getting them to finish reading the entire New Testament was no easy task. Moreover, I had to lecture about money and wealth, a topic in which these teens have no interest, for three whole hours in the morning. The anxiety induced indigestion eventually became a fast of sorts.

Because I had a son who had gone through the same adolescent period, I knew that kneeling before the Lord was all I could do. I was powerless; I was at my wit's end. But, on the other hand, my heart burned with the anticipation of meeting these children in the most passionate time of their lives.

Lecturers, leaders, and parents included, thousands of intercessors engaged in a relay fast. Acting leaders who served the camp fasted for 100 days, eating only one half-portioned meal a day. Everyone bowed down before the Lord and waited. The results were truly stunning! The energy of the Youth Hero Camp just exploded.

I cannot forget the last night of dedication to this day. On that night, I saw the hope for Korea. Children who are of the Lord cannot go far from the Lord. And yet if they do, they, always and without fail, return to Him. Parents must always give their children a chance to meet the Lord. Dear parents, academics are not everything; you need to provide your children with the opportunity to attend camps that are organized by churches and sound organizations.

The Name That Was Not Erased for Three Days Cho YiGyeong

I grew up in a Buddhist household. At the end of December 2019, a friend said to me, "Kim MiJin, Kim MiJin" without any further explanations. I had no idea what it meant, but I wrote in on my palm before heading back home. After three days, the name had not been erased from my palm. Out of curiosity, I looked up the name on the internet.

That was the day I began watching the King's Finances lectures. The more I listened to the lectures, the more I felt a growing urge to attend church. So I made my way to the church across from my house only to find its doors locked. I went again, but it was still locked. Then in April 2017, I found out about the church I am currently attending and started going there. But I found it hard to fully immerse myself in my faith because I had a hard time understanding the Bible. I would go to church, come straight back home, and watch TV lying on the couch.

Feeling that things could not go on as they were, I signed up for the NCMN King's Finances School in Daegu. They gave us assignments. We had to upload a recording of ourselves reading aloud ten chapters of the Bible as well as a summary of our daily devotions and the lecture we watched each day.

What others did without the slightest problem, even with their fulltime jobs, I, as a former Buddhist, found to be a challenge. But at the same time, I found the assignments quite interesting and enjoyed doing them. I stopped watching TV and spent 5-6 hours a day in my room, reading the Bible out loud.

Initially, my husband was humored that I had given up my favorite activity of watching TV to study like a student preparing for her university exams. But seeing my consistent dedication, that humor eventually changed to bewilderment. Each day, he saw the positive changes my training had on me, and this sparked an interest in him.

Members of my small group visited my home during the King's Finances School outreach period. They must have left quite an impression on him because later my husband said: "Dear, I think I want to try out that King's Finances School as well." It was a miracle. My husband, who would reply, "You do your thing, it's not for me. Be sure to pray that my business makes a lot of money, though!" whenever I asked him to come to church with me, had told me voluntarily that he wanted to attend the King's Finances School.

Wanting to seize this window of opportunity, I said to my husband, "Dear, you first need to start attending church if you want to get into the King's Finances School." And because he likes everything to be new, I bought him a brand new Bible of his own. My husband began following me to church despite feeling quite out of place at first. After he had begun attending church regularly, I told him, "Dear, you first need to serve the poor to get into the King's Finances School." He replied, "Why are admissions so complicated?"

Now, that husband of mine wears his little red vest and serves the poor with the 5K relief ministry, picking up cigarette butts off the streets and serving food to those in need.

Although attending church was something my husband initially did just to get into the King's Finances School, his attitude completely changed after he enrolled in the 3rd session of the King's Finances School. He became more attuned to the Word than even I was and dedicated 51 percent of our finances toward building the next generation of God's kingdom. My husband dedicated himself to the work of bringing the next generation back to the Lord after witnessing firsthand the Holy Spirit's powerful work in our high school senior daughter after the Hero camp.

PART IV Awaken the Next Generation of Faith

My parents still practice jesa[15], but I am determined to spread the Gospel to them no matter what. I thank Kyujang Publishing House, Rev. Hong SungGun, and Sister Kim MiJin for publishing *The King's Finances* and leading me to Jesus. My husband and I will surrender the rest of our lives to the expansion of God's kingdom.

— Rev. Hong and I met Sister Cho YiGyeong and her husband in person and heard their testimonies at a joint conference in the Jinhae region. Her husband gave his testimony with spectacular humor. Although there are many other funny stories we could share, we unfortunately cannot realistically record them all. Many who know this couple have attested to the truthfulness of their testimonies.

---

15 Ancestral rites practiced in memorial to the ancestors of the participants, usually held on the anniversary of the ancestor's death.

Epilogue

Catch the Timing of the Movement of Wealth

Prepare The Movement of Wealth

Before I began my ministry, the Lord showed me a colossal mountain gilded in gold.

'Lord, what is this?'

'A great movement of wealth will take place. Prepare.'

'How should I prepare?'

'Write the King's Finances, build the King's Finances School, and found the King's Business Group. Build up businesses of which God is the sole owner. There will be a great movement of wealth.'

'What will be the purpose of this movement of wealth?'

'Prepare a Korea that serves the world and in which the South and North are one.'

These were the words the Lord spoke to me in the initial stages of my ministry.

During one lecture, when I told the audience to buy land in the locations which God has shown us to prepare for His kingdom, someone asked if I was asking them to make a speculative land purchase. Investment and speculation are two different things. Although they are both profit-seeking activities, investment seeks profits through productive activities while speculation is only after profits without offering anything productive in return.

Explained in biblical terms, speculation is 'to buy out of greed using debt,' and investment is 'to buy legitimately using surplus funds.' The best investment is a deposit made in the Heavenly Bank.

What I meant when I said to buy land was for them to buy plots in a good location and donate it to a church or mission organization. I wanted for us to acquire good locations so that the first buildings to be built in those good locations could be churches. This is because buildings for the expansion of God's kingdom must take their place before buildings of worldly pleasure settle in. It is in these places that we must execute the projects of the kingdom of God.

I personally bought and donated a parcel of land in the place God showed me at a very reasonable price. Real estate prices in that area have since gone up so much that buying land there right now would be unthinkable. That is what I meant when I told people to buy land. We must be mindful when we buy and sell property because an increase in property prices could make the lives of ordinary citizens much more difficult.

I prayed and fasted for seven days at a prayer retreat center before beginning to write *The King's Finances II*. During that time, the Lord showed me the events that would unfold in the nations.

- First, the Lord will overhaul the world's finances in the end of days. There will be a movement of wealth. The ownership over land and buildings will change hands at the time of this movement of wealth.
- Second, awaken a holy generation within this obscene generation. Baal and Asherah must be taken down.
- Third, prepare for reunification and, furthermore, for a Korea which serves the world.

The Lord said that there will be a vast movement of wealth. He showed me a vision of all the riches of the world being poured into Korea. And when the Lord overhauls the world's finances, people and companies with debt will be shaken to their cores. Those with debt must first repay their debts above all else. Make sure to look for and plan your business ideas within the context of reunification. Open your eyes to the Lord and catch the timing of this movement of wealth.

God's Love Pushes Me Forward

God's love has transformed me. He continually renews a merciful spirit in my heart. The love of Jesus flows inside me every time I see those who are weak and sick. Many times, He has allowed me to be a witness to the Holy Spirit rescue them from their fears and illnesses when I whisper in their ears, "Jesus loves you."

The love of Jesus frees those who are taken captive wherever it flows. I have witnessed the darkness flee, overpowered by His love.

'A deficiency of love' is what causes weakness and illness. This lack gives darkness the chance to create fear and hold them captive. This is why parents must often, and as much as they can, say the words, "I love you," to their children.

"I love you with the love of our Lord."

When I tell people to say this to each other, some respond with, "I cannot because I don't have the Lord's love in me." Such statements are words of arrogance that stem from a lack of knowledge of the Bible.

> A new command I give you: Love one another. As I have loved you, so you must love one another. By this everyone will know that you are my disciples, if you love one another
> John 13:34-35

The Lord gave us a new commandment.

"Love one another. As I have loved you, so you must love one another."

Though we may not have love in us, the Lord's love is ever in us. The moment we obey the Word and stretch out our hands, saying, "I love you with the love of our Lord," Jesus' love begins flowing out of us. When we obey the Word and respond with faith, His love flows through us to others.

> There is no fear in love. But perfect love drives out fear
> 1 John 4:18

He, who is the Prince of Peace, came to this world. He, who is Jesus, came in love.

> There will be no more gloom for those who were in distress... The people walking in darkness have seen a great light; on those living in the land of deep darkness a light has dawned... you have shattered the yoke that burdens them, the bar across their shoulders, the rod of their oppressor... For to us a child is born... And he will be called Wonderful Counselor, Mighty God, Everlasting Father, Prince of Peace.
> Isa. 9:1-6

The Prince of Peace, who came to us, tells us:
−I will remove the gloom over those in distress. I will remove their suffering.

—I will shine a light upon those living in the land of deep darkness. I will give them joy, hope, and life.
—I will shatter their heavy yoke and the rod of their oppressor. I will set them free.

There is freedom where the spirit of Jesus is. Be free in Jesus. He has come as the Prince of Peace. Jesus! He is love itself!

Very truly I tell you, whoever believes in me will do the works I have been doing, and they will do even greater things than these, because I am going to the Father. And I will do whatever you ask in my name, so that the Father may be glorified in the Son. You may ask me for anything in my name, and I will do it John 14:12-14

Ever since elementary school, I had a hard time understanding these verses.

"Can I really do everything that Jesus did and even more if I only have faith?"

So, just as Jesus did, I would pray and share pieces of the bread in my hand with my friends. But I was always left with nothing.

1. Jesus fed 5,000 people with 5 loaves of barley bread and 2 small fish and had 12 baskets of food leftover.
2. Jesus brought the putrefying corpse of Lazarus, who had been dead for four days, back to life.

For 20 years, the meaning of these Scriptures was kept a secret from me (Maybe this is why the kingdom of God is said to be a secret).

After my bankruptcy, I endured many days in hunger. I helped with the dishes in the kitchen on Sundays and brought the leftovers home. I remember scooping a spoonful of rice to eat it but crying instead because I felt so sorry for myself. I remembered the homeless who were no better off than I was. Unable to bring myself to eat the rice, I cooked up a porridge, adding kimchi and water to the rice, and took it to the homeless so we could share.

It being winter, the underground passage where the homeless were was bitterly cold. They had nothing to sleep on but cardboard boxes and nothing to use as a blanket but sheets of newspaper. I gave them each a warm bowl of porridge; tears rolled down my face as I sat there eating together with a homeless sister.

'Thank you, my daughter. Look around you. See the miracle of the five loaves and two fishes wrought by your hands.'

That voice was one I can never forget; that voice was an immense source of encouragement and a new revelation. On that night, 50 people soothed their hunger with the rice that I otherwise would have had on my own.

Each year, I go to Africa on a mission trip. On my 2018 trip, I met a child who was dying from heart disease. I remembered these words of God, "Whoever believes in me will do the works I have been doing." My company helped the child receive surgery, and the boy survived. Now that Muslim child is attending a Christian school.

Jesus' love was delivered to that little child. We did the works that our Lord had done. I finally understood what John Chapter 12 Verses 13-14 meant by "I will do whatever you ask in my name, so that the Father may be glorified in the Son," regarding "the works" in John Chapter 12 Verse 12.

Moreover, God further deepened my understanding by connecting these verses with Nehemiah Chapter 9 Verses 10: "You sent signs and wonders… You made a name for yourself." Many of the things we ask from the Lord require a miracle. And through these miracles, the Lord is glorified, and His name is honored.

The life which our Lord wants us to live is a life that works the miracle of the five loaves and two fishes. If 50 people gather and buy milk and bread to feed the poor on the streets, they will have 12 baskets leftover after feeding 5,000. We can be the agents of this miracle just as we are today. Whatever we ask for the purpose of giving glory to God, He will provide. The works of Jesus, that miracle will be wrought by your hands! I invite you to be the agent of this miracle.

Final Words

In Seventy Years, I Will Make You Return

Sometimes, a cycle of 70 years appears in the Bible.

Babylonian Exile and the Return to Zion
Jeremiah was active during the time of Judah's fall. He pleaded with the king and people of Judah to surrender to the Babylonians countless times. This was because God had brought the Babylonians upon His people as judgment for their disobedience. I imagine that it must have been extremely difficult for Jeremiah to be the deliverer of these words. Nevertheless, his hopes were high; his hope was in God's mercy and grace.

I well remember them, and my soul is downcast within me.

Yet this I call to mind and therefore I have hope: Because of the Lord's great love we are not consumed, for his compassions never fail. They are new every morning; great is your faithfulness. I say to myself, "The Lord is my portion; therefore I will wait for him." Lam. 3:20-24

God commands Jeremiah to declare:

This whole country will become a desolate wasteland, and these nations will serve the king of Babylon seventy years. Jer. 25:11

This is what the Lord says: "When seventy years are completed for Babylon, I will come to you and fulfill my good promise to bring you back to this place." Jer. 29:10

God limited the number of years His people would live in Babylonian captivity to 70 years. This is a historical fact. Judah's captivity began in 606 BC, and their return began 70 years after that in 536 BC. Solomon's Temple in Jerusalem was destroyed in 586 BC, and Zerubabbel's Temple was built in 516 BC by those who had returned from exile. Again, 70 years.

Daniel was exiled to Babylon in the first phase of the Babylonian captivity. Daniel was yet just a young boy of ten years at the time. One day, as he was reading the Book of Jeremiah, he understood the Scriptures and began pleading with the Lord in prayer and fasting that the Scriptures would be fulfilled (see Dan. Chapter 9).

Then, there was the Prophet Ezekiel, who prophesied during his exile in Babylon. Through him, God promised the restoration of Israel and said that prayer was the key to fulfilling this prophecy.

> This is what the Sovereign Lord says: Once again I will yield to Israel's plea and do this for them Ezek. 36:37

The Beginning and End of Communism

Karl Marx and Lenin drew inspiration from the Bible when coming up with the idea of communism. They sought to create a classless society in which there was no gap between the rich and poor. The revolution that started under these ideals succeeded and marked the creation of the communist society. At the time of this revolution, the West was faced with the collapse of the feudal system and the rise of the industrial revolution.

But the structure of the economy did not change at all. The relationship between feudal lords and tenant farmers fundamentally remained the same; it only changed in name to the relationship between employers and employees. Wealth distribution was largely skewed toward the wealthy, and this created a severe wealth inequality in society. Ninety percent of all wealth belonged to the richest ten percent of employers, and the remaining 90 percent majority had to share what was left of the last ten percent.

Citizens who were outraged by this inequality led the 1917 communist revolution and succeeded in 1920. We call this the Bolshevik Revolution. The Bolshevik Revolution began in Russia, a Christian country. And although the idea of communism was taken from the Bible, its founders ironically removed the Bible, God, and church completely from the equation.

These revolutionaries targeted not employers but Christians. The Gospel really began to spread around Europe in the 4th century AD. By the early 20th century, most countries in Europe were Christian countries. Communists blamed the rampant inequality on Christianity. Although the communists had it all wrong, the so-called "Christian" countries themselves also had no excuse. The Christian countries of Europe were, in fact, built on a biblical foundation in many areas.

But these Christian countries made one fatal mistake; they turned a blind eye to the gap between the rich and poor. Royals, aristocrats, and clergy comprised the ten percent who owned 90 percent of all wealth.

The early church recorded in the Book of Acts paints a completely different picture. The church was the first to share. Christians always worked hard to earn money and tried to decrease the wealth inequality by attending to the needs of the poor. But over time, such biblical financial principles were forgotten in the Western church. They ignored what was the most important.

The great Russian Empire, which was a Christian nation, disappeared into the pages of history and in its place the great Union of Soviet Socialist Republics (Soviet Union) was born. Then in 1987, the General Secretary of the Communist Party of the Soviet Union Mikhail Gorbachev declared the end of communism. The world was in shock. These were his words:

"We have championed communism for the past 70 years and tried to create an ideal world. But now, we have reached a verdict. This ideology is in no way feasible. It is nothing but an impossible theory; it is as worthless as a piece of paper."

In 1990, the Soviet Union collapsed, leading to rapid changes in global politics. The enormous Soviet Union was instantly broken into 20 independent countries. Churches in Europe had long been praying for the fall of communism as churches were destroyed, Bibles burned, and ministers imprisoned under the ideology.

Despite all their prayers, there was no answer. That is why they called communism, the "iron curtain." In the 1980s, many countries around the world adopted communism. But in the depths of their despair, God reminded His praying people of the work He did in the past, the work of "70 years," as prophesied by Jeremiah. The Western church held on to this during their prayers; their prayers were answered, and God's work was fulfilled.

Bolshevik Revolution 1917
The fall of communism 1987

The emergence of Soviet Communist suzerainty 1920
The Dissolution of Soviet Communist suzerainty 1990

God heard the cries of His people.

Now, It Is Our Turn

Everyone welcomed communism in theory. A classless society, a society in which wealth is equally distributed! How magnificent would such a society be? But why then, did it fail? Although Karl Marx and Lenin got the idea of communism from the Bible, they missed the most important aspect. To use a metaphor, they bathed a newborn baby and threw the baby out with the water they used to wash it.

The ability of the early church in the Book of Acts to share came only from the power of the Holy Spirit. Such a society is only possible if the society is centered around the Bible, God, and the Holy Spirit. We now understand. God's plan is to create such a society. Such a society is only possible through a life of sharing, giving, and doing good deeds; such a society takes shape when its constituents take it upon themselves to look after the poor.

But as I have said before, we must not miss the central aspect that this is only possible when we are centered on God and the Bible. This is why NCMN pursues the 5K Movement. It is to rid ourselves of our greed, avarice, selfishness, and egotism.

The world tells us to work hard to earn money. It says, "Why make money just to give to others?" In short, it claims: "The money I made is mine; the ownership of this money is my right, and I will spend it as I please." But the Bible tells a different story. It says, "Let's earn money and give to others." But my understanding of Scripture is even more powerful.

"Let's earn money to give to others."

I call this the "spirit of the breadwinner." The breadwinner of a household works tirelessly from dawn to dusk. They sacrifice themselves to meet the needs of their family. This is the spirit by which we Christians must live.

The King's Finances School run by NCMN was founded for this purpose, and the 5K Movement puts this purpose into practice. It is the Christian Civilization Reform Movement. This movement does not require grandiose works. Anyone who has enough clothes to wear and food to eat can take part in the movement. It is not a movement for the mighty rich, nor is it a movement that requires people of high status.

Korea, Arise!

Realizing that the 70-year cycle takes place not just in the Bible but also in contemporary Western societies, I began praying earnestly before the Lord in 2012.

"Father, allow this cycle to take place in our country, Korea, as well!"

Before Korea even had a chance to appreciate its liberation from Japanese colonial rule fully, an immense conflict divided the country into two pieces. 1948 is the year of the formal establishment of the Republic of Korea in the South and also the year of South and North division in absolute terms. I prayed that 2018 would be the year we overcome this separation and engage in meaningful talks with the North.

But rather than move towards reconciliation, the two Koreas appeared as though they were on the brink of nuclear war at the end of 2017. Then came 2018, and with it, a great transformation: two Koreas began engaging in talks about denuclearization. This is merely the beginning. Again, 70 years.

The Korean war broke out it 1950. That year is the most tragic year in history of our nation. More than ten million people fled to the South during the war. I pray for this war to end in 2020. 70 years. In 1953, the two Koreas signed an armistice, which completely separated the South from the North. I pray that the two Koreas will be able to exchange with each other freely in 2023. Again, 70 years.

But there is one prerequisite.

This is what the Sovereign Lord says: Once again I will yield to Israel's plea and do this for them Ezek. 36:37

We, too, must fast and pray and desperately seek the face of the Lord, just as Daniel did. This is the prayer we should pray:

I well remember them, and my soul is downcast within me. Yet this I call to mind and therefore I have hope: Because of the Lord's great love we are not consumed, for his compassions never fail. They are new every morning; great is your faithfulness. I say to myself, "The Lord is my portion; therefore I will wait for him." Lam. 3:20-24

Hong SungGun

About NCMN Ministries

God shows me a vision amid my preparations for NCMN ministries

A new road was paved inside Korea. This road passed through big cities, small cities, the countryside, farming and fishing communities, and extended beyond islands as far as the eyes could see into the nations. And water, whose source lay in Korea, filled up this paved road and flowed out, gushing into the nations. The strong current swallowed up the Buddhists, Hindus, and Muslims who were standing on its path. Then, this water flowed and covered all the nations, and I saw a school of large fish with big jaws singing praises to the sky.

For the earth will be filled
With the knowledge of the glory of the Lord
As the waters cover the sea Hab. 2:14

NCMN is an organization that leads the Christian Civilization Reform Movement. Having marked the 500 anniversary of the Reformation in October 2017, NCMN is preparing for the next 500 years.

○ **The King's Finances Movement**
− The King's Finances School
   The King's Finances School in Seoul – 15 sessions completed (May 2019)
   → Number of students and leaders in each session 500; total 7,500
   The King's Finances School in Gwangju 3 sessions completed
   → Number of students and leaders in each session 350-400; total 1,050-1,200
   The King's Finances School in Daegu 3 sessions completed
   → Number of students and leaders in each session 400; total 1,200
   The King's Finances School in Sydney – 4 sessions

The King's Finances School in Cambodia – 3 sessions

The King's Finances School in Kenya, Africa – 2 sessions

The King's Finances School in Tokyo, Japan – 3 sessions

- The Changer Leadership School (A leadership school that champions change)

  Seoul Cherry School 9 sessions, 500 students and leaders in each session; total 4,500

- Shema Bible School (2019)

  Seoul Shema Bible Schoo 9 sessions, 500 students and leaders in each session; total 4,500

  Seoul Kids Shema Bible School 3 sessions, 90 students and leaders in each session; total 270

○ Seminars

- A Life That Hears the Voice of God

  Seoul – 6 sessions, Gwangju – 1 session; total 3,400 in Seoul and Gwangju

- Spiritual Warfare and Intercessory Prayer

Seoul – 4 sessions, Daejeon, Daegu, Japan, London (England), Sydney (Australia); total 3,000

– The Holy Spirit Festival (Living by the power of the Holy Spirit)
Seoul – 5 sessions, Gwangju, Daegu, Sydney (Australia), Japan; total 3,500

– Spiritual Authority (A channel of blessing and life)
Seoul, Gwangju; total 1,000

○ Next Generation
– King's Finances School for Kids
Seoul – 11 sessions completed, 70 students and leaders in each session; total 770
Gwangju – 2 sessions completed, 70 students and leaders in each session; total 140
Daegu – 3 sessions completed, 70 students and leaders in each session; total 210
King's Finances School for Kids in Sydney, Australia – 1 session
King's Finances School for Kids in London, England – 1 session

King's Finances School for Kids in Malaysia – 1 session

King's Finances School for Kids in Tokyo, Japan – 1 session

– Changer Leadership School for Kids
Seoul – 1 session, 80 participants

○ **Camps**
– **Hero 300 Camp for Youth** (Hero camp for adolescents)
Seoul – 2 sessions, 700 students (May 2019)

– **Hero 300 Camp for Young Adults** (Hero camp for young adults and college students)
Seoul – 4 sessions; 1,200 participants
Sydney – 1 session; 300 participants

○ **The Scripture Multiplier Movement**
This is a movement to read ten chapters of the Bible a day using the book, *The Word, Cover to Cover in 100 Days*. Thousands of small groups are participating in the movement in alliance with churches, and the numbers continue to multiply.

- **100,000 Intercessors Movement**
  We are raising 100,000 intercessors to engage in intercessory prayer for Korea and the nations.

- **Cherry Multiplier Movement**
  It is a movement to raise sound leaders who can stand upright in society, equipped with the leadership skills to create change in their respective fields.

- **The King's Business Group**
  - God is the sole owner of all things
  - A company owned by God
  - The "Give 51 Percent of Corporate Net Income to Others" Movement
  - The "Give 90 percent of Corporate Net Income to Others" Club for Holy Rich Companies
  - The movement to establish God's character of "Uprightness" as the foundation of the realm of economics
  - Currently, there are approximately 400 corporate participants in the training

○ **The 5K Movement**
Practicing Jesus' four main ministries (education, medicine, relief, evangelism) in a 5km radius around each church, a 5km radius around a location in North Korea, and a 5km radius around a location in front line mission fields. Currently, this movement is being carried out in alliance with countless churches in about 300 locations at home and dozens of countries abroad.

○ **The NCMN Vision Center**
Currently under construction on a 50,000 pyeong parcel of land in Gosung, Gangwondo, the NCMN Vision Center will serve as a center to carry out the Christian Civilization Reform Movement. The center is expected to open its doors in March 2022.

− Multiply NCers (Nations-Changers) and deployment for missions in various fields of society both at home and abroad.
− Reeducation for pastors
− Theological education
− Camp operations

○ NCMN Christian School
− Offers elementary, middle, and high school education

Homepage www.ncmn.kr
NCMN Support Account Shinhan Bank 140-012-482733 NCMN
ARS Support Number 060 707 0500 10,000 won/1 call

WHO IS THE MASTER OF YOUR LIFE?
GOD OR MONEY?